5th International Workshop for Computational Linguistics of Uralic Languages (IWCLUL 2019)

Tartu, Estonia
7 - 8 January 2019

ISBN: 978-1-5108-8132-7

Printed by Curran Associates, Inc. (2019)

For permission requests, please contact the Association for Computational Linguistics
at the address below.

Association for Computational Linguistics
209 N. Eighth Street
Stroudsburg, Pennsylvania 18360

Phone: 1-570-476-8006
Fax: 1-570-476-0860

acl@aclweb.org

Additional copies of this publication are available from:

Curran Associates, Inc.
57 Morehouse Lane
Red Hook, NY 12571 USA
Phone: 845-758-0400
Fax: 845-758-2633
Email: curran@proceedings.com
Web: www.proceedings.com

IWCLUL 2019

**The fifth International Workshop on
Computational Linguistics for Uralic Languages**

Proceedings of the Workshop

January 7—January 8, 2019
Tartu, Estonia

Introduction

These are the proceedings for the fifth international workshop on computational linguistics of Uralic languages, with a special focus on neural methods. Uralic languages are interesting from the computational-linguistic perspective, and also less-researched in the up-and-coming methodology of neural networks in natural language processing. The Uralic languages share large parts of morphological and morphophonological complexity that is not present in the Indo-European language family, which has traditionally dominated computational-linguistic research. This can be seen for example in number of morphologically complex forms belonging to one word, which in Indo-European languages is in range of ones or tens whereas for Uralic languages, it can be in the range of hundreds and thousands. Furthermore, Uralic language situations share a lot of geo-political aspects: the three national languages—Finnish, Estonian and Hungarian—are comparably small languages and only moderately resourced in terms of computational-linguistics while being stable and not in threat of extinction. The recognised minority languages of western-European states, on the other hand—such as North Sámi, Kven and Võro—do clearly fall in the category of lesser resourced and more threatened languages, whereas the majority of Uralic languages in the east of Europe and Siberia are closer to extinction. Common to all rapid development of more advanced computational-linguistic methods is required for continued vitality of the languages in everyday life, to enable archiving and use of the languages with computers and other devices such as mobile applications.

Computational linguistic research inside Uralistics is being carried out only in a handful of universities, research institutes and other sites and only by relatively few researchers. Our intention with organising this conference is to gather these researchers from scattered institutions together in order to share ideas and resources, and avoid duplicating efforts in gathering and enriching these scarce resources. We want to initiate more concentrated effort in collecting and improving language resources and technologies for the survival of the Uralic languages and hope that our effort today will become an ongoing tradition in the future.

For the current proceedings of The Fifth International Workshop on Computational Linguistics for Uralic Languages, we accepted 15 high-quality submissions about topics including semantic parsing, neural models, language documentation, tokenisation, corpora and lexicons, optical character recognition, morphological analysis and disambiguation. The range of languages covered this year again is wide, stretching over large part of Uralic languages including Finnish, Hungarian and Estonian as well as North Sámi, Livonian and Votic, and some multilingual papers touching methods and corpora for also Udmurt, Komi, Erzya, Moksha, Mari, Kildin Sámi, Khanty, Mansi and many others.

The conference was organised in collaboration with Tartu Ülikool, Estonia, on January 7–8 2019. The program consisted of an invited speech by Måns Huldén, a poster session, and six talks during the first day and an open discussion and individual project workshops during the second day. The current proceedings include the written versions all oral and poster presentations.

—Tommi A. Pirinen, Heiki-Jaan Kaalep, Francis M. Tyers
Conference organisers,
January 8, 2019, Tartu

Organizers:

ACL SIGUR, the special interest group for Uralic Languages, and the local organisers:
Anneli Vainumäe, University of Tartu
Heiki-Jaan Kaalep, University of Tartu

Program Committee:

Tommi Pirinen, University of Hamburg
Francis Tyers, Indiana University and Higher School of Economics
Eszter Simon, Research Institute for Linguistics, Hungarian Academy of Sciences
Anna Volkova, School of Linguistics, National Research University, Higher School of Economics, Moscow
Heiki-Jaan Kaalep, University of Tartu
Lene Antonsen, University of Tromsø
Trond Trosterud, University of Tromsø
Thierry Poibeau, LaTTiCe-CNRS
Veronika Vincze, Hungarian Academy of Sciences, Research Group on Articial Intelligence
Kadri Muischnek, University of Tartu
Csilla Horvath, Research Institute for Linguistics, Hungarian Academy of Sciences
Filip Ginter, University of Turku
Mark Fišel, University of Tartu
Kaili Müürisep, University of Tartu
Michael Rießler, Albert-Ludwigs-Universität Freiburg
Jeremy Bradley, Ludwig Maximilian University of Munich

Invited Speaker:

Mans Hulden, University of Colorado in Boulder

Table of Contents

Conference Program

Monday, January 7, 2019

8:30–9:00   *Registration*

9:00–9:15   *Opening Remarks*

9:15–10:15   *Invited Talk by Måns Huldén*

10:15–11:15   **Presentations 1**

10:15–10:45   *Data-Driven Morphological Analysis for Uralic Languages*
Miikka Silfverberg and Francis Tyers

10:45–11:15   *North Sámi morphological segmentation with low-resource semi-supervised sequence labeling*
Stig-Arne Gronroos, Sami Virpioja and Mikko Kurimo

11:15–11:45   **Poster Boasters**

11:15–11:18   *What does the Nom say? An algorithm for case disambiguation in Hungarian*
Noémi Ligeti-Nagy, Andrea Dömötör and Noémi Vadász

11:18–11:21   *A Contrastive Evaluation of Word Sense Disambiguation Systems for Finnish*
Frankie Robertson

11:21–11:24   *Elliptical Constructions in Estonian UD Treebank*
Kadri Muischnek and Liisi Torga

11:24–11:27   *FiST –towards a free Semantic Tagger of modern standard Finnish*
Kimmo Kettunen

11:27–11:30   *An OCR system for the Unified Northern Alphabet*
Niko Partanen and Michael Rießler

11:30–11:33   *ELAN as a search engine for hierarchically structured, tagged corpora*
Joshua Wilbur

Monday, January 7, 2019 (continued)

15:00   **Posters and Demos**

20:00   *Social Dinner*

Tuesday, January 8, 2019

10:00–11:00   *ACL SIGUR Business Meeting*

11:00–   **Tutorials and Hands-On Session**

Data-Driven Morphological Analysis for Uralic Languages

Miikka Silfverberg
University of Helsinki
Department of Digital Humanities
00014-FI Helsinki
miikka.silfverberg@helsinki.fi

Francis M. Tyers
Indiana University
Department of Linguistics
Bloomington, IN 47408
ftyers@indiana.edu

Abstract

This paper describes an initial set of experiments in data-driven morphological analysis of Uralic languages. The paper differs from previous work in that our work covers both lemmatization and generating ambiguous analyses. While hand-crafted finite-state transducers represent the state of the art in morphological analysis for most Uralic languages, we believe that there is a place for data-driven approaches, especially with respect to making up for lack of completeness in the lexicon. We present results for nine Uralic languages that show that, at least for basic nominal morphology for six out of the nine languages, data-driven methods can achieve an F-score of over 90%, providing results that approach those of finite-state techniques. We also compare our system to an earlier approach to Finnish data-driven morphological analysis (Silfverberg and Hulden, 2018) and show that our system outperforms this baseline.

Abstract

Tämä artikkeli esittelee kokeita uralilaisten kielten morfologisessa analyysissä koneoppimismenetelmin. Artikkeli eroaa aiemmista lähestymistavoista, koska se tuottaa lemmoja morfologisten analyysien osana ja pystyy tuottamaan useampia analyysejä monitulkintaisille sanoille. Vaikka sääntöpojaiset käsin tehdyt analysaattorit vielä selkeästi päihittävät koneoppimismenetelmin rakennetut analysaattorit, uskomme että koneoppimismenetelmillä on sija morfologisen analyysin alalla varsinkin perinteisten analysaatorien sovellusalan kasvattamisessa. Tässä artikkelissa esittelemme koetuloksia yhdeksälle uralilaiselle kielelle. Osoitamme että on mahdollista oppia analysoimaan substantiivien perusmorfologiaa 90% F1-score tasolla, mikä lähestyy olemassa olevia sääntöpohjaisten järjestelmien tasoa. Vertaamme myös järjestelmäämme aiemmin esiteltyyn koneoppimismenetelmin rakennettuun morfologiseen jäsentimeen (Silfverberg and Hulden, 2018) ja osoitamme, että meidän järjestelmämme on parempi.

1

1   Introduction

Morphological analysis is the task of producing, for a given surface form, a list of all and only the valid analyses in the language. For example, given the surface form *voisi* in Finnish, a morphological analyser must produce not only the most frequent analysis `voida+VERB|Mood=Cond|Number=Sg|Person=3` 'can they?' but also the less frequent `voida+VERB|ConNeg=Yes` 'can-NEG', or theoretical/rare ones `voi+NOUN|Number=Sg|Case=Nom|Possessor=Sg2` 'your butter'.

Morphological analysis is a cornerstone of language technology for Uralic and other morphologically complex languages, where type-to-token ratio becomes prohibitive for purely word based methods. Rule-based morphological analyzers (Beesley and Karttunen, 2003) represent the current state-of-the-art for this task. The analyses returned by such systems are typically very accurate, however, rule-based systems suffer from low coverage since novel lexical items often need to be manually added to the system.[1]

We explore the task of data-driven morphological analysis, that is, learning a model for analyzing previously unseen word forms based on a morphologically analyzed text corpus. This can help with the coverage problem encountered with rule-based analyzers. Morphological guessers based on existing rule-based analyzers represent a classical approach to extending the coverage of a rule-based analyzer. These are constructed by transforming an original analyzer typically using weighted finite-state methods (Lindén, 2009). In practice, this limits the range of data-driven models that can be applied. For example, models which do not incorporate a Markov assumption (such as RNNs) can be difficult to apply due to the inherent finite-state nature of rule-based analyzers.

Our system[2] is a neural encoder-decoder which is learned directly from morphologically analyzed text corpora. It is inspired by previous approaches to morphological analysis by Moeller et al. (2018) and Silfverberg and Hulden (2018). In contrast to these existing neural morphological analyzers, our system produces full morphological analyses: it provides both morphological tags and lemmas as output and it can return multiple alternative analyses for one input word form using beam search.

We present experiments on morphological analysis of nouns for nine Uralic languages: Estonian, Finnish, Komi-Zyrian, Moksha, Hill Mari, Meadow Mari, Erzya, North Sámi and Udmurt. We show that our system achieves roughly 90% F1-score for most of the tested languages. Additionally, we compare our system to the Finnish data-driven morphological analyzer presented by Silfverberg and Hulden (2018). As seen in Section 5, our system clearly outperforms the earlier approach.

2   Related Work

There is a strong tradition of work on rule-based morphological analysis for Uralic languages. Recent examples include Pirinen et al. (2017), Trosterud et al. (2017) and Antonsen et al. (2016), although work in the area has been going on for many years (cf. Koskenniemi (1983)). There is also a growing body of work on data-driven morphological tagging for Uralic languages, especially Finnish. Here, a system is trained to find a single contextually appropriate analysis for each token in a text. Examples of

---

[1] Although novel lexical items can cause problems for data-driven systems as well, most data-driven systems are still able to analyze any word form in principle.

[2] Code available at `https://github.com/mpsilfve/morphnet`.

work exploring morphological tagging for Finnish include Kanerva et al. (2018) and Silfverberg et al. (2015). However, work on full data-driven morphological analysis, where the task is to return all and only the valid analyses for each token irrespective of sentence context, is almost non-existent for Uralic languages. The only system known to the authors is the recent neural analyzer for Finnish presented by Silfverberg and Hulden (2018). The system first encodes an input word form into a vector representation using an LSTM encoder. It then applies one binary logistic classifier conditioned on this vector representation for each morphological tag (for example NOUN|Number=Sg|Case=Nom). The classifier is used to determine if the tag is a valid analysis for the given input word form. Similarly to Silfverberg and Hulden (2018), our system is also a neural morphological analyzer but unlike Silfverberg and Hulden (2018) we incorporate lemmatization. Moreover, the design of our system considerably differs from their system as explained below in Section 3.

The lack of work on morphological analysis for Uralic languages is unsurprising because the field of data-driven morphological analysis in general remains underexplored at the present time. Classically, morphological analyzers have been extended using morphological guessers (Lindén, 2009), however, the premise for such work is quite different—An existing analyzer is modified to analyze unknown word forms based on orthographically similar known word forms. In contrast, we explore a setting, where the starting point is a morphologically analyzed corpus and the aim is to learn a model for analyzing unseen text.

Outside of the domain of Uralic languages, Nicolai and Kondrak (2017) frame morphological analysis as a discriminative string transduction task. They present experiments on Dutch, English, German and Spanish. In contrast to Nicolai and Kondrak (2017), Moeller et al. (2018) use a neural encoder-decoder system for morphological analysis of Arapaho verbs. Their system returns both lemmas and morphological tags but it cannot handle ambiguous analyses in general.[3] Our work is inspired by the neural encoder-decoder approach presented by Moeller et al. (2018) but we do handle unrestricted ambiguity.

In contrast to data-driven morphological analysis, data-driven morphological generation has received a great deal of attention lately due to several shared tasks organized by CoNLL and SIGMORPHON (Cotterell et al., 2016, 2017, 2018). The most successful approaches (Kann and Schütze, 2016; Bergmanis et al., 2017; Makarov et al., 2017; Makarov and Clematide, 2018) to the generation task involve different flavors of the neural encoder-decoder model. Therefore, we opted for applying it in our morphological analyzer.

3 Model

This section presents the encoder-decoder model used in the experiments.

3.1 An Encoder-Decoder Model for Morphological Analysis

Following Moeller et al. (2018), we formulate morphological analysis as a character-level string transduction task and use an LSTM (Hochreiter and Schmidhuber, 1997) encoder-decoder model with attention (Bahdanau et al., 2014) for performing the string transduction. To this end, we train our model to translate input word forms

---

[3] The system can handle ambiguity in limited cases by using underspecified tags. For example an ambiguity between singular and dual number could be expressed using a tag [SG/DPL].

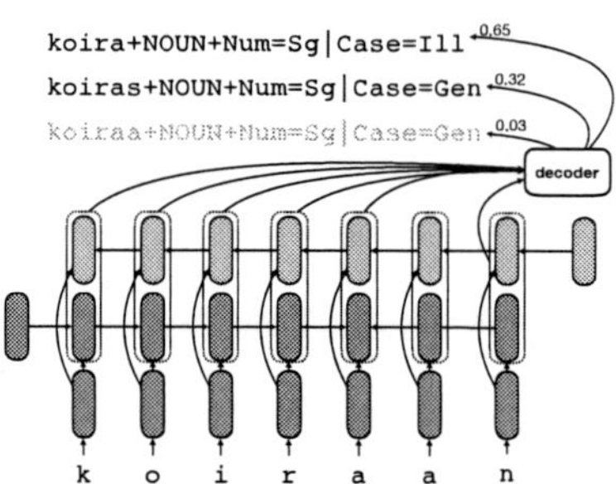

Figure 1: We use a bidirectional LSTM encoder for encoding an input word form into forward and backward states (pink and green bars) one character at a time. We then use an attentional LSTM decoder for generating output analyses one symbol at a time. We return the least number of most probable analyses whose combined mass is greater than a threshold p. In this example, for $p = 0.9$, the analyzer would return `koira+NOUN+Num=Sg|Case=Ill` and `koiras+NOUN+Num=Sg|Case=Gen` whose combined probability mass is 0.97, given the input form `koiraan`.

like *koiraan* (singular illative for *koira* 'dog' or singular genitive for *koiras* 'male' in Finnish) into a set of output analyses:

`koira+NOUN+Number=Singular|Case=Ill`
`koiras+NOUN+Number=Singular|Case=Gen`

Each analysis consists of a lemma (`koira` 'dog'), a part-of-speech (POS) tag (`NOUN`) and a morphosyntactic description (MSD) (`Number=Singular|Case=Gen`). The procedure is illustrated in Figure 1.

Above, we presented an example from Finnish, *voisi*, which can be both an inflected form of a noun and an inflected form of a verb. This shows that a word form may have multiple valid morphological analyses with different lemmas, POS tags and MSDs. Therefore, our model needs to be able to generate multiple output analyses given an input word form. We accomplish this by extracting several output candidates from the model using beam search and selecting the most probable candidates as model outputs. The number of outputs is controlled by a probability threshold hyperparameter p. We extract the least number of top scoring candidates whose combined probability mass is greater than p. Additionally, we restrict the maximal number of output candidates using a single hyperparameter N. The hyperparamaters p and N are tuned on the development data.

3.2 Implementation Details

We implement our LSTM encoder-decoder model using the OpenNMT neural machine translation toolkit (Klein et al., 2017). We use 500-dimensional character and tag embeddings for input and output characters as well as POS and MSD tags. These are processed by a 2-layer bidirectional LSTM encoder with hidden state size 500. Encoder representations are fed into a 2-layer LSTM decoder with hidden state size 500. During inference, we use beam search with beam width 10.

When training, we use a batch size of 64 and train for 10,000 steps where one step corresponds to updating on a single mini-batch. Model parameters are optimized using the Adam optimization algorithm (Kingma and Ba, 2014).

4 Data

We use two datasets in the experiments. The first dataset is created by using the morphological transducers from Giellatekno to analyze wordforms in a frequency list from Uralic Wikipedias. The second one is created using data from the Turku Dependency Treebank. This dataset was originally presented by Silfverberg and Hulden (2018). We explicitly do not use any data from the Unimorph project.

4.1 Uralic Wikipedia Data

We applied the models to nine Uralic languages: Erzya (myv), Estonian (est), Finnish (fin), Komi-Zyrian (kpv), Hill Mari (mhr), Meadow Mari (mrj), Moksha (mdf), North Sámi (sme) and Udmurt (udm). These languages were chosen as they had both a moderately-sized free and open text corpus (Wikipedia) and an existing free/open-source morphological analyser from the Giellatekno infrastructure (Moshagen et al., 2014). Hungarian (hun) was omitted as there was no functional analyser in the Giellatekno infrastructure, while the remainder of the Sámi languages (i.e. South (sma), Lule (smj), Inari (smn), ...) and Kven (fkv) were left out as they have as yet no Wikipedia. The remainder of the Uralic languages have neither wide-coverage analyser nor Wikipedia.

The data used in the experiments consisted of tab separated files with five columns: language code, surface form, lemma, part-of-speech and list of morphological tags expressed as Feature=Value pairs (see Figure 2). Both the parts of speech and the morphological tags broadly follow the conventions of the Universal Dependencies project (Nivre et al., 2016), with one exception: The tags are given in the same order they appear in the original morphological analyses (largely morpheme order) as opposed to in alphabetical order by feature name.

Each file was generated as follows: First we downloaded the relevant Wikipedia dump[4] and extracted the text using `WikiExtractor`.[5] This gave us a plain-text corpus of the language in question. We then used the morphological transducers from Giellatekno (Moshagen et al., 2014) to both tokenize and analyze the text. This was then made into a frequency list using standard Unix utilities. We then extracted only the forms with noun analyses and removed all non-noun analyses, along with noun analyses that included numerals, abbreviations, acronyms, spelling errors or dialectal forms. All derived and compound analyses were also removed, in addition to analyses that included clitics (e.g. Finnish *-kään, -kaan*). The exclusion of these phenomena makes the task less applicable to a real-world setting, but at the same time makes it tractable for initial experiments such as the ones presented in this paper.

After creating the frequency list, we converted the format of the analyses by means of a simple lookup table (e.g. +Gen $\rightarrow$ Case=Gen). An example from the training data of North Sámi can be found in Figure 2 and details about the size of the training data for each of the languages can be found in Table 1.

All data sets were randomly split into 80% training data, 10% development data and 10% test data. The splits are disjoint in the sense that the training and development set never include word forms seen in the test set. They may, however, include other inflected forms of lemmas that do occur in the test set.

---

[4] Available from `https://dumps.wikimedia.org`.
[5] `https://github.com/apertium/WikiExtractor`

sme	čuđiid	čuhti	NOUN	Number=Plur|Case=Acc
sme	čuđiid	čuhti	NOUN	Number=Plur|Case=Gen
sme	čuđiid	čuohti	NOUN	Number=Plur|Case=Acc
sme	čuđiid	čuohti	NOUN	Number=Plur|Case=Gen
sme	čuđiid	čuđđi	NOUN	Number=Plur|Case=Acc
sme	čuđiid	čuđđi	NOUN	Number=Plur|Case=Gen

Figure 2: Example from the North Sámi (sme) training data for the forms of the word *čuđiid*, which could be a form of *čuhti* 'Chud', *čuohti* 'hundred' or *čuđđi* 'enemy'.

Language	Code	Data			Ambig.	Lemmas	Tags	MSDs	Th. forms
		train	dev	test					
Estonian	est	87930	10991	10991	1.11	17814	16	26	32
Finnish	fin	153603	19200	19200	1.17	44644	21	142	180
Komi-Zyrian	kpv	9413	1176	1176	1.44	3602	25	113	312
Moksha	mdf	3456	431	431	1.16	1479	23	66	156
Hill Mari	mhr	7789	973	973	1.11	4650	17	20	120
Meadow Mari	mrj	6885	860	860	1.11	2923	13	55	108
Erzya	myv	11384	1423	1423	1.50	5204	23	90	288
North Sámi	sme	9328	1166	1166	1.90	6032	16	54	126
Udmurt	udm	6344	792	792	1.23	3115	23	100	150

Table 1: Quantitative description of the Uralic Wikipedia datasets. For each language, we give its ISO 639-3 code (**Code**), the number of unique `train`, `dev` and `test` word forms, as well as, the average number of analyses per word form (**Ambig.**), the number of unique lemmas (**Lemmas**), the number of unique tags such as `NOUN` and `Number=Sing` (**Tags**) and the number of unique morphosyntactic descriptions such as `NOUN|Number=Sing|Case=Nom` (**MSDs**) in the dataset. In addition we provide an approximate number of possible theoretical forms in the noun paradigm for each language (**Th. forms**). Note that both the **Ambig.** and **Th. forms** columns give the theoretical maximum only for the morphological features of number, case and possession and does not include forms generated by productive derivation or addition of clitics.

| Language | Code | Data | | | Ambig. | Lemmas | Tags | MSDs | Th. forms |
		train	dev	test					
Finnish UD	—	162827	18311	21070	1.80	—	137	2452	—

Table 2: Quantitative description of the Finnish treebank dataset. We give the number of unique `train`, `dev` and `test` word forms, as well as, the average number of analyses per word form (**Ambig.**), the number of unique lemmas (**Lemmas**), the number of unique tags such as `NOUN` and `Number=Sing` (**Tags**) and the number of unique morphosyntactic descriptions such as `NOUN|Number=Sing|Case=Nom` (**MSDs**).

4.2 Finnish Treebank Data

Our second dataset was presented by Silfverberg and Hulden (2018). It is the Finnish part of the Universal Dependencies treebank v1 (Pyysalo et al., 2015) which has been analyzed using the OMorFi morphological analyzer (Pirinen et al., 2017). We used the splits into training, development and test sets provided by Silfverberg and Hulden (2018).

In contrast to the Uralic Wikipedia datasets, which is a type-level resource consisting of analyses for unique word forms, the Finnish treebank data is a token-level resource consisting of morphologically analyzed running text. Therefore, the same word form can occur multiple times in the dataset. This means that the training, development and test sets are not disjoint which makes the task somewhat easier. However, the dataset contains word forms from all Finnish word classes. It also contains derivations and clitics. This, in turn, makes it more versatile than the Uralic Wikipedia data. The dataset is described in Table 2.

5   Experiments and Results

We present results for two experiments. In the first experiment, we train analyzers for the Uralic Wikipedia data presented in Section 4. In the second experiment, we train an analyzer on the Finnish Treebank data used by Silfverberg and Hulden (2018) and compare our system to theirs.

Because an input word form can have several alternative analyses, we present results for precision, recall and F1-score on analyses. These are defined with regard to the quantities *true positives* (tp) which is the number of gold standard analyses that our system recovered, *false positives* (fp) which is the number of incorrect analyses that our system produced and *false negatives* (fn) which is the number of gold standard analyses which our system was unable to recover. Definitions for recall, precision and F1-score are given below:

$$\text{Recall} = \tfrac{tp}{tp+fn}, \text{Precision} = \tfrac{tp}{tp+fp} \text{ and F1-score} = 2 \cdot \tfrac{\text{Recall}\cdot\text{Precision}}{\text{Recall}+\text{Precision}}$$

5.1 Experiment on Uralic Wikipedia Data

We present three different evaluations of the results. Table 3 shows results on complete analyses including the lemma, POS tag and MSD. The results are above 90% F1-score for most languages. The exception to this are Finnish and Northern Sámi where results fall below 90%. Recall is higher than precision for most languages with the exception of Northern Sámi and Komi-Zyrian. Our model achieves the best F1-score for Udmurt (95.09%)

Language	Recall	Precision	F1-Score
est	92.97	89.26	91.08
fin	89.30	87.37	88.32
kpv	88.13	92.14	90.09
mdf	93.91	90.78	92.32
mhr	89.98	89.48	89.73
mrj	93.95	91.65	92.78
myv	91.19	89.79	90.48
sme	85.95	87.12	86.53
udm	96.41	93.81	95.09

Table 3: Results for full analyses (lemma + POS + MSD) on the Uralic Wikipedia data.

Language	Recall	Precision	F1-Score
est	95.69	91.06	93.32
fin	93.41	87.72	90.48
kpv	96.51	92.81	94.62
mdf	95.15	91.96	93.53
mhr	90.69	89.84	90.26
mrj	93.71	91.25	92.46
myv	95.40	90.91	93.10
sme	91.47	87.45	89.42
udm	97.26	94.32	95.77

Table 4: Results for lemmas on the Uralic Wikipedia data.

Language	Recall	Precision	F1-Score
est	95.21	94.04	94.62
fin	93.62	95.11	94.36
kpv	90.43	95.10	92.70
mdf	96.95	95.78	96.36
mhr	96.28	95.32	95.80
mrj	97.65	96.72	97.18
myv	94.62	94.39	94.50
sme	92.12	94.30	93.20
udm	97.84	96.25	97.03

Table 5: Results for tags (POS + MSD) on the Uralic Wikipedia data.

Error category	Count	% Total
1. Loan words in *-ue*, *-ье* or *-ья*	18	18.6
2. Other Russian loan word mistake	2	2.1
3. Plural morpheme part of stem	6	6.2
4. Loan words ending in *ь*	10	9.7
5. Overenthusiastic lemmatization	2	2.1
6. Underenthusiastic lemmatization	3	3.1
7. Impossible lemma	4	4.1
8. Words containing hyphen	6	6.2
9. Other	46	47.4
Total:	97	100.0

Table 6: Qualitative evaluation of the errors in the output of the system for Udmurt. The majority of errors can be classified with loan words from Russian making a good proportion.

Table 4 shows results for plain lemmas without POS or MSD. Here all languages except Northern Sámi receive F1-score over 90% and, as in the case of full analyses, recall is again higher than precision for all languages. For lemmas, the best F1-score is again attained on Udmurt (95.77%)

The final evaluation is shown in Table 5. This table shows results for POS and MSD tag. Overall results here are higher than for the lemma or full analysis: in excess of 92% for all languages. Similarly as in the case of full analyses and lemmas, our model again delivers the best F1-score for Udmurt (97.03%).

For the Udmurt data, given that only 97 analyses were incorrect we were able to do a partial qualitative evaluation shown in Table 6. We looked at all the analyses and categorised them into nine error classes: (1) Russian loan words ending in *-ue*, *-ье* or *-ья* that do not receive the right lemma; (2) Other mistakes in loan words from Russian; (3) Plural morpheme is considered part of the stem; (4) Words ending in soft sign *-ь* that were mislemmatized; (5) Overenthusiastic lemmatization — i.e. the system produced a lemma that did not exist in the data; (6) Under enthusiastic lemmatization — i.e. a lemma in the data was not produced by the system, (7) Impossible lemma — i.e. the singular nominative did not have the same form as the lemma; (8) Words with hyphen in; (9) Other.

A typical error of the first type can be found in the lemmatization of the word *путешествие* 'travel', the lemma given by the network was **путешestви*,[6] similarly **междометия* was given for *междометие* 'interjection'. The second error class included errors like the lemma **республик* for the form *республиказы* 'to/in our republic'. The system also sometimes generated lemmas in the plural form (third error type), for example *бурдъёсаз* 'on/to its wings' generated two correct analyses with the lemma *бурд* 'wing' and one incorrect with the lemma *бурдъёс* 'wings'. For errors of the fourth type we can consider the form *пристане* 'wharf-ɪʟʟ' which has the lemma *пристань* 'wharf' (as in Russian), but for which the system produced both **пристан* and **пристане*, neither of which exist as lemmas in Udmurt or Russian.

For the fifth type we have *спортэ* giving the lemma **спор*[7] instead of *спорт* 'sport'

---

[6]According to some Udmurt authors this is the preferred nominative singular form, but we count it as an error as the analyser we based the gold standard on uses *путешествие* as the lemma.

[7]Note that this could potentially be a loan of *спор* 'dispute, argument' from Russian, but as it was not in the gold standard counted it as an error.

System	Recall	Precision	F1-Score
Our System	93.45	96.47	94.94
Silfverberg and Hulden (2018)	89.66	94.03	91.79

Table 7: Comparison between our system and Silfverberg and Hulden (2018). We present results for tags only (POS + MSD) since the system by Silfverberg and Hulden (2018) does not lemmatize.

and sixth type *берлань* we get the noun lemma *берлань* instead of *бер* 'back-APPROX'. Note that there is a much more frequent reading of *берлань* as an adverb 'ago, back' (rus. *назад*), but as this was not a nominal reading it was excluded from the experiments.

For the seventh type consider the word *пияш* 'boy, lad' which generated nominative singular analyses with the lemmas *пи* 'son' and **пиеш*.

The system was also confused by compound words written with a hyphen (error type 8). Three out of seven of these had various different kinds of errors, for example losing part of the compound *ваньмыз-ӧвӧлэз* → *ваньмыз*, making compound-internal vowel changes *тодон-эскеронъя* → **тодон-ӧскерон* or considering an affix part of the lemma *музей-коркан* 'village-house museum' → *музей-коркан*.

While the 'Other' class makes up almost half of the data, we can see that over half of the errors should in principle be able to be solved with simply adding more data. That is, the model has not received enough information about how Russian loan words, or words with hyphens work as they compose a small fraction of the data.

5.2   Experiment on Finnish Treebank Data

In our second experiment, we compare our system against the neural morphological analyzer proposed by Silfverberg and Hulden (2018). We trained a morphological analyzer on the Finnish treebank training data used by Silfverberg and Hulden (2018) and report results on their test data. Similarly to Silfverberg and Hulden (2018), we also return the set of analyses seen in the training set for those test word forms which were seen in the training data.

Table 7 shows results on the Finnish treebank dataset. We only report results for precision, recall and F1-score with regard to tags (POS + MSD) because the system by Silfverberg and Hulden (2018) is not capable of lemmatization. As Table 7 shows, our system clearly outperforms the system proposed by Silfverberg and Hulden (2018) with regard to F1-Score on tags. Results on the Finnish treebank data are also far better than results on the Finnish Wikipedia data.

6   Discussion and Conclusions

On the Uralic Wikipedia data, F1-score for full analyses ranges from 86% for Northern Sámi to 95% for Udmurt with most languages receiving an F1-score around 90%. The weaker performance on Northern Sámi is understandable since the language is known to have an intricate system of morphophonological alternations (see for example the description in Sammallahti (1998)).

Our system clearly outperforms the system by Silfverberg and Hulden (2018) on the Finnish Wikipedia data. In contrast to the Uralic Wikipedia data, the Finnish Treebank dataset, represents continuous text with word forms belonging to a mix of word classes. It also covers clitics and derivations which are missing from the Uralic Wikipedia dataset.[8] Therefore, this experiment indicates that our system is also applicable to analysis of running text for Finnish.

The overall better performance on the Finnish Treebank dataset is explained by the fact that it is a token-level resource where frequent words, which are easy to analyze, can substantially improve performance.

In contrast to what Silfverberg and Hulden (2018) found, our results on the Finnish Wikipedia data indicate that recall is higher than precision for most languages. However, on the Finnish treebank data, we also get higher precision than recall although our system delivers more balanced recall and precision than the system proposed by Silfverberg and Hulden (2018). It is not immediately clear, why it is advantageous to prefer precision over recall but this may be related to the large number of possible POS + MSD combinations in the Finnish Treebank dataset. Many of these could potentially be applicable judging purely on the basis of the orthographical form of a particular word form but only a small number of the combinations will actually result in a valid analysis. Therefore, it may be advantageous to return a more restricted set of highly likely analyses.

As there are other treebanks for Uralic languages, i.e. Hungarian (Vincze et al., 2010), Estonian (Muischnek et al., 2016), North Sámi (Sheyanova and Tyers, 2017) and Erzya (Rueter and Tyers, 2018), we would like to run the equivalent experiments as on the Finnish treebank.

As explained in Section 3, we return analyses based on probability mass. It could be better to predict how many forms are going to be included based on the input word form. For example, if the input word form is markedly different than most forms seen in the training data, the model may assign lower confidence to output analyses. Applying a probability mass threshold in this case may result in a very large number of outputs.

Large training sets are available for only a few Uralic languages, Therefore, we should explore using a hard attention model similar to Makarov and Clematide (2018) in our encoder-decoder. The results from CoNLL SIGMORPHON shared tasks (Cotterell et al., 2018) show that a hard attention model can be a far stronger learner in a low-resource setting.

We presented a data driven morphological analyzer and evaluated its performance on morphological analysis of nouns for nine Uralic languages. Moreover, we evaluated the performance on Finnish running text. Our system delivers encouraging results. F1-score for analysis of nouns is around 90% for most of our languages. In addition, our system substantially improves upon the baseline presented by Silfverberg and Hulden (2018). In future work, we need to explore hard attention models for morphological analysis since these deliver strong performance in low-resource settings which are typical for Uralic languages. Moreover, we need to explore more principled ways to handle ambiguous analyses.

---

[8] Recall that clitics and derivations are missing as they were removed during processing of the Wikipedia data (§4) to make the data easier to process and more comparable cross-linguistically, as clitics are treated differently in the different analysers.

Acknowledgements

We wish to thank the anonymous reviewers for their insightful comments. The first author has received funding from the European Research Council (ERC) under the European Union's Horizon 2020 research and innovation programme (grant agreement No 771113).

References

Lene Antonsen, Trond Trosterud, Marja-Liisa Olthuis, and Erika Sarivaara. 2016. Modelling the Inari Saami morphophonology as a finite state transducer. In *The Second International Workshop on Computational Linguistics for Uralic Languages, Szeged, January 2016*.

Dzmitry Bahdanau, Kyunghyun Cho, and Yoshua Bengio. 2014. Neural machine translation by jointly learning to align and translate. *CoRR* abs/1409.0473. http://arxiv.org/abs/1409.0473.

Kenneth R Beesley and Lauri Karttunen. 2003. *Finite state morphology*. CSLI publications.

Toms Bergmanis, Katharina Kann, Hinrich Schütze, and Sharon Goldwater. 2017. Training data augmentation for low-resource morphological inflection. In *Proceedings of the CoNLL SIGMORPHON 2017 Shared Task: Universal Morphological Reinflection*. Association for Computational Linguistics, pages 31–39. https://doi.org/10.18653/v1/K17-2002.

Ryan Cotterell, Christo Kirov, John Sylak-Glassman, Géraldine Walther, Ekaterina Vylomova, Arya D McCarthy, Katharina Kann, Sebastian Mielke, Garrett Nicolai, Miikka Silfverberg, et al. 2018. The CoNLL–SIGMORPHON 2018 shared task: Universal morphological reinflection. *arXiv preprint arXiv:1810.07125* .

Ryan Cotterell, Christo Kirov, John Sylak-Glassman, Géraldine Walther, Ekaterina Vylomova, Patrick Xia, Manaal Faruqui, Sandra Kübler, David Yarowsky, Jason Eisner, et al. 2017. CoNLL-SIGMORPHON 2017 shared task: Universal morphological reinflection in 52 languages. *arXiv preprint arXiv:1706.09031* .

Ryan Cotterell, Christo Kirov, John Sylak-Glassman, David Yarowsky, Jason Eisner, and Mans Hulden. 2016. The SIGMORPHON 2016 shared task—morphological reinflection. In *Proceedings of the 14th SIGMORPHON Workshop on Computational Research in Phonetics, Phonology, and Morphology*. pages 10–22.

Sepp Hochreiter and Jürgen Schmidhuber. 1997. Long short-term memory. *Neural computation* 9:1735–80. https://doi.org/10.1162/neco.1997.9.8.1735.

Jenna Kanerva, Filip Ginter, Niko Miekka, Akseli Leino, and Tapio Salakoski. 2018. Turku neural parser pipeline: An end-to-end system for the CoNLL 2018 shared task. In *Proceedings of the CoNLL 2018 Shared Task: Multilingual Parsing from Raw Text to Universal Dependencies*. Association for Computational Linguistics, Brussels, Belgium, pages 133–142. http://www.aclweb.org/anthology/K18-2013.

Katharina Kann and Hinrich Schütze. 2016. MED: The LMU system for the SIG-MORPHON 2016 shared task on morphological reinflection. In *Proceedings of the 14th SIGMORPHON Workshop on Computational Research in Phonetics, Phonology, and Morphology*. Association for Computational Linguistics, pages 62–70. https://doi.org/10.18653/v1/W16-2010.

Diederik P. Kingma and Jimmy Ba. 2014. Adam: A method for stochastic optimization. *CoRR* abs/1412.6980. http://arxiv.org/abs/1412.6980.

G. Klein, Y. Kim, Y. Deng, J. Senellart, and A. M. Rush. 2017. OpenNMT: Open-Source Toolkit for Neural Machine Translation. *ArXiv e-prints* .

Kimmo Koskenniemi. 1983. Two-level model for morphological analysis. In *IJCAI*. volume 83, pages 683–685.

Krister Lindén. 2009. Guessers for finite-state transducer lexicons. In *Proceedings of the 10th International Conference on Computational Linguistics and Intelligent Text Processing*. Springer-Verlag, Berlin, Heidelberg, CICLing '09, pages 158–169.

Peter Makarov and Simon Clematide. 2018. UZH at CoNLL-SIGMORPHON 2018 shared task on universal morphological reinflection. *Proceedings of the CoNLL SIG-MORPHON 2018 Shared Task: Universal Morphological Reinflection* pages 69–75.

Peter Makarov, Tatiana Ruzsics, and Simon Clematide. 2017. Align and copy: UZH at SIGMORPHON 2017 shared task for morphological reinflection. In *Proceedings of the CoNLL SIGMORPHON 2017 Shared Task: Universal Morphological Reinflection*. Association for Computational Linguistics, pages 49–57. https://doi.org/10.18653/v1/K17-2004.

Sarah Moeller, Ghazaleh Kazeminejad, Andrew Cowell, and Mans Hulden. 2018. A neural morphological analyzer for Arapaho verbs learned from a finite state transducer. In *Proceedings of the Workshop on Computational Modeling of Polysynthetic Languages*. pages 12–20.

Sjur Moshagen, Jack Rueter, Tommi Pirinen, Trond Trosterud, and Francis M. Tyers. 2014. Open-source infrastructures for collaborative work on under-resourced languages. In *Proceedings of the 1st Workshop on Collaboration and Computing for Under-Resourced Languages in the Linked Open Data Era (CCURL-2014)*. pages 71–77.

Kadri Muischnek, Kaili Müürisep, and Tiina Puolakainen. 2016. Estonian Dependency Treebank: from Constraint Grammar tagset to Universal Dependencies. In *Proceedings of LREC 2016*.

Garrett Nicolai and Grzegorz Kondrak. 2017. Morphological analysis without expert annotation. In *Proceedings of the 15th Conference of the European Chapter of the Association for Computational Linguistics: Volume 2, Short Papers*. volume 2, pages 211–216.

Joakim Nivre, Marie-Catherine de Marneffe, Filip Ginter, Yoav Goldberg, Jan Hajič, Chris Manning, Ryan McDonald, Slav Petrov, Sampo Pyysalo, Natalia Silveira, Reut Tsarfaty, and Dan Zeman. 2016. Universal Dependencies v1: A Multilingual Treebank Collection. In *Proceedings of Language Resources and Evaluation Conference (LREC'16)*.

Tommi A Pirinen, Inari Listenmaa, Ryan Johnson, Francis M. Tyers, and Juha Kuokkala. 2017. Open morphology of Finnish. LINDAT/CLARIN digital library at the Institute of Formal and Applied Linguistics, Charles University. http://hdl.handle.net/11372/LRT-1992.

Sampo Pyysalo, Jenna Kanerva, Anna Missilä, Veronika Laippala, and Filip Ginter. 2015. Universal Dependencies for Finnish. In *NODALIDA*.

Jack Rueter and Francis M. Tyers. 2018. Towards an open-source universal-dependency treebank for Erzya. In *Proceedings of the 4th International Workshop for Computational Linguistics for Uralic Languages*. pages 108–120.

Pekka Sammallahti. 1998. Saamic. In Daniel Abondolo, editor, *The Uralic Languages*, Routledge.

Mariya Sheyanova and Francis M. Tyers. 2017. Annotation schemes in North Sámi dependency parsing. In *Proceedings of the 3rd International Workshop for Computational Linguistics of Uralic Languages*. pages 66–75.

Miikka Silfverberg and Mans Hulden. 2018. Initial experiments in data-driven morphological analysis for Finnish. In *Proceedings of the Fourth International Workshop on Computatinal Linguistics of Uralic Languages*. pages 98–105.

Miikka Silfverberg, Teemu Ruokolainen, Krister Lindén, and Mikko Kurimo. 2015. Finnpos: an open-source morphological tagging and lemmatization toolkit for finnish. *Language Resources and Evaluation* 50. https://doi.org/10.1007/s10579-015-9326-3.

Sindre Reino Trosterud, Trond Trosterud, Anna-Kaisa Räisänen, Leena Niiranen, Mervi Haavisto, and Kaisa Maliniemi. 2017. A morphological analyser for kven. In *Proceedings of the Third Workshop on Computational Linguistics for Uralic Languages*. Association for Computational Linguistics, pages 76–88. https://doi.org/10.18653/v1/W17-0608.

Veronika Vincze, Dóra Szauter, Attila Almási, György Móra, Zoltán Alexin, and János Csirik. 2010. Hungarian Dependency Treebank. In *Proceedings of the Seventh Conference on International Language Resources and Evaluation (LREC'10)*.

North Sámi morphological segmentation with low-resource semi-supervised sequence labeling

Stig-Arne Grönroos
stig-arne.gronroos@aalto.fi
Aalto University, Finland

Sami Virpioja
sami.virpioja@aalto.fi
Aalto University, Finland
Utopia Analytics, Finland

Mikko Kurimo
mikko.kurimo@aalto.fi
Aalto University, Finland

December 14, 2018

Abstract

Semi-supervised sequence labeling is an effective way to train a low-resource morphological segmentation system. We show that a feature set augmentation approach, which combines the strengths of generative and discriminative models, is suitable both for graphical models like conditional random field (CRF) and sequence-to-sequence neural models. We perform a comparative evaluation between three existing and one novel semi-supervised segmentation methods. All four systems are language-independent and have open-source implementations. We improve on previous best results for North Sámi morphological segmentation. We see a relative improvement in morph boundary F_1-score of 8.6% compared to using the generative Morfessor FlatCat model directly and 2.4% compared to a seq2seq baseline. Our neural sequence tagging system reaches almost the same performance as the CRF topline.

Tiivistelmä

Puoliohjattu sekvenssiluokitus on tehokas tapa opettaa morfologinen pilkontajärjestelmä kielelle, jolle on saatavilla niukasti lingvistisiä resursseja. Osoitamme, että generatiivisen mallin tuottamien piirteiden käyttäminen soveltuu paitsi graafisille malleille kuten ehdollinen satunnaiskenttä (CRF), myös sekvenssistäsekvenssiin (seq2seq) -neuroverkkomalleille. Vertailemme kolmea olemassaolevaa ja yhtä uutta puoliohjattua menetelmää. Kaikki menetelmät ovat kieliriippumattomia, ja niille on avoimen lähdekoodin toteutus. Parannamme aikaisempia tuloksia pohjoissaamen morfologisen pilkonnan tehtävässä. Suhteelliset parannukset morfirajojen osumien F_1-mittaan ovat 8.6% verrattuna generatiiviseen Morfessor FlatCat -malliin ja 2.4% verrattuna seq2seq-verrokkimalliin. Ehdottamamme uusi neuroverkkomalli saavuttaa lähes saman tason kuin paras CRF-malli.

Proceedings of the fifth Workshop on Computational Linguistics for Uralic Languages, pages 15–26,
Tartu, Estonia, January 7 - January 8, 2019.

1 Introduction

Subword models have enjoyed recent success in many natural language processing (NLP) tasks, such as machine translation (Sennrich et al., 2015) and automatic speech recognition (Smit et al., 2017). Uralic languages have rich morphological structure, making morphological segmentation particularly useful for these languages. While rule-based morphological segmentation systems can achieve high quality, the large amount of human effort needed makes the approach problematic for low-resource languages. As a fast, cheap and effective alternative, data-driven segmentation can be learned based on a very small amount of human annotator effort. Using active learning, as little as some hundreds of annotated word types can be enough (Grönroos et al., 2016).

Adopting neural methods has lead to a large performance gain for many NLP tasks. However, neural networks are typically data-hungry, reducing their applicability to low-resource languages. Most research has focused on high-resource languages and large data sets, while the search for new approaches to make neural methods applicable to small data has only recently gained attention. For example, the workshop Deep Learning Approaches for Low-Resource NLP (DeepLo[1]) was arranged first time in the year of writing. Neural methods have met with success in high-resource morphological segmentation (e.g. Wang et al., 2016). We are interested to see if data-hungry neural network models are applicable to segmentation in low-resource settings, in this case for the Uralic language North Sámi.

Neural sequence-to-sequence (seq2seq) models are a very versatile tool for NLP, and are used in state of the art methods for a wide variety of tasks, such as text summarization (Nallapati et al., 2016) and speech synthesis (Wang et al., 2017). Seq2seq methods are easy to apply, as you can often take e.g. existing neural machine translation software and train it with appropriately preprocessed data. Kann et al. (2018) apply the seq2seq model for low-resource morphological segmentation.

However, arbitrary length sequence-to-sequence transduction is not the optimal formulation for the task of morphological surface segmentation. We return to formulating it as a a sequence tagging problem instead, and show that this can be implemented with minor modifications to an open source translation system.

Moreover, we show that the semi-supervised training approach of Ruokolainen et al. (2014) using feature set augmentation can also be applied to neural networks to effectively leverage large unannotated data.

2 Morphological processing tasks

There are several related morphological tasks that can be described as mapping from one sequence to another. Morphological segmentation is the task of splitting words into morphemes, meaning-bearing sub-word units. In morphological *surface* segmentation, the word w is segmented into a sequence of surface morphs, substrings whose concatenation is the word w.

$$\text{e.g.} \quad \textit{achievability} \mapsto \textit{achiev} \circ \textit{abil} \circ \textit{ity}$$

Canonical morphological segmentation (Kann et al., 2016) instead yields a sequence of standardized segments. The aim is to undo morphological processes that result in

---

[1] https://sites.google.com/view/deeplo18/home

allomorphs, i.e. different surface morphs corresponding to the same meaning.

$$w \mapsto y; \quad w \in \Sigma^*, y \in (\Sigma \cup \{\circ\})^*$$

e.g. $\quad achievability \mapsto achieve \circ able \circ ity$

where Σ is the alphabet of the language, and $\circ$ is the boundary marker.

Morphological analysis yields the lemma and tags representing the morphological properties of a word.

$$w \mapsto yt; \quad w, y \in \Sigma^*, t \in \tau^*$$

e.g. $\quad took \mapsto take$ PAST

where τ is the set of morphological tags.

Two related morphological tasks are reinflection and lemmatization. In *morphological reinflection* (see e.g. Cotterell et al., 2016), one or more inflected forms are given to identify the lexeme, together with the tags identifying the desired inflection. The task is to produce the correctly inflected surface form of the lexeme.

$$wt \mapsto y; \quad w, y \in \Sigma^*, t \in \tau^*$$

e.g. $\quad taken$ PAST $\mapsto took$

In *lemmatization*, the input is an inflected form and the output is the lemma.

$$w \mapsto y; \quad w, y \in \Sigma^*$$

e.g. $\quad better \mapsto good$

Morphological surface segmentation can be formulated in the same way as canonical segmentation, by just allowing the mapping to canonical segments to be the identity. However, this formulation fails to capture the fact that the segments must concatenate back to the surface form. The model is allowed to predict any symbol from its output vocabulary, although only two symbols are valid at any given timestep: the boundary symbol or the actual next character. If the labeled set for supervised training is small, the model may struggle with learning to copy the correct characters. Kann et al. (2018) address this problem by a multi-task training approach where the auxiliary task consists of reconstructing strings in a sequence auto-encoder setting. The strings to be reconstructed can be actual words or even random noise.

Surface segmentation can alternatively be formulated as structured classification

$$w \mapsto y; \quad w \in \Sigma^k, y \in \Omega^k, k \in \mathbb{N}$$

e.g. $\quad uses \mapsto BMES$

where Ω is the segmentation tag set. Note that there is no need to generate characters from the original alphabet, instead a small tag set Ω is used. The fact that the sequence of boundary decisions is of the same length k as the input has also been made explicit.

Different tag sets Ω can be used for segmentation. The minimal sets only include two labels: BM/ME (used e.g. by Green and DeNero, 2012). Either the beginning (B) or end (E) of segments is distinguished from non-boundary time-steps in the middle (M). A more fine-grained approach BMES[2] (used e.g. by Ruokolainen et al., 2014) uses

---

[2]Also known as BIES, where I stands for internal.

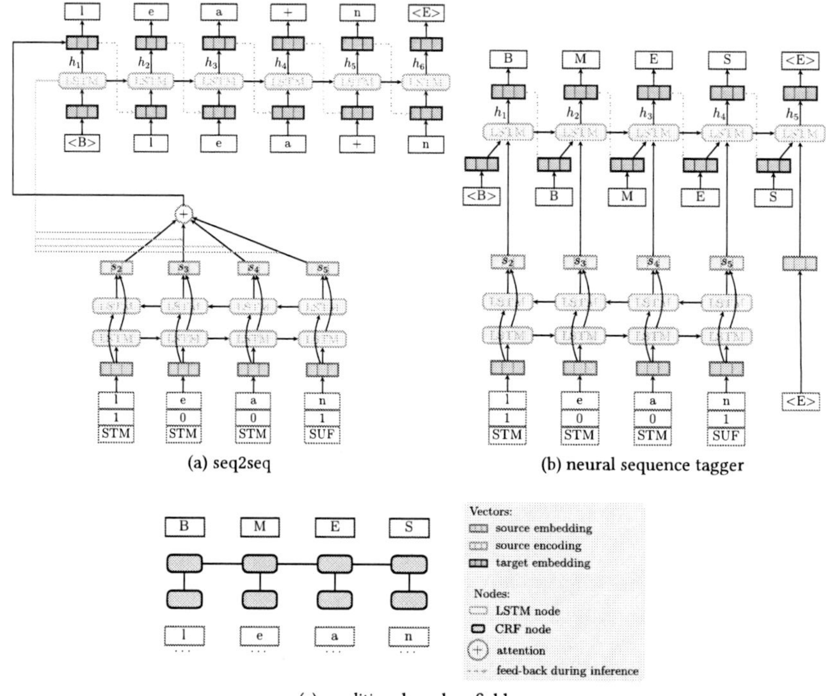

(a) seq2seq   (b) neural sequence tagger

(c) conditional random field

Figure 1: Model architectures. To prevent the figure from becoming too large, the seq2seq model is drawn with only one LSTM layer in both encoder and decoder. The attention is only shown for the fist time step.

four labels. In addition to marking both beginning and end of segments, a special label is used for single-character (S) segments.

Morphological analysis or canonical segmentation resolve ambiguity, and are more informative than surface segmentation. Learning to resolve such ambiguity is a more challenging task to learn than surface segmentation. Surface segmentation may be preferred over the other tasks e.g. when used in an application that needs to generate text in a morphologically complex language, such as when it is the target language in machine translation. If surface segments are generated, the final surface form is easily recovered through concatenation.

To summarize, arbitrary-length sequence transduction is a formulation well suited for many morphological tasks. Morphological surface segmentation is an exception, being more appropriately formulated as sequence tagging.

3   Models for semi-supervised segmentation

Our semi-supervised training follows the approach of Ruokolainen et al. (2014). The training data consists of a large unlabeled set, and a smaller labeled training set. The labeled training set is further divided into two parts. A generative model, in our

Factor	Emb																	
character	350	b	i	e	b	m	o	r	á	h	k	a	d	e	a	m	i	s
boundary	10	0	0	0	0	0	0	1	0	0	0	0	0	1	0	0	0	1
category	10	M	M	M	M	M	M	M	M	M	M	M	M	f	f	f	f	f

Table 1: Example input factors with embedding dimension. The example word biebmoráhkadeamis is segmented as biebmo/STM ráhkad/STM eami/SUF s/SUF. Stem (STM) is abbreviated M, and suffix (SUF) is f.

case Morfessor FlatCat, is trained in a semi-supervised fashion using the first part of the labeled training set. The words in the second part of the labeled training set are segmented using the generative model. Now these words are associated with two segmentations: predicted and gold standard. A discriminative model is then trained on the second part of the labeled training set. The predictions of the generative model are fed into the discriminative model as augmented features. The gold standard segmentation is used as the target sequence.

At decoding time a two-step procedure is used: first the features for the desired words are produced using the generative model. The final segmentation can then be decoded from the discriminative model.

The idea is that the features from the generative model allow the statistical patterns found in the large unannotated data to be exploited. At the same time, the capacity of the discriminative model is freed for learning to determine when the generative model's predictions are reliable, in essence to only correct its mistakes.

3.1 Morfessor FlatCat

We produce the features for our semi-supervised training using Morfessor FlatCat (Grönroos et al., 2014). Morfessor FlatCat is a generative probabilistic method for learning morphological segmentations. It uses a prior over morph lexicons inspired by the Minimum Description Length principle (Rissanen, 1989). Morfessor FlatCat applies a simple Hidden Markov model for morphotactics, providing morph category tags (stem, prefix, suffix) in addition to the segmentation. The segmentations are more consistent compared to Morfessor Baseline, particularly when splitting compound words.

Morfessor FlatCat produces morph category labels in addition to the segmentation decisions. These labels can also be used as features. An example of the resulting 3-factor input is shown in Table 1.

3.2 Sequence-to-sequence

Our sequence-to-sequence (seq2seq) baseline model follows Kann et al. (2018) with some minor modifications. It is based on the encoder-decoder with attention (Bahdanau et al., 2014). The encoder is a 2-layer bidirectional Long Short-Term Memory (LSTM) layer (Hochreiter and Schmidhuber, 1997), while the decoder is a 2-layer LSTM. The model is trained on the character level.

Figure 1a shows the basic structure of the architecture. For simplicity a single layer is shown for both encoder and decoder.

3.3 Conditional random fields

Conditional random fields (CRF) are discriminative structured classification models for sequential tagging and segmentation (Lafferty et al., 2001). They are expressed as undirected probabilistic graphical models. Figure 1c shows the model structure. CRFs can be seen as generalizing the log-linear classifier to structured outputs. They bear a structural resemblance to hidden Markov models, while relaxing the assumption of the observations being conditionally independent given the labels.

We use the implementation of linear-chain CRFs by Ruokolainen et al. (2014)[3].

3.4 Neural sequence tagger

The encoder is a standard single-layer bidirectional LSTM. The decoder is a single-layer LSTM, which takes as input at time t the concatenation of the encoder output at time t and an embedding of the predicted label at $t - 1$. There is no attention mechanism. However, the time-dependent connection to the encoder could be described as a hard-coded diagonal monotonic attention that always moves one step forward. The architecture can be seen in Figure 1b.

The most simple fixed-length decoding strategy is to forego structured prediction and instead make a prediction at each time-step based only on the encoder output s_t. The prediction at each time-step is then conditionally independent given the hidden states. We choose to instead feed the previous decision back in, causing a left-to-right dependence on previous decisions.

The proposed model has only 5% of the number of parameters of the seq2seq model (469 805 versus 8 820 037). The proposed model requires no attention mechanism, and the target vocabulary is much smaller. We also found that the optimal network size in terms of number of layers and vector dimensions was smaller.

We use factored input for the additional features. The FlatCat segmentation decision and morph category label are independently embedded. These factor embeddings are concatenated to the character embedding.

Because our human annotations include the category labels, we use a simple target-side multi-task setup to predict them in addition the the segmentation boundaries. The output vocabulary is extended to cover all combinations of segmentation decision and category label. Because our data set contains two morph categories, STM and SUF, this only increases the size of the output vocabulary from 5 (BMES + end symbol) to 10.

We use a modified beam search to ensure that the output sequence is of the correct length. This is achieved by manipulating the probability of the end symbol, setting it to zero if the sequence is still too short and to one when the correct length is reached.

The system is implemented by extending OpenNMT (Klein et al., 2017). Our implementation is open source[4].

4 North Sámi

North Sámi (davvisámegiella) is a Finno-Ugric language, spoken in the northern parts of Norway, Sweden, Finland and Russia. With around 20 000 speakers, it is biggest of the nine Sámi languages.

---

[3]Available from `http://users.ics.tkk.fi/tpruokol/software/crfs_morph.zip`
[4]Available from `https://github.com/Waino/OpenNMT-py/tree/same_length_decoder`

Purpose	Subset	Component	Word types	Labels
Training	Unlabeled	FlatCat	691190	No
Training	Feature train	FlatCat	200	Yes
	Main train	System	844	Yes
Development		Both	199	Yes
Testing			796	Yes

Table 2: Subdivision of data sets, with size in word types. The component column indicates which components use the data during training.

North Sámi is a morphologically complex language, featuring both rich inflection, derivation and productive compounding. It has complicated although regular morphophonological variation. Compounds are written together without an intermediary space. For example nállošalbmái ("into the eye of the needle"), could be segmented as nállo ∘ šalbmá ∘ i.

The morphology of Sámi languages has been modeled using finite state methods (Trosterud and Uibo, 2005; Lindén et al., 2009). The Giellatekno research lab[5] provides rule-based morphological analyzers both for individual word forms and running text, in addition to miscellaneous other resources such as wordlists and translation tools. A morphological analyzer is not a direct replacement for morphological segmentation, as there is no trivial way to map from analysis to segmentation. In addition to this, rule-based analyzers are always limited in their coverage of the vocabulary.

For an overview into the Giellatekno/Divvun and Apertium projects, including their work on Sámi languages, see Moshagen et al. (2014).

5   Data

We use version 2 of the data set collected by (Grönroos et al., 2015; Grönroos et al., 2016) as the labeled data, and as unlabeled data a word list extracted from *Den samiske tekstbanken* corpus[6].

The labeled data contains words annotated for morphological segmentation with morph category labels. The annotations were produced by a single Sámi scholar, who is not a native speaker of Sámi. In total 2311 annotated words were available. The development and test sets contain randomly selected words. The training set set of 1044 annotations is the union of 500 randomly selected words and and 597 using different active learning approaches. There was some overlap in the sets. Due to the active learning, it should be assumed that the data set is more informative than a randomly selected data set of the same size.

Table 2 shows how the data was subdivided. The unlabeled data, the development set and the test set are the same as in Grönroos et al. (2016). To produce the two labeled training sets, we first combined the labeled training data collected with different methods. From this set, 200 word types were randomly selected for semi-supervised training of Morfessor FlatCat, and the remaining 844 were used for training the dis-

---

criminative system. These two labeled data sets must be disjoint to avoid the system overestimating the reliability of the FlatCat output.

6   Training details

Tuning of FlatCat was performed following Grönroos et al. (2016). The corpus likelihood weight α was set to 1.4. The value for the annotation likelihood weight β was set using a heuristic formula optimized for Finnish:

$$\log \beta = 1.9 + 0.8 \log |\boldsymbol{D}| - 0.6 \log |\boldsymbol{A}|, \tag{1}$$

where $|\boldsymbol{D}|$ and $|\boldsymbol{A}|$ are the numbers of word types in the unannotated and annotated training data sets, respectively. Using this formula resulted in setting β to 13000. Perplexity threshold for suffixes was set to 40. For prefixes we used a high threshold (999999) to prevent the model from using them, as there are no prefixes in North Sámi.

The neural networks were trained using SGD with learning rate 1.0. Gradient norm was clipped to 5.0. Batch size was set to 64 words. Embeddings were dropped out with probability 0.3. Models were trained for at most 5000 steps, and evaluated for early stopping every 250 steps.

For the neural sequence tagger, the embedding size was 350 for characters and 10 for other input factors, and 10 for target embeddings. The encoder single bi-LSTM layer size was set to 150.

All neural network results are the average of 5 independent runs with different seeds.

7   Evaluation

The segmentations generated by the model are evaluated by comparison with annotated morph boundaries using *boundary precision*, *boundary recall*, and *boundary F_1-score* (see e.g., Virpioja et al., 2011). The boundary F_1-score equals the harmonic mean of precision (the percentage of correctly assigned boundaries with respect to all assigned boundaries) and recall (the percentage of correctly assigned boundaries with respect to the reference boundaries).

$$\text{Precision} = \frac{\#(\text{correct})}{\#(\text{proposed})}; \qquad \text{Recall} = \frac{\#(\text{correct})}{\#(\text{reference})} \tag{2}$$

Precision and recall are calculated using macro-averages over the words in the test set. In the case that a word has more than one annotated segmentation, we take the one that gives the highest score.

In order to evaluate boundary precision and recall, a valid segmentation is needed for all words in the test set. The seq2seq model can fail to output a valid segmentation, in which case we replace the output with the input without any segmentation boundaries. To include an evaluation without this source of error we also report word type level accuracy. A word in the test set is counted as correct if all boundary decisions are correct. Output that does not concatenate back to the input word is treated as incorrect.

system	Pre	Rec	F_1	w-acc
FlatCat (200 words)	78.20	77.60	77.90	57.20
Seq2seq (s)	86.94	78.62	82.54	64.60
NST (s)	83.26	83.92	83.58	69.12
CRF (s)	**87.70**	83.30	85.40	69.30
FlatCat (full)	74.30	84.10	78.90	61.80
Seq2seq (ss)	87.66	80.16	83.72	68.36
NST (ss)	84.28	**85.58**	84.94	71.02
CRF (ss)	86.30	85.20	**85.70**	**71.10**

Table 3: Results on the test set. Boundary precision (Pre), recall (Rec), and F_1-scores, together with word-type level accuracy (w-acc). NST is short for neural sequence tagger. FlatCat (200 words) shows the performance of the FlatCat system used to produce the input features. FlatCat (full) line shows FlatCat trained using the full training set. Fully supervised models, i.e. without using FlatCat features, are marked (s). Semi-supervised models are marked (ss).

	STM	STM + STM			STM + SUF			STM + SUF + SUF		
	Pre	Pre	Rec	F_1	Pre	Rec	F_1	Pre	Rec	F_1
FlatCat (200)	71.50	78.50	70.90	74.50	77.60	69.90	73.50	78.90	56.70	66.00
Seq2seq (s)	82.02	89.82	66.54	76.08	88.22	74.78	80.94	81.44	56.10	66.32
NST (s)	76.74	83.84	78.20	80.90	86.04	79.82	82.82	80.30	58.34	67.58
CRF (s)	79.80	95.50	60.00	73.70	**89.40**	**82.70**	**85.90**	83.30	62.70	71.60
FlatCat (full)	62.70	82.50	**92.70**	87.30	76.70	76.40	76.60	72.90	61.90	67.00
Seq2seq (ss)	**82.46**	91.08	68.00	77.80	88.46	76.46	82.00	84.74	57.60	68.56
NST (ss)	78.78	87.90	86.56	87.20	85.28	80.12	82.60	78.20	59.54	67.58
CRF (ss)	77.20	**96.40**	85.50	**90.60**	86.60	79.40	82.80	**88.60**	**67.90**	**76.90**

Table 4: Boundary precision (Pre), recall (Rec), and F_1-scores for different subsets of the evaluation data. NST stands for Neural sequence tagger. (s) stands for fully supervised, (ss) for semi-supervised.

8   Results

Table 3 shows results on the full test set. The semi-supervised CRF shows the best performance both according to F_1-score and word-type level accuracy. Semi-supervised seq2seq has high precision but low recall, indicating under-segmentation. The neural sequence tagger shows the opposite behavior, with the highest recall.

All semi-supervised methods improve on the quality of the semi-supervised Flat-Cat trained on 200 annotated words which is used as input features. All three discriminative methods also outperform FlatCat trained on the whole training set, on F_1 and accuracy. All three semi-supervised methods outperform their fully supervised variants. These results show that two-step training is preferable over using only Morfessor FlatCat or one of the discrinative methods.

The seq2seq model frequently fails to output a valid segmentation, either generating incorrect characters, stopping too early, or getting stuck repeating a pattern of characters. For 10.7% of the test set, the seq2seq output does not concatenate back to the input word.

Table 4 shows results for subsets of the evaluation data. The subsets include all words were the gold standard category labels follow a particular pattern: No internal structure (STM), uninflected compound (STM+STM), single-suffix inflected word (STM+SUF) and two-suffix inflected word (STM+SUF+SUF).

The seq2seq model has the best performance for the STM-pattern. This is only partly explained by the bias towards not segmenting at all caused by the replacement procedure for the invalid outputs.

The seq2seq model has high precision for all category patterns. Fully supervised CRF has superior precision and recall for the STM+SUF pattern, while semi-supervised CRF is superior for the STM+SUF+SUF pattern. CRF is good at modeling the boundaries of suffixes. Adding the FlatCat features improves the modeling of the boundary between multiple suffixes, while slightly deteriorating the modeling of the boundary between stem and suffix. The left-to-right decoding is a possible explanation for the weaker performance of the neural sequence tagger on the STM+SUF+SUF pattern. Fully supervised CRF is poor at splitting compound words, evidenced by the low recall for the STM+STM pattern. This deficiency is effectively alleviated by the addition of the FlatCat features.

The neural sequence tagger is good at modeling the ends of stems, indicated by high recall on the STM+STM and STM+SUF patterns.

9   Conclusions and future work

Semi-supervised sequence labeling is an effective way to train a low-resource morphological segmentation system. We recommend training a CRF sequence tagger using a Morfessor FlatCat-based feature set augmentation approach. This setup achieves a morph boundary F_1-score of 85.70, improving on previous best results for North Sámi morphological segmentation. Our neural sequence tagging system reaches almost the same word-type level accuracy as the CRF system, while having better morph boundary recall.

The bidirectional LSTM-CRF model (Huang et al., 2015) uses the power of a recurrent neural network to combine contextual features, and stacks a CRF on top for sequence level inference. The performance of this architecture on the North Sámi morphological segmentation task should be explored in future work.

Acknowledgments

This research has been supported by the European Union's Horizon 2020 Research and Innovation Programme under Grant Agreement No 780069. Computer resources within the Aalto University School of Science "Science-IT" project were used.

References

Dzmitry Bahdanau, Kyunghyun Cho, and Yoshua Bengio. 2014. Neural machine translation by jointly learning to align and translate. In *ICLR15*.

Ryan Cotterell, Christo Kirov, John Sylak-Glassman, David Yarowsky, Jason Eisner, and Mans Hulden. 2016. The sigmorphon 2016 shared task—morphological reinflection. In *Proceedings of the 14th SIGMORPHON Workshop on Computational Research in Phonetics, Phonology, and Morphology*. pages 10–22.

Spence Green and John DeNero. 2012. A class-based agreement model for generating accurately inflected translations. In *Proceedings of the 50th Annual Meeting of the Association for Computational Linguistics: Long Papers-Volume 1*. Association for Computational Linguistics, pages 146–155.

Stig-Arne Grönroos, Katri Hiovain, Peter Smit, Ilona Erika Rauhala, Päivi Kristiina Jokinen, Mikko Kurimo, and Sami Virpioja. 2016. Low-resource active learning of morphological segmentation. *Northern European Journal of Language Technology* .

Stig-Arne Grönroos, Kristiina Jokinen, Katri Hiovain, Mikko Kurimo, and Sami Virpioja. 2015. Low-resource active learning of North Sámi morphological segmentation. In *Proceedings of 1st International Workshop in Computational Linguistics for Uralic Languages*. pages 20–33.

Stig-Arne Grönroos, Sami Virpioja, Peter Smit, and Mikko Kurimo. 2014. Morfessor FlatCat: An HMM-based method for unsupervised and semi-supervised learning of morphology. In *Proceedings of COLING 2014, the 25th International Conference on Computational Linguistics*. Association for Computational Linguistics, Dublin, Ireland, pages 1177–1185.

Sepp Hochreiter and Jürgen Schmidhuber. 1997. Long short-term memory. *Neural Computation* 9(8):1735–1780.

Zhiheng Huang, Wei Xu, and Kai Yu. 2015. Bidirectional LSTM-CRF models for sequence tagging. *CoRR arXiv:1508.01991* .

Katharina Kann, Ryan Cotterell, and Hinrich Schütze. 2016. Neural morphological analysis: Encoding-decoding canonical segments. In *Proceedings of the 2016 Conference on Empirical Methods in Natural Language Processing*. Association for Computational Linguistics, pages 961–967.

Katharina Kann, Manuel Mager, Ivan Meza, and Hinrich Schütze. 2018. Fortification of neural morphological segmentation models for polysynthetic minimal-resource languages. In *Proceedings of NAACL 2018*. Association for Computational Linguistics, New Orleans, Louisiana, USA.

Guillaume Klein, Yoon Kim, Yuntian Deng, Jean Senellart, and Alexander M. Rush. 2017. OpenNMT: open-source toolkit for neural machine translation. In *Proc. ACL*.

John Lafferty, Andrew McCallum, and Fernando CN Pereira. 2001. Conditional random fields: Probabilistic models for segmenting and labeling sequence data. In *Proceedings of ICML*. pages 282–289.

Krister Lindén, Miikka Silfverberg, and Tommi Pirinen. 2009. HFST tools for morphology—an efficient open-source package for construction of morphological analyzers. In *State of the Art in Computational Morphology*, Springer, pages 28–47.

Sjur Moshagen, Jack Rueter, Tommi Pirinen, Trond Trosterud, and Francis M. Tyers. 2014. Open-source infrastructures for collaborative work on under-resourced languages. In *Collaboration and Computing for Under-Resourced Languages in the Linked Open Data Era. LREC 2014.*. pages 71–77.

Ramesh Nallapati, Bowen Zhou, Caglar Gulcehre, and Bing Xiang. 2016. Abstractive text summarization using sequence-to-sequence rnns and beyond. In *in Proceedings of The 20th SIGNLL Conference on Computational Natural Language Learning*. pages 280–290.

Jorma Rissanen. 1989. *Stochastic Complexity in Statistical Inquiry*, volume 15. World Scientific Series in Computer Science, Singapore.

Teemu Ruokolainen, Oskar Kohonen, Sami Virpioja, and Mikko Kurimo. 2014. Painless semi-supervised morphological segmentation using conditional random fields. In *European Chapter of the Association for Computational Linguistics (EACL)*. Association for Computational Linguistics, Gothenburg, Sweden, pages 84–89.

Rico Sennrich, Barry Haddow, and Alexandra Birch. 2015. Neural machine translation of rare words with subword units. In *ACL16*.

Peter Smit, Sami Virpioja, Mikko Kurimo, et al. 2017. Improved subword modeling for WFST-based speech recognition. In *In INTERSPEECH 2017–18th Annual Conference of the International Speech Communication Association.*.

Trond Trosterud and Heli Uibo. 2005. Consonant gradation in Estonian and Sámi: two-level solution. In *Inquiries into Words, Constraints and Contexts–Festschrift for Kimmo Koskenniemi on his 60th Birthday*, Citeseer, page 136.

Sami Virpioja, Ville T Turunen, Sebastian Spiegler, Oskar Kohonen, and Mikko Kurimo. 2011. Empirical comparison of evaluation methods for unsupervised learning of morphology. *Traitement Automatique des Langues* 52(2):45–90.

Linlin Wang, Zhu Cao, Yu Xia, and Gerard de Melo. 2016. Morphological segmentation with window LSTM neural networks. In *AAAI*. pages 2842–2848.

Yuxuan Wang, RJ Skerry-Ryan, Daisy Stanton, Yonghui Wu, Ron J Weiss, Navdeep Jaitly, Zongheng Yang, Ying Xiao, Zhifeng Chen, Samy Bengio, Q Le, Y Agiomyrgiannakis, R Clark, and R. A. Saurous. 2017. Tacotron: Towards end-to-end speech synthesis. In *Proc. Interspeech*. pages 4006–4010.

What does the Nom say?
An algorithm for case disambiguation in Hungarian

Noémi Ligeti-Nagy
MTA-PPKE
Hungarian Language Technology Research Group
ligeti-nagy.noemi@itk.ppke.hu

Andrea Dömötör
MTA-PPKE
Hungarian Language Technology Research Group
domotor.andrea@itk.ppke.hu

Noémi Vadász
Research Institute for Linguistics
Hungarian Academy of Sciences
vadasz.noemi@nytud.mta.hu

Abstract

In this paper, we present our algorithm called nom-or-not designed for dissolving case-disambiguation in Hungarian. By case, we mean an abstract syntactic case, a kind of syntactic role of the given token. Nouns and proper names, adjectives, participles and numerals without a case suffix are always tagged as Nom, although the lack of case ending may represent various functions: it may mark the subject of the sentence or a possessor or the nominal part of a nominal predicate or the vocative case; on top of that, a modifier of a nominal or a nominal combined with a postposition lacks a case suffix as well; proper names consisting of two or more elements are also caseless. Our algorithm is motivated by the needs of a psycholinguistically motivated parser which aims to process sentences from left to right. Therefore, our case disambiguator follows the basic principles of the parser and analyses the sentences from left to right, always making a decision based on the information of the previously processed elements and the elements in a two token wide look-ahead parsing window. Our preliminary results show that if some modifications and new rules are added and it's run on a more precisely annotated corpus, it can improve the disambiguator algorithm. The preliminary results were obtained from a manually annotated corpora of 500 sentences.

Proceedings of the fifth Workshop on Computational Linguistics for Uralic Languages, pages 27–41,
Tartu, Estonia, January 7 - January 8, 2019.

Kivonat

Tanulmányunkban bemutatjuk a `nom-or-not` névre keresztelt algoritmust, amely az esetrag nélküli névszók mondatbeli szerepének egyértelműsítését végzi. A magyarban a testes esetrag hiánya nem egyértelműen a nominatívuszi esetet kódolja; egy testes esetragot magán nem viselő névszó többféle szerepet betölthet a mondatban: lehet valóban alany, lehet birtokos, lehet névszói állítmány névszói része, lehet névszó módosítója vagy névutó előtt álló névszói elem, lehet vokatívuszi esetben álló névszó, vagy lehet több elemből álló tulajdonnév egyik belső eleme. Algoritmusunk háttere egy az emberi szövegfeldolgozást modellálni szándékozó elemzőrendszer. Ennek szellemében az eset-egyértelműsítést az elemzőrendszer működési elvei alapján végezzük: balról jobbra haladva dolgozzuk fel a szöveget, mindig csak az eddig már olvasott szavakon, illetve a kételemű, előretekintő elemzési ablakban látható információra támaszkodva. Szabályalapú algoritmusunkat egy 500 mondatból álló korpuszon értékeljük ki, melyben kézzel annotálunk minden testes esetrag nélküli névszót. Eredményeink azt mutatják, hogy eljárásunk – két előzmény-algoritmusához hasonlóan, melyek egy-egy részfeladat kezelésére születtek – pontossága néhány szabály beillesztésével és pontosabban annotált korpusz használatával könnyedén javítható lehet.

1 Introduction

Here we present a rule-based algorithm offering a case disambiguation method designed primarily for the ANAGRAMMA parsing system (Prószéky and Indig, 2015; Prószéky et al., 2016). Following a brief description of the parsing system and its principles we turn to the discussion of the possible functions of nominals in the sentence and finally we introduce our algorithm disambiguating caseless nominals in Hungarian sentences.

The current algorithm is an upgraded and extended version of two previously described algorithms presented in Ligeti-Nagy et al. (2018) and Dömötör (2018), to be described in details below.

It is inevitable to clarify some terminological questions. Throughout this article, by nominals we mean nouns, adjectives, participles and numerals – words able to fill the role of a subject or a possessor, words that may be modifiers of another nominal etc. This also applies to pronouns that substitute these lexical word classes.

With case, and more specifically, with *function in the sentence* on the one hand we refer to the set of syntactic roles in the sentence, on the other hand we use *function in the sentence* to identify nominal positions inside a noun phrase (NP) as well. Therefore, when we aim to specify the function of a caseless nominal in the sentence, we want to determine if it is the argument of a verb. Otherwise we specify its role inside an NP.

2 Background

Our algorithm fits into the frame of ANAGRAMMA, a psycholinguistically motivated parsing system which tries to model human sentence processing with its left-to-right and word-by-word parsing design. The context of a word often influences its interpretation, therefore ANAGRAMMA uses a two token wide look-ahead window that provides information of the right context of the word, while the information of the previously processed elements is always available in the so-called *pool*. The theoretical background of ANAGRAMMA is based on a two-phased sentence processing model, the *Sausage Machine* where the parsing process consists of two main phases. The first phase is – as Frazier and Fodor (Frazier and Fodor (1978)) calls it – the *Preliminary Phrase Packager* which assigns the lexical and phrasal nodes to groups of words within the string input. The look-ahead window of ANAGRAMMA implements this first phase. In this phase the components of the sentence are prepared, e.g. disambiguation of case-ambiguous nominals presented in this paper. Then, in the second phase, these packaged phrases get their roles in the sentence by adding non-terminal nodes. The second phase is called the *Sentence Structure Supervisor*, as the packages – the pieces of the sausage – receive their role in the sentence.

2.1 Caseless nominals in Hungarian

Our basic assumption about caseless nominals is that their function in a sentence may be one of the followings: subject (1a), unmarked possessor (1b), argument of a postposition[1] (1c), element in vocative case (where the noun or the pronoun is used to address a person directly, (1d)), modifier of another nominal (1e), part of a proper name consisting of more than one component (1f) or part of a nominal predicate (discussed in detail later). In the examples (1a)-(1f), the third row illustrates the current morphological annotation of the words.

(1)   a.   *A*   *szomszéd* *tegnap*   *érkez-ett.*
            the   neighbour   yesterday arrive-PST.3SG
            DET|ART.DEF   N.NOM   ADV   V.PST.NDEF.3SG

            'The neighbour arrived yesterday.'

      b.   *A*   *szomszéd* *kutyá-ja*   *ugat.*
            the   neighbour   dog-Poss.3SG   bark.3SG
            DET|ART.DEF   N.NOM   N.POSS.3SG.NOM V.PRS.NDEF.3SG

            'The neighbour's dog barks.'

      c.   *A*   *szomszéd* *után*   *érkez-t-ünk.*
            the   neighbour   after   arrive-PST-1PL
            DET|ART.DEF   N.NOM   POST   V.PRS.NDEF.1SG

            'We arrived after the neighbour.'

      d.   *Jó*   *reggel-t,*   *szomszéd!*
            good   morning-Acc   neighbour
            ADJ.NOM N.ACC   N.NOM

            'Good morning, neighbour!'

      e.   *Az*   *előző*   *szomszéd* *kedves* *volt.*
            the   previous   neighbour kind   be.PST.3SG
            DET|ART.DEF   ADJ.NOM   N.NOM   ADJ.NOM V.PST.NDEF.3SG

            'The previous neighbour was kind.'

---

[1]Considering the noun to be the argument of the postposition is a simplification and is motivated by ANAGRAMMA being a dependency-parser. In our system, the noun is a dependent of the postposition. A detailed argument for this, however, is beyond the scope of this paper.

f. ***Máris*** *szomszéd* *tegnap* *érkez-ett.*
   Máris   neighbour yesterday arrive-Pst.3sg
   N.Nom N.Nom   Adv   V.Pst.NDef.3sg

'Neighbour Máris arrived yesterday.'

As mentioned above, the emphasised nominals in (1a)-(1f) are either arguments of the verb or parts of an NP. The role of predicative nominals, however, is different. Sentence parsing in computational linguistics is usually based on the verb and its argument frame. However, in Hungarian, it is possible to make well-formed, complete and non-elliptic sentences without a finite verb. This is due to the so-called zero copula phenomenon. The copula in Hungarian can be defined as 'an expletive' which is present "if and only if its presence is required by a morphophonological constraint" (É. Kiss (2002):72). This morphophonological constraint is related to the Third Person Parameter of Stassen (1994) which means that the (verbal) copula can only be omitted in the third person in present tense. See examples in (2).

(2) a.   *A*   *szomszéd-om*   *ügyvéd.*
          the neighbour-Poss.1sg lawyer

          'My neighbour is a lawyer.'

     b.   *A*   *szomszéd-om*   *ügyvéd volt.*
          the neighbour-Poss.1sg lawyer be.Pst.3sg

          'My neighbour was a lawyer.'

     c.   *Ügyvéd vagyok.*
          lawyer be.1sg

          'I am a lawyer.'

In nominal sentences like (2a) the parsing tool needs to be able to identify whether or not the sentence contains a nominal predicate as the nominal this should be the head of the whole sentence.

Predicative nominals can be nouns, adjectives, occasionally numerals, and pronouns that substitute these elements. If the predicate is a noun phrase, then the nominal, which is the head of the phrase, is considered predicative. According to Higgins (1973) and others there are various types of copular clauses. The two main categories are predicative and equative sentences. By the former one, we mean those copular sentences in which the nominal predicate is a bare noun or adjective, an indefinite noun phrase or adjectival phrase which denotes an attribute of the subject. In contrast, the latter sentence type states the equality of two individuals. In this case, both the predicate and the subject must be a referential, therefore a determiner phrase (DP) – which encodes definiteness in Hungarian. DPs can be NPs with definite article, proper names or possessive NPs.

The predicative nominal is morphologically unmarked in both types of copular sentences, therefore it shows no difference in form to nominative, genitive and caseless nominals mentioned above. The issue of the case of predicative nominals could be subject of theoretical debate. There are three main approaches to this question. We could either 1) assume a phonologically zero predicative nominal, 2) claim that the nominal predicate is nominative which gets its case by the agreement with its subject (Szécsényi, 2000), or 3) simply consider it caseless. This study does not intend to take sides in this issue. With respect to automatic parsing, we may consider the predicative role as a functional feature indicating that the nominal in question needs a subject and optionally a copula as complement. The question of abstract cases does not have special importance for our purposes, therefore in the following, predicative nominals will simply be considered nominals with predicative feature and without case marking.

Based on the above described roles it can be stated that caseless nominals either bear a phonologically zero case suffix (when functioning as a subject as in (1a), an unmarked possessor (1b) or being in vocative case (1d)) or bearing nothing (when modifying another nominal (1e), being followed by a postposition (1c), being part of a complex proper name (1f), or functioning as a predicative nominal (2)).

Throughout this paper the following annotation is used to distinguish the previously detailed functions:

- phonologically zero case suffix (marking either a Nom or a Gen): α

- real 'caselessness' (marking the true lack of case ending): 0

- tag marking the predicative nominal: Pred

- Nom, Gen, and Voc stands for the nominative, genitive, and vocative case, respectively

2.2   Previous algorithms

nom-or-what presented in (Ligeti-Nagy et al., 2018) is a rule-based algorithm primarily built on the ideas drawn up in (Vadász and Indig, 2018) where a basic method was introduced to identify unmarked possessors in a sentence (nomorgen). nom-or-what aims to identify the roles of caseless nominals in the sentence solely based on the information seen in the two token wide look-ahead window and was essentially planned to be a module of the ANAGRAMMA parser. This algorithm does not disambiguate nouns in vocative case and only operates on sentences with a verb present (meaning that it does not intend to identify nominal predicates). The algorithm was designed by analysing the caseless nominals both inside and in the final position of an NP in a syntactically annotated corpus of Hungarian (Szeged Treebank 2.0, Csendes et al. (2005)).

Three sets of rules were created for nouns, adjectives, and numerals. The rules attempt to define the precise role of the token under examination based on its morphological annotation and on the information gained from the parsing window. If no solid decision can be made and more information is needed to further specify an element, default tags were used. The performance of the algorithm was evaluated on a manually annotated corpus of 500 sentences collected from the Hungarian Gigaword Corpus (Oravecz et al., 2014). The high precision (97.73%) indicated that the basic principles of the algorithm are correct. The relatively low recall (67.63%) was explained by the authors as a sign of the excessive use of default values.

The algorithm described in Dömötör (2018) (named is-pred) was also designed to constitute a part of the ANAGRAMMA parser. It follows the principles of the sausage machine model described in section 2. nom-or-what was basically the implementation of the first phase of this two-phased parsing model. The second phase carried out by is-pred uses the whole left context, the so-called *pool*. Besides, the is-pred algorithm strongly relies on the output of nom-or-what, as there would be little chance to identify predicative nominals based exclusively on the left context without taking into account the local decisions of the first phase.

In sum, the input of `is-pred` is a sequence that consists of the nominal in question and the part of the sentence that precedes it. The left context of the current word is already analysed and disambiguated by `nom-or-what` (if possible), thus the algorithm can use various pieces of morphosyntactic information from the pool. The output is a value, similar to trivalent logic: `Pred` if the nominal is obviously a predicate, `Nonpred` if it is obviously not a predicate, and `Undefined` if its syntactic role is still unclear from the given information.

The `is-pred` algorithm achieved high precision on its test, however, it has some deficiencies that should be improved. On the one hand, its responses are binary which do not complete the analysis in the `Nonpred` cases. On the other hand, `is-pred` only handles the predicative copular clauses, therefore the recognition of nominal predicates in equative sentences is a significant gap that this study intends to fill.

The idea behind the current algorithm – called `nom-or-not`, referring to its role as a synthesis of its antecedents – is, on the one hand, to merge all working and tested rules of the previous algorithms, and, on the other hand, to fill as many gaps left as possible.

3 Method

The method of `nom-or-not` follows `nom-or-what` and `is-pred` in being rule-based which means that the algorithm does not use machine learning approaches rather it is built on linguistically grounded, hand-crafted rules. The main difference among the three is that `nom-or-not` merges the two phases of parsing and aims to disambiguate each possible role of caseless nominals in one step. For this task, it is necessary to use both the window and the pool at the same time, therefore the algorithm operates with both forward- and back-looking rules. In either case, the principal source of information is the morphological annotation with only a small scent of lexical information. That is, the disambiguation of caseless nominals is carried out primarily based on the syntactic structure.

The algorithm is designed to process sentences annotated by the *emMorph* morphological analyser (Novák (2003), Novák (2014), Novák et al. (2016)), where the token, the lemma and the morphological tags are separated by a /, and the morphological tags are in square brackets (*USA/USA/[/N][NOM]*). The algorithm processes the sentences from left to right, word by word. The rules are only applied if the token under examination is tagged as `Nom`. As the targeted parsing method has a psycholinguistic motivation, the case disambiguation algorithm first gathers all the information of the given nominal that is deductible from the pool (the collection of the information of the already processed elements). The back-looking rules are used for preliminary disambiguation of predicative nominals, and they are the following:

- If there is a non-copular finite verb in the pool → the current token is not Pred

- If there is a nominative in the pool → the current token is Pred, if other cases will be ruled out based on the window, and only Nom and Pred remains as an option

- If the word is the possible head of a DP and there is no nominative in the pool → it is not Pred

- If proper name → Head of DP

- If possessive → Head of DP

- If preceded by a determiner and optionally one or more NP-modifiers →
  Head of DP

- If demonstrative pronoun ('this', 'that') → Head of DP

The rule to detect vocative case on nominals is rather simple at the moment: if
the pool contains a verb in 1st or 2nd person singular or plural, and now we see a 3rd
person singular or plural noun assigned nominative case Nom (see example (3), where
the morphological annotation of the words can be seen in the third line), then it is a
Voc.

(3) *Jövök,*   *apám!*
     come.Prs1Sg   father.Poss3Sg
     [/V][Prs.NDef.1Sg] [/N][Nom]

     I'm coming, father!

Having exploited the left context the algorithm refines its judgment about the
nominal in question using the information gathered from the window. The forward-
looking rules are displayed in decision trees in Figures 1-3. Obviously, only those
branches will be activated that are relevant considering the conclusions drawn up
from the information coming from the pool; and every non-final decision is finalised
if the knowledge based on the pool makes it possible to rule out a part of the outcome.
(E.g. an edge leads us to a leaf with the tag *nom_or_pred* on it, but the pool already
made it clear that the actual token cannot be a Pred, therefore here the tag Nom will
be assigned to this token.)

As the algorithm does not exploit the whole sentence, there necessarily may remain cases where no certain decision can be made. We use the following tags for
these cases:

- α: this is the default case of nouns; if no final tag can be assigned to a noun,
  but the predicative function is ruled out, the token in question is marked with
  an α, which can later be further specified as Nom or Gen

- *Nom/Pred*: a tag signaling that the given word may either be the subject of the
  sentence or the nominal predicate

- 0/*Pred*: a tag signaling that the given word may either be a modifier element in
  an NP or the nominal predicate of the sentence

We assume that nouns and proper names share the same default role – the one
marked by α – with the default case of adjectives, participles, and numerals being 0.

Figure 1 shows the forward-looking rules activated when the token in question
is a noun, a proper name, or a plural adjective or participle. The root of the tree
is the POS-tag of the given word. The edges on the first level of the tree contain
information gathered from the first element in the parsing window. As an example, if
the first token in the window contains the tag of a postposition (Post), the algorithm
assigns the tag 0 to the word in question, deleting its original Nom tag. The edges
on the second level contain information seen on the second element in the parsing

window. These edges are only activated if no final decision could be made based on the first token in the window and only a default tag was assigned to the given token.

A special distinction is made during the process not visible on the decision trees. If the given word has a possessive case suffix on it, no Gen tag can be assigned to it based on a possessive suffix on the second element in the window. It is a simplification with which we intend to rule out cases like (4a). The genitive case of a word like the one in bold in (4b) remain identifiable for the algorithm by detecting the possessive suffix on the first element in the window (*megbízásából* ('on behalf of the government')).

(4) a. *Magyarország* **kormány-a**   *mostani*   *nyilatkozat-á-ból*
         Hungary   government-Poss.3sg current   statement-Poss.3sg-out.of
         N.Nom   N.Poss.3sg.Nom   Adj.Nom   N.Poss.3sg.Ela

     'from the current statement of the government of Hungary'

     b. *Magyarország* **kormány-a**   *nyilatkozat-á-ból*
         Hungary   government-Poss.3sg statement-Poss.3sg-out.of
         N.Nom   N.Poss.3sg.Nom   N.Poss.3sg.Ela

     'from the statement of the government of Hungary'

The rules for singular adjectives and participles are displayed in Figure 2. The same distinction explained above is valid for the analysis of these tokens as well. Finally, the rules for numerals can be seen in Figure 3. Throughout the figures we use the macro NPMod for adjectives and participles as nom-or-gen started to tag every adjective and participle as NPMod referring to their ability to modify an NP.

The algorithm implemented in Python is available with the test corpus containing the gold standard annotation at `https://github.com/ppke-nlpg/nom-or-not`.

4   Results

For the evaluation of the performance of the algorithm we used a randomly composed subcorpus of the Hungarian Gigaword Corpus. The test corpus contains 500 sentences with no restriction to genre, content or quality. We carried out the morphological analysis of the sentences with the *emMorph* tool integrated in e-magyar language processing system (Váradi et al. (2018)).

The testcorpus contains 2 255 tokens tagged as Nom by the morphological analyser. We manually annotated them with tags from the set described above. The output of the algorithm was compared to this gold standard. It is important to note that the human annotation took the whole sentence into consideration and no default tags were allowed (unless the whole sentence was ambiguous). As the algorithm operates without analysing the whole sentence, it necessarily provides ambiguous responses in some cases meaning that we cannot expect 100% recall. The algorithm was consciously designed to work with high precision instead of high recall.

The evaluation follows the rules described in Table 1. The true positive (TP) matches are the correct ones. The erroneous or overspecified results are considered false positives (FP). Finally, we refer to the uncertain (underspecified) responses of the algorithm as false negatives (FN). The results are shown in Table 2. By precision we mean the percentage of $TP/(TP + FP)$ and by recall we mean $TP/(TP + FP + FN)$.

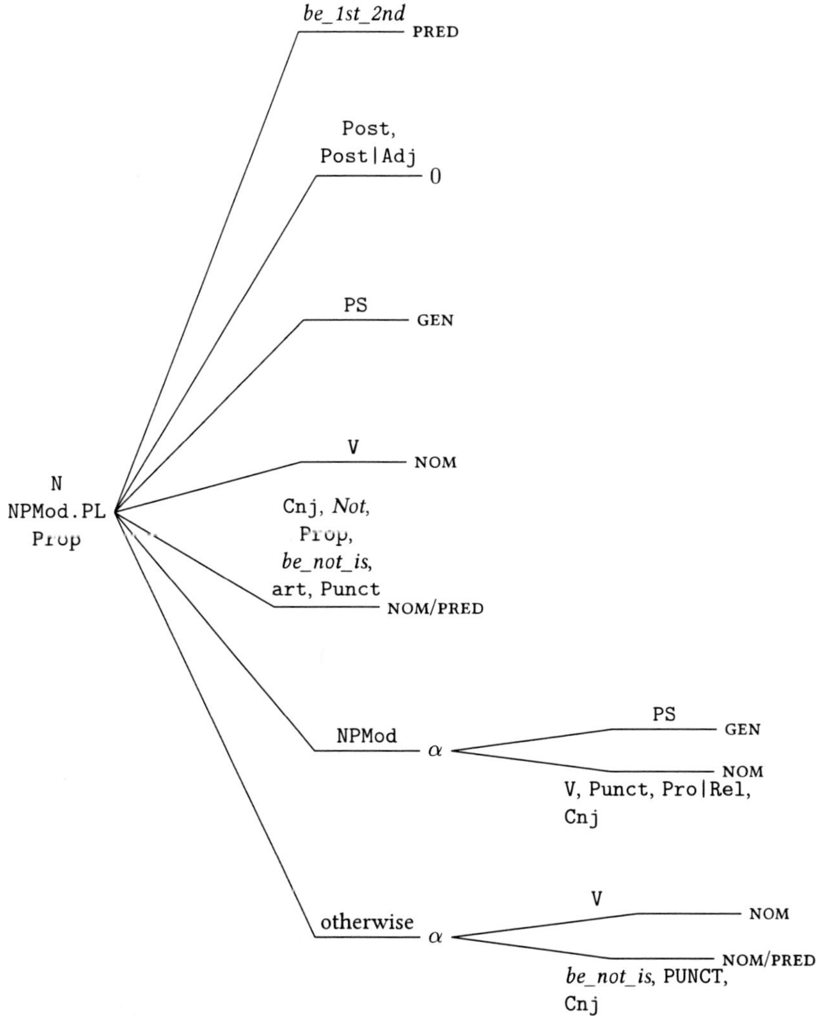

Figure 1: Decision tree summarising the rules concerning nouns, proper names, and plural adjectives, numerals and participles. The root of the tree is the POS-tag of the token under examination. The edges on the first level contain information seen on the first element in the parsing window. The edges on the second level contain information seen on the second element in the parsing window. *be_1st_2nd* is a macro for the 1st and 2nd person forms of the copula. *Not* is a macro for negation. *be_not_is* is a macro for any copula except for the singular and plural 3rd person form of *be*.

As can be seen, the algorithm achieved moderately good recall and a precision lower than expected. We analysed the results in more detail in a confusion matrix (Table 3). The rows display the responses of the algorithm, while the columns show

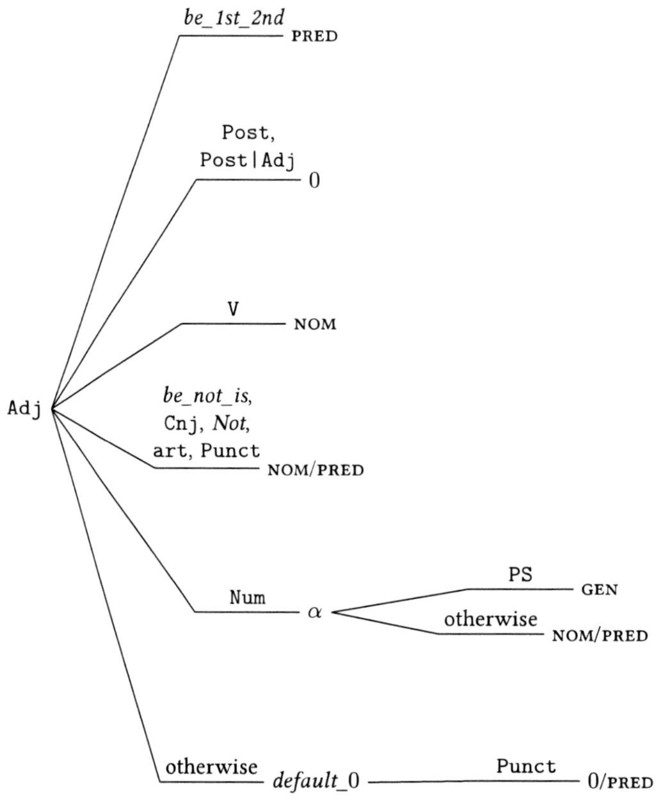

Figure 2: Decision tree summarising the rules concerning (singular) adjectives and participles. The root of the tree is the POS-tag of the token under examination. The edges on the first level contain information seen on the first element in the parsing window. The edges on the second level contain information seen on the second element in the parsing window. *be_1st_2nd* is a macro for the 1st and 2nd person forms of the copula. *Not* is a macro for negation. *be_not_is* is a macro for any copula except for the singular and plural 3rd person form of *be*.

the gold standard annotation.

A significant part of the errors (102) is due to an erroneous morphological annotation of the surrounding tokens. We eliminated those from the final results.

5 Discussion

As expected, the algorithm performs with a moderately high recall compared to that of nom-or-what (67.63%) which is due to the fact that some of the default tags were eliminated from the algorithm. Recall is influenced by the number of false negative hits (361 in the results). Considering that the algorithm does not have the whole sentence available when deciding, underspecification (resulting in false negative hits)

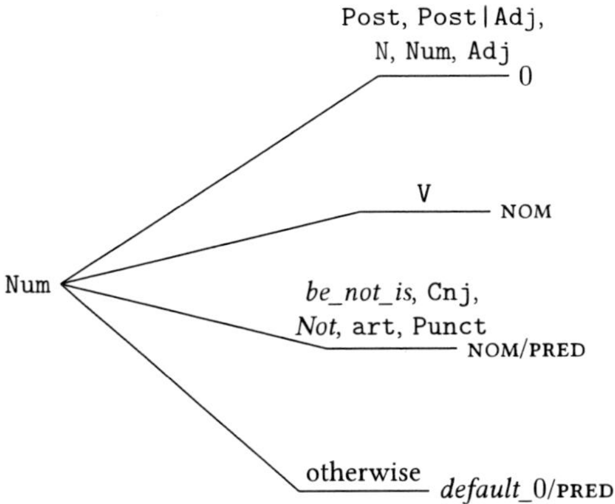

Figure 3: Decision tree summarising the rules concerning numerals. The root of the tree is the POS-tag of the token under examination. The edges on the first level contain information seen on the first element in the parsing window. *be_not_is* is a macro for any copula except for the singular and plural 3rd person form of *be*.

category	result	standard
	NOM	NOM
	GEN	GEN
TP	PRED	PRED
	0	0
	VOC	VOC
	α	α
	NOM	α
	GEN	α
FP	0	0/PRED
	PRED	0/PRED
	NOM	NOM/PRED
	PRED	NOM/PRED
	every other non-matching tags	
	α	NOM
	α	GEN
FN	0/PRED	0
	0/PRED	PRED
	Nom/Pred	Nom
	NOM/PRED	PRED

Table 1: Rules of evaluation. The tags in the *result* column are the ones assigned by the algorithm. The tags in the *standard* column are the gold standard annotation.

is comprehensible in many of the cases. These results are not as problematic for the whole parsing task as the false positive ones, since the uncertain tags can still be specified at a later point of parsing with the scanning of further words.

Precision	Recall	F-measure
77.82%	79.3%	78.55%

Table 2: Test results of the nom-or-not algorithm evaluated on 500 randomly selected and manually annotated sentences

	Nom	Gen	0	Pred	Voc	α	*Nom/Pred*
Nom	281	9	54	57	0	0	0
Gen	3	229	8	0	0	0	0
0	1	1	811	3	0	0	0
Pred	105	0	2	62	0	0	5
Voc	0	0	0	0	0	0	0
alpha	83	27	79	5	0	0	0
Nom/Pred	143	2	26	69	1	1	0
0/Pred	0	0	39	0	0	0	0

Table 3: Confusion matrix. The rows refer to the tags assigned by the algorithm. The columns represent the gold standard annotation.

The confusion matrix in Table 3 reveals that the majority of FP hits (268) is in connection with Nom or Pred, and more than half of them (162) is caused by a swap of these two tags. This can be explained on the one hand with the fact that our rules detecting predicative nominals are highly dependent on our preceding decisions on nominals: if a Nom was found we assume that no more Nom should be identified. However, our rules do not take clause boundaries into consideration, although a previously found Nom may be the subject of another clause other than the clause under examination . Stopping the backwards-looking rules on clause boundaries is a rather important issue to solve later. Obviously, any erroneously annotated Nom can lead to further mistakes during the analysis, even within the same clause. On the other hand, transposing Nom with Gen or vice versa is often caused by a verb falsely considered a copular verb. *Lehet* (may be) or *lesz* (will be) are just two examples of verbs that can either be a copular verb or a normal verb. This distinction is not available in their current morphological annotation, therefore the algorithm always assumes them to be a copular verb.

Another source of errors (159 cases) is the undiscovered inner structure of constructions like (5a) and (5b). Here we assume that there is no case suffix on the first element, therefore a 0 would be the correct tag for it. However, detecting these names is challenging and currently not solved in nom-or-not. There is no visible sign of the connection between the words in these constructions, especially not in their morphological analysis. Therefore, the first element most often receives a default tag. Presumably, these cases should be referred to a module responsible for world knowledge.

(5) a. *elnök   úr*
       president sir
       N.Nom   N.Nom

       'Mr. President'

b.   *Kinaesthetics termék*
    Kinaesthetics product
    Prop.Nom   N.Nom

    'the product Kinaesthetics'

Finally, cases like (6a) present a challenge to our algorithm as well: these are some kind of exclamations without any particular case suffix on them, as they play no role in the sentence. We would assign a 0 tag for them, but their distinction is quite problematic and at the moment unsolved in a sentence.

(6)   a.   *Támadás!*
        attack
        N.Nom

        'Attack!'

Setting the unsolved problems and all the errors aside, we can see that the algorithm performs well with genitive case and with tokens not bearing any suffix at all (tagged with 0). With Pred, on the other hand, nom-or-not is quite uncertain, but never assigns any Gen or 0 tag to the nominal predicates of a sentence.

A part of the underspecification (FN results) may be solved by inserting a final step at the end of the analysis of each sentence: any verb following the tokens tagged as *Nom/Pred* can clarify its role as Nom.

6   Conclusion

We presented our rule-based algorithm called nom-or-not designed to disambiguate the role of caseless nominals for Hungarian. It is the successor of some related algorithms, each of which were implemented to solve a small part of the complex problem. Here we intended to provide an algorithm able to deal with every possible role of caseless nominals.

In this paper, we presented the design of the algorithm accompanied by the preliminary results obtained by evaluating the algorithm's performance on a test corpus containing 500 manually annotated sentences. Although we expected a higher precision, the majority of FP results is not a random mistake but a systematic error that can and should be solved by extending our rules or by evaluating the algorithm on a more precisely annotated test corpus. The recall is higher than our expectations proving that eliminating the default tags of adjectives, participles and numerals results in a better performance.

There are numerous tasks ahead of us: we need to revise our rules concerning predicative nominals as they seem to cause a significant amount of FP results. After inserting a final check in the algorithm that makes it able to clarify the role of tokens temporarily annotated with a tag of a default value, nom-or-not will hopefully provide a solution of high precision and recall for this case-disambiguation task for Hungarian.

References

Dóra Csendes, János Csirik, Tibor Gyimóthy, and András Kocsor. 2005. The Szeged Treebank. In Václav Matoušek, Pavel Mautner, and Tomáš Pavelka, editors, *Text, Speech and Dialogue: 8th International Conference, TSD 2005, Karlovy Vary, Czech Republic, September 12-15, 2005. Proceedings*. Springer Berlin Heidelberg, Berlin, Heidelberg, pages 123–131.

Andrea Dömötör. 2018. Nem mind VP, ami állít – A névszói állítmány azonosítása számítógépes elemzőben [All that Predicates is not VP – The Identification of Nominal Predicate in Automatic Parsing]. In Zsófia Ludányi, Valéria Krepsz, and Tekla Etelka Gráczi, editors, *Doktoranduszok tanulmányai az alkalmazott nyelvészet köréből 2018*. pages 3–10.

Katalin É. Kiss. 2002. *The Syntax of Hungarian*. Cambridge University Press.

Lyn Frazier and Janet Dean Fodor. 1978. The Sausage Machine: A New Two-stage Parsing Model. *Cognition* 6(4):291–325.

Francis Roger Higgins. 1973. *The Pseudo-Cleft Construction in English*. Garland Press, New York.

Noémi Ligeti-Nagy, Noémi Vadász, Andrea Dömötör, and Balázs Indig. 2018. Nulla vagy semmi? Esetegyértelműsítés az ablakban [Zero or Nothing? Case Disambiguation in the Window]. In Veronika Vincze, editor, *XIV. Magyar Számítógépes Nyelvészeti Konferencia*. pages 25–37.

Attila Novák. 2003. Milyen a jó Humor? [What is Good Humor Like?]. In *I. Magyar Számítógépes Nyelvészeti Konferencia*. SZTE, Szeged, pages 138–144.

Attila Novák. 2014. A New Form of Humor – Mapping Constraint-Based Computational Morphologies to a Finite-State Representation. In Nicoletta Calzolari, Khalid Choukri, Thierry Declerck, Hrafn Loftsson, Bente Maegaard, Joseph Mariani, Asuncion Moreno, Jan Odijk, and Stelios Piperidis, editors, *Proceedings of the Ninth International Conference on Language Resources and Evaluation (LREC'14)*. European Language Resources Association (ELRA), Reykjavik, Iceland.

Attila Novák, Borbála Siklósi, and Csaba Oravecz. 2016. A New Integrated Opensource Morphological Analyzer for Hungarian. In Nicoletta Calzolari, Khalid Choukri, Thierry Declerck, Sara Goggi, Marko Grobelnik, Bente Maegaard, Joseph Mariani, Helene Mazo, Asuncion Moreno, Jan Odijk, and Stelios Piperidis, editors, *Proceedings of the Tenth International Conference on Language Resources and Evaluation (LREC 2016)*. European Language Resources Association (ELRA), Paris, France.

Csaba Oravecz, Tamás Váradi, and Bálint Sass. 2014. The Hungarian Gigaword Corpus. In Nicoletta Calzolari (Conference Chair), Khalid Choukri, Thierry Declerck, Hrafn Loftsson, Bente Maegaard, Joseph Mariani, Asuncion Moreno, Jan Odijk, and Stelios Piperidis, editors, *Proceedings of the Ninth International Conference on Language Resources and Evaluation (LREC'14)*. European Language Resources Association (ELRA), Reykjavik, Iceland.

Gábor Prószéky and Balázs Indig. 2015. Magyar szövegek pszicholingvisztikai indíttatású elemzése számítógéppel [Psycholingvistically Motivated Analysis of Hungarian Texts with Computer]. *Alkalmazott Nyelvtudomány* 15(1-2):29–44. Original document in Hungarian.

Gábor Prószéky, Balázs Indig, and Noémi Vadász. 2016. Performanciaalapú elemző magyar szövegek számítógépes megértéséhez [A Performance-based Parser to the Comprehensive Understanding of Hungarian Texts]. In Kas Bence, editor, *"Szavad ne feledd!": Tanulmányok Bánréti Zoltán tiszteletére*, MTA Nyelvtudományi Intézet, Budapest, pages 223–232. Original document in Hungarian.

Leon Stassen. 1994. Typology Versus Mythology: The Case of the Zero-Copula. *Nordic Journal of Linguistics* 17(2):105–126.

Tibor Szécsényi. 2000. Esetegyeztetés a predikatív főnévi csoportban [Case agreement in the predicative noun phrase]. In László Büky and Márta Maleczki, editors, *A mai magyar nyelv leírásának újabb módszerei IV.*, Szegedi Tudományegyetem, Szeged, pages 189–202.

Noémi Vadász and Balázs Indig. 2018. A birtokos esete az ablakkal [Possessor's Case with the Window]. In György Scheibl, editor, *LingDok: Nyelvész-doktoranduszok dolgozatai 17.*, SZTE Nyelvtudományi Doktori Iskola, Szeged, pages 85–99.

Tamás Váradi, Eszter Simon, Bálint Sass, Iván Mittelholcz, Attila Novák, Balázs Indig, Richárd Farkas, and Veronika Vincze. 2018. E-magyar – A Digital Language Processing System. In Nicoletta Calzolari (Conference chair), Khalid Choukri, Christopher Cieri, Thierry Declerck, Sara Goggi, Koiti Hasida, Hitoshi Isahara, Bente Maegaard, Joseph Mariani, Hélène Mazo, Asuncion Moreno, Jan Odijk, Stelios Piperidis, and Takenobu Tokunaga, editors, *Proceedings of the Eleventh International Conference on Language Resources and Evaluation (LREC 2018)*. European Language Resources Association (ELRA), Miyazaki, Japan.

A Contrastive Evaluation of Word Sense Disambiguation Systems for Finnish

Frankie Robertson
University of Jyväskylä
Faculty of Information Technology
`frankie.r.robertson@student.jyu.fi`

Abstract

Previous work in Word Sense Disambiguation (WSD), like many tasks in natural language processing, has been predominantly focused on English. While there has been some work on other languages, including Uralic languages, up until this point no work has been published providing a contrastive evaluation of WSD for Finnish, despite the requisite lexical resources, most notably FinnWord-Net, having long been in place. This work rectifies the situation. It gives results for systems representing the major approaches to WSD, including some of the systems which have performed best at the task for English. It is hoped these results can act as a baseline for future systems, including both multilingual systems and systems specifically targeting Finnish, as well as point to directions for other Uralic languages.

Tiivistelmä

Aiempi saneiden alamerkitysten yksiselitteistämistä käsittelevä työ, kuten monet muut luonnollisen kielen käsittelyyn liittyvät tehtävät, on enimmäkseen keskittynyt englannin kieleen. Vaikka hieman työtä on tehty myös muilla kielillä, mukaan lukien uralilaiset kielet, vertailevaa arviointia suomen kielen saneiden alamerkitysten yksiselitteistämisestä ei ole tähän mennessä julkaistu huolimatta siitä, että tarvittavat leksikaaliset resurssit, erityisesti FinnWordNet, ovat jo pitkään olleet saatavilla. Tämä työ pyrkii korjaamaan tilanteen. Se tarjoaa tuloksia merkittävimpiä lähestymistapoja saneiden alamerkitysten yksiselitteistämiseen edustavista ohjelmista, sisältäen joitakin parhaiten englanninkielellä samasta tehtävästä suoriutuvia ohjelmia. Näiden tulosten toivotaan voivan toimia lähtökohtana tuleville, sekä monikielisille että erityisesti suomen kieleen kohdentuville, ohjelmille ja tarjota suuntaviivoja muihin uralilaisiin kieliin keskittyvään työhön.

1 Introduction

Like many natural language understanding tasks, Word Sense Disambiguation (WSD) has been referred to as AI-complete (Mallery, 1988, p. 57). That is to say, it is considered as hard as the central problems in artificial intelligence, such as passing the

---

Proceedings of the fifth Workshop on Computational Linguistics for Uralic Languages, pages 42–54,
Tartu, Estonia, January 7 - January 8, 2019.

Turing test (Turing, 1950). While in the general case this may be true, the best current systems can at least do better than the (quite tough to beat) Most Frequent Sense (MFS) baseline. Evaluations against common datasets and dictionaries, largely following procedures set out by the shared tasks under the auspices of the SensEval and SemEval workshops, have been key to creating measurable progress in WSD.

For English, Raganato et al. (2017) present a recent comparison of different WSD systems across harmonised SensEval and SemEval data sets. Within the Uralic languages, Kahusk et al. (2001) created a manually sense annotated corpus of Estonian so that it could be included in SensEval-2. Two systems based on supervised learning were submitted, presented by Yarowsky et al. (2001) and Vider and Kaljurand (2001). Both systems failed to beat the MFS baseline (Edmonds, 2002, Table 1). For Hungarian, Miháltz (2010) created a sense tagged corpus by translating sense tagged data from English into Hungarian and then performed WSD with a number of supervised systems. Precision was compared with an MFS baseline, but the comparison was only given on a per-word basis. Up until this point, however, no work providing this type of a contrastive evaluation of WSD has been published for Finnish. This work rectifies the situation, giving results for systems representing the major approaches to WSD, including some of the systems which have performed best at the task for other languages.

2   Data and Resources

The minimum resources required to conduct a WSD evaluation are a Lexical Knowledge Base (LKB) and an evaluation corpus. Supervised systems require additionally a training corpus. The current generation of NLP systems make copious usage of word embeddings as lexical resources, as do some of the systems evaluated here, and so these are also needed. Here, the FinnWordNet (FiWN) (Lindén and Carlson, 2010) LKB is used, while both the evaluation and training corpus are based on the EuroSense corpus (Bovi et al., 2017). The rest of this section describes these linguistic resources and their preparation in more depth.

2.1   Obtaining a Sense Tagged Corpus

EuroSense (Bovi et al., 2017) is a multilingual sense tagged corpus, obtained by running the knowledge based Babelfy (Moro et al., 2014) WSD algorithm on multilingual texts. To use this corpus in a way which is compatible with the maximum number of systems and in line with the standards of previous evaluations, it first has to be preprocessed. The preprocessing pipeline is shown in Figure 1.

In the first stage, *drop non-Finnish*, all non Finnish text and annotations are removed from the stream. EuroSense is tagged with synsets from the BabelNet LKB (Navigli and Ponzetto, 2012). This knowledge base is based on the WordNets of many languages enriched and modified according to other sources, such as Wikipedia and Wikitionary. However, here the LKB to be used is FinnWordNet. A mapping file was extracted from BabelNet using its Java API and a local copy, obtained through direct communication with its authors[1]. The *Babelnet lookup* stage applies this mapping. The stage will drop annotation which do not exist in FiWN according to the mapping. A BabelNet synset can also map to multiple FiWN synsets, and in this case an ambiguous annotation can be produced.

---

[1] Made available at `https://github.com/frankier/babelnet-lookup`.

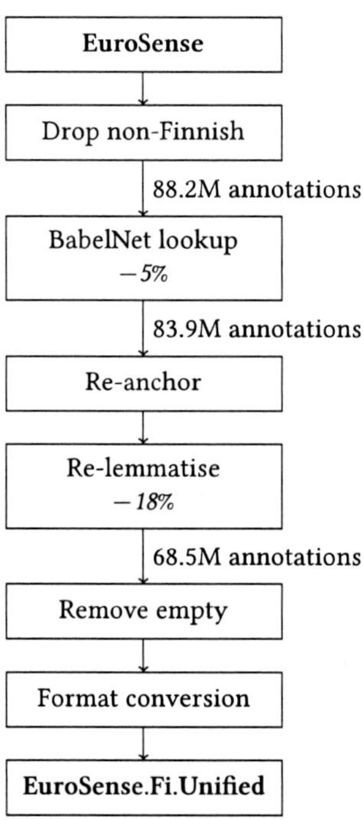

Figure 1: A diagram showing the pipeline to convert EuroSense to the unified format used for training and evaluation data. The number of annotations after various pipeline stages in millions are given, as are the proportion of annotations dropped by individual pipeline stages. The total proportion of Finnish annotations dropped is 22%.

The *re-anchor* and *re-lemmatise* stages clean up some problems with the grammatical analyses in EuroSense. EuroSense anchors sometimes include help words associated with certain verb conjugations, for example negative forms, e.g. "ei mene", or the perfect construction "on käynyt". *Re-anchor* removes these words from the anchor, taking care of the cases in which the whole anchor could actually refer to a lemma form in WordNet, e.g. "olla merkitystä". *Re-lemmatise* checks that the current lemma is associated with the annotated synsets in FiWN. In case there is no matching synsets, we look back at the surface form and check all possible lemmas obtained from OMorFi (Pirinen, 2015)[2] for matches against FiWN. At this point, any annotations which do not have exactly one lemma and one synset which exist in FiWN are dropped. In the penultimate stage, *remove empty*, any sentences without any annotations are removed entirely. Finally, the XML format is converted from the back-off annotations of the EuroSense format to the inline annotations of the unified format of Raganato et al. (2017).

The corpus is then split into testing and training sections. The testing corpus is made up of the first 1000 sentences, resulting in 4507 tagged instances. The resulting corpus is already sentence and word segmented. Additionally, the instance to be disambiguated is passed to each system with the correct lemma and part of speech tag, meaning the evaluation only tests the disambiguation stage of a full WSD pipeline and not the candidate extraction or POS tagging stage. The corpus is further processed with FinnPOS (Silfverberg et al., 2016)[3] for systems that need POS tags and/or lemmas for the words in the context.

2.2 Enriching FinnWordNet with frequency data

Many WSD techniques based on WordNet, including the typical implementation of the MFS baseline, assume it is possible to pick the most frequent sense of a lemma by picking the first sense. The reason this works with Princeton WordNet (PWN) (Miller et al., 1990) is because word senses are numbered according to the descending order of sense occurrence counts based on the part of the Brown corpus used during its creation[4]. FinnWordNet senses on the other hand are randomly ordered.

Since this data is potentially needed even by knowledge based systems, which should not have access to a training corpus, it is estimated here based on the frequency data in PWN. Unlike most PWN aligned WordNets, which are aligned at the synset level, FinnWordNet is aligned with PWN at the lemma level. An example of when this distinction takes effect is when lemmas are structurally similar. For example, in the synset "singer, vocalist, vocalizer, vocaliser", the Finnish lemma laulaja is mapped only to singer rather than to every lemma in the synset. When there is no clear distinction to be made, whole synsets are mapped. This reasoning fits with the existing structure of PWN: Relations between synsets encode purely semantic concerns, whereas relations between lemmas encode so-called morpho-semantic relationships, such as morphological derivation.

Let the Finnish-English lemma mapping be denoted $\mathcal{L}$, the specific frequency estimate for a Finnish lemma is then defined like so:

$$\text{freq}(l_{\text{fin}}) = \sum_{(l_{\text{fin}},\, l_{\text{eng}}) \in \mathcal{L}} \frac{\text{freq}(l_{\text{eng}})}{\left|\left\{(l_{\text{fin}_2},\, l_{\text{eng}}) \in \mathcal{L}\right\}\right|}$$

---

[2] `https://github.com/flammie/omorfi`
[3] `https://github.com/mpsilfve/FinnPos`
[4] This data is overlapping with, but distinct from SemCor (Miller et al., 1993).

Table 1: Word embeddings used

Name	Training data	Dim	Represents	Subword	Cross-lingual
MUSE Supervised fastText[a][b]	Wikipedia & bilingual dictionary	300	Word forms	Yes	Yes
ConceptNet Numberbatch 17.06[c][d]	Wikipedia & ConceptNet	300	Lemmas & Multiwords	—	Yes
NLPL Word2Vec[e][f]	Wikipedia & CommonCrawl[g]	100	Word forms	No	No

[a] Conneau et al. (2017)
[b] `https://github.com/facebookresearch/MUSE`
[c] Speer et al. (2016)
[d] `https://github.com/commonsense/conceptnet-numberbatch`
[e] Fares et al. (2017)
[f] `http://vectors.nlpl.eu/repository/`
[g] `https://lindat.mff.cuni.cz/repository/xmlui/handle/11234/1-1989`

The rationale of this approach is that this causes the frequencies of English lemmas to be evenly distributed across all the Finnish lemmas which they map to.

To integrate the resulting synthetic frequency data into as many applications as possible, it is made available in the WordNet format[5]. The WordNet format requires sense occurrence counts, meaning the frequency data must be converted to integer values. To perform this conversion all frequencies are multiplied by the lowest common multiple of the divisors in the above formula. Some care must be taken in downstream applications since the resulting counts are no longer true counts, but rescaled probabilities. The main consequence here is that systems which use +1 smoothing are reconfigured to use +1000 smoothing.

2.3 Word embeddings

Table 1 summarises the word embeddings used here. Due to the large number of word forms a Finnish lemma can take, it is of note here whether the word embedding represents word forms or lemmas. In the case an embedding represents word forms, it is additionally of note whether it uses any subword or character level information during its training, which should help to combat data sparsity. Despite the use of subword information, none of these embeddings can analyse out of vocabulary word forms. Cross-lingual word embeddings embed words from multiple languages in the same space, a property utilised in Section 3.2.2.

To extend word representations to sequences of words such as sentences, taking the arithmetic mean of word embeddings (AWE) has been commonly used as a baseline. Various incremental modifications have been suggested. Rücklé et al. (2018)

---

[5]Made available at `https://github.com/frankier/fiwn`.

Table 2: Results of experiments

Family	System	Variant	F_1
Baseline	Limits	Floor	13.1%
		Ceiling	99.9%
	Random sense	-	29.8%
	MFS	-	50.4%
Knowledge	UKB	No freq	51.8%
		No freq + Extract	52.2%
		Freq	54.5%
		Freq + Extract	54.9%
	Cross-lingual Lesk	No freq	32.6% – 48.2%[a]
		Freq	48.2% – 52.4%[a]
Supervised	SupWSD	No embeddings	72.9%
		Word2Vec$_{-s}$	73.6%
		Word2Vec	73.1%
		fastText$_{-s}$	73.3%
		fastText	73.4%
	AWE-NN	—	72.9% – 75.8%[b]

[a] See Table 3
[b] See Table 4

suggest concatenating the vectors formed by multiple power means, including the arithmetic mean. Variants CATP3 and CATP4 are used here. The former is the concatenation of the minimum, arithmetic mean, and the maximum, while the latter contains also the 3rd power mean. Arora et al. (2017) proposed Smooth Inverse Frequency (SIF), by taking a weighted average according to $\frac{a}{a+p(w)}$, where a is a parameter and $p(w)$ is the probability of the word. Arora et al. (2017) perform common component removal on the resulting vector. In the variant used here, (referred to as pre-SIF) a is set to the suggested value of 10^{-3} and common component removal is not performed, while $p(w)$ is estimated based upon the word frequency data of Speer et al. (2018)[6].

3   Systems and Results

This evaluation is based on the all-words variant of the WSD task. In this task, the aim is to identify and disambiguate all words in some corpus. This is contrasted with the lexical sample approach, where a fixed set of words are chosen for evaluation. There are many systems and approaches which have been proposed for performing WSD. To select techniques for this evaluation, the following criteria were used:

- Prefer techniques which have been used in previous evaluations for English.

- Prefer techniques with existing open source code that can be adapted.

- Apart from this, include also simple schemes, especially if they represent an approach to WSD not covered otherwise.

---

[6] https://github.com/LuminosoInsight/wordfreq

The last criterion has led to the inclusion of multiple techniques based upon representation learning, where some representation of words or groups of words is learned in an unsupervised manner from a large corpus. To perform WSD based on these representations a relatively simple classifier, such as a nearest neighbour classifier, is then used. This approach to WSD additionally acts as a grounded extrinsic evaluation of the quality of the representations. The results of the evaluation are summarised in Table 2, with variants of the *Cross-lingual Lesk* and *AWE-NN* systems broken down in Tables 3 and 4. The rest of this section describes each of the systems in more detail.

3.1 Baseline

We can define limits for the performance of the WSD systems. The floor is defined by the proportion of unambiguous test instances. It is the F_1 score obtained by a system which makes correct guesses for unambiguous instances and incorrect guesses for every other instance. The ceiling is for systems based upon supervised learning, and is the proportion of test instances for which the true sense exists in the training data. It is the F_1 score obtained by a system which correctly associated every item in the test data with the true class seen in the training data, and makes an incorrect guess for every other instance.

The *random sense* baseline picks a random sense by picking the first sense according to a version of FinnWordNet without the frequency data from Section 2.2 i.e. the original sense order in FinnWordNet is assumed to be random. This also gives us a rough estimate of the average ambiguity of the gold standard, $\frac{1}{29.8\%} \approx 3$. The *MFS* baseline also picks the first sense, but uses the estimated frequencies from Section 2.2.

3.2 Knowledge based systems

Knowledge based WSD systems use only information in the LKB. In almost all dictionary style resources, this can include the text of the definitions themselves. In WordNet style resources, this can include also the graphical structure of the LKB.

3.2.1 UKB

UKB (Agirre et al., 2014) is a knowledge based system, representing the graph based approach to WSD. Since it works on the level of synsets, the main algorithm is essentially language independent, with the candidate extraction step being the main language dependent component. UKB can also make use of language specific word sense frequencies.

As noted in Agirre et al. (2018), depending on the particular configuration, it is easy to get a wide range of results using UKB. The configurations used here are based on the recommended configuration given by Agirre et al. (2018). For all configurations, the *ppr w2w* algorithm is used, which runs personalised page rank for each target word. One notable configuration difference here is that the contexts passed to UKB are fixed to a single sentence. This is the same input as is given to the other systems in this evaluation. Variations with and without access to word sense frequency information are given, (freq & no freq) with the latter assumed to be similar to the configuration given in Raganato et al. (2017).

By default, the lemmas and POS tags in the contexts given to UKB are from the sense tagged instances of EuroSense. Since some instances have been filtered from

Table 3: Results for variants of Lesk with cross-lingual word embeddings

Freq	Embedding	Agg	No expand		Expand	
			No filter	Filter	No filter	Filter
No	fastText	AWE	37.6%	34.9%	40.1%	40.0%
		CATP3	37.5%	35.5%	45.9%	46.9%
		CATP4	37.2%	35.2%	44.0%	45.2%
		pre-SIF	35.3%	34.5%	41.8%	40.1%
	Numberbatch	AWE	34.3%	*32.6%*	33.1%	34.3%
		CATP3	35.9%	35.6%	47.0%	47.7%
		CATP4	35.6%	35.4%	45.5%	46.2%
		pre-SIF	33.3%	33.3%	35.3%	36.0%
	Concatenated	AWE	36.7%	33.1%	37.1%	38.3%
		CATP3	36.3%	35.1%	47.6%	**48.2%**
		CATP4	36.3%	35.3%	45.9%	46.6%
		pre-SIF	33.8%	33.9%	40.0%	39.1%
Yes	fastText	AWE	49.4%	49.5%	50.1%	50.1%
		CATP3	49.3%	*48.2%*	49.2%	49.1%
		CATP4	49.3%	48.3%	49.5%	49.4%
		pre-SIF	52.2%	52.2%	52.4%	52.3%
	Numberbatch	AWE	49.7%	49.9%	50.5%	50.1%
		CATP3	49.3%	48.7%	48.8%	49.0%
		CATP4	49.5%	49.1%	49.0%	49.2%
		pre-SIF	52.0%	51.9%	51.9%	51.9%
	Concatenated	AWE	49.4%	49.6%	50.6%	50.3%
		CATP3	49.2%	48.5%	48.9%	49.1%
		CATP4	49.3%	48.9%	49.1%	49.3%
		pre-SIF	52.3%	52.0%	51.6%	51.7%

EuroSense so as to retain high precision, it may that UKB is hamstrung by an insufficient context size. To increase the information in the context without extending it beyond the sentence boundary, a high recall, low precision lemma extraction procedure based on OMorFi is performed. The procedure (referred to in Table 2 as *extract*) adds to the context all possible lemmas from each word form, including parts of compound words, and also extracts multiwords that are in FiWN.

3.2.2 Lesk with cross-lingual word embeddings

A variant of Lesk, referred to hereafter as Lesk with cross-lingual word embeddings (Cross-lingual Lesk) is included to represent the gloss based approach to WSD. The variant presented here is loosely based upon Basile et al. (2014). The technique is a derivative of simplified Lesk (Kilgarriff and Rosenzweig, 2000) in that words are disambiguated by comparing contexts and glosses. For each candidate definition, the word vectors of each word in the definition text are aggregated to obtain a definition vector. The word vectors of the words in the context of the word being disambiguated are also aggregated to obtain a context vector. Definitions are then ranked from best to worst in descending order of cosine similarity between their definition vector and the context vector. Frequency data (freq) can be incorporated by multiplying the obtained cosine similarities by the smoothed probabilities of the synset given the lemma.

Since the words in the context are Finnish, but the words in the definitions are English, cross-lingual word vectors are required. The embeddings used are fastText, Numberbatch and the concatenation of both. Other variations are made by the choice of aggregation function, choosing whether or not to only include words which occur in FiWN, and whether glosses are expanded by adding also the glosses of related synsets. The gloss expansion procedure follows Banerjee and Pedersen (2002, Chapter 6). The results are summarised in Table 3.

3.3 Supervised systems

Supervised WSD systems are based on supervised machine learning. Most typically in WSD a separate classifier is learned for each individual lemma.

3.3.1 SupWSD

SupWSD (Papandrea et al., 2017) is a supervised WSD system following the traditional paradigm of combining hand engineered features with a linear classifier, in this case a support vector machine. SupWSD is largely a reimplementation of It Makes Sense (Zhong and Ng, 2010), and as such uses the same feature templates and its results should be largely comparable. It was chosen over It Makes Sense since it can handle larger corpora.

All variants include the POS tag and local colocation feature templates, and the default configuration includes also the set of words in the sentence. Variants incorporating the most successful configuration of Iacobacci et al. (2016), exponential decay averaging of word vectors with a window size of 10, are also included for each applicable word embedding from Section 2.3. For each configuration incorporating word vectors, variants without the set of words in the sentence are included, denoted e.g. Word2Vec$_{-s}$.

3.3.2 Nearest neighbour using word embeddings

Nearest neighbour using word embeddings has been used previously by Melamud et al. (2016) as a baseline. This system is very similar to the one outlined in Section 3.2.2. The main difference is that word senses are now represented by all memorised training instances, each themselves represented by the aggregation of word embeddings in their contexts. When a training instance is the nearest neighbour of a test instance, based on cosine distance, its tagged sense is applied to the test instance. This moves the technique from the realm of knowledge based WSD to supervised WSD. Since both tagged instances and the untagged context to be disambiguated are in Finnish, the constraint that word embeddings must be cross-lingual is removed. The results are summarised in Table 4.

4 Discussion & Conclusion

This paper has presented the first comparative WSD evaluation for Finnish. In the results presented here, several systems beat the MFS baseline. Of the knowledge based systems, both UKB and some variants of cross-lingual Lesk incorporating frequency

Table 4: Nearest neighbour using word embeddings

	AWE	CATP3	CATP4	pre-SIF
fastText	74.1%	74.1%	74.2%	74.1%
Numberbatch	74.5%	75.0%	74.9%	74.3%
Word2Vec	73.6%	72.9%	73.1%	73.8%
Concat 2[a]	75.1%	75.8%	75.5%	75.0%
Concat 3[b]	73.9%	73.2%	73.4%	74.5%

[a] Concatenation of fastText and Numberbatch
[b] Concatenation of fastText, Numberbatch and Word2Vec

information managed to clear the baseline. All the supervised systems tested beat it by a 20% margin. For techniques incorporating aggregates of word vectors, CATP3 reliably outperformed a simple arithmetic mean across a variety of configurations.

This evaluation may be limited by a number of issues. Multiple issues stem from the use of EuroSense. Due to the way it is automatically induced, it contains errors, making its use problematic, especially its use as a gold standard. First we model these errors as occurring in an essentially random manner. In this case a perfect WSD system would get a less than perfect score, and in fact the performance of all systems would be expected to decrease. It is worth noting that since inter-annotator agreement can be relatively low for word sense annotation, manual annotations can also be modelled as having this type of problem to some degree. Random errors in the training data would also cause the supervised systems to perform worse, however this does not effect the overall integrity of the evaluation. However, it is likely that EuroSense in fact contains systematic errors. One type of systematic error is an error of omission: EuroSense assigns senses to a subset of all possible candidate words, filtering out those which the Babelfy algorithm cannot assign sufficient confidence to, meaning that the gold standard may be missing words which are in some sense more difficult, artificially increasing the score of systems which would also have problems with these same words. Perhaps worse are systematic errors which bias certain lemmas within certain types of contexts to certain incorrect senses. In this case, supervised systems may seem to perform better, but only because they are essentially learning to replicate the systematic errors in EuroSense rather than because they are performing WSD more accurately.

Another factor which may cause this evaluation to present too optimistic a picture of the performance of supervised systems is that the evaluation corpus and training corpus are from the same domain, parliamentary proceedings, which could result in an inflated score in comparison to an evaluation corpus from another domain. Finally, since the corpus is derived from EuroParl, the original language of most text is likely not Finnish. Particular features of translated language, sometimes referred to as translationese may affect the applicability of the results to non translated Finnish[7].

Finally, the MFS baseline may have been handicapped in terms of its performance. On the one hand, the MFS baseline may be reasonably analagous with MFS baselines in WSD evaluations for other languages in that it is ultimately derived from frequency data which is out of domain. On the other hand, estimating the frequencies based on English frequency data is likely quite inaccurate when compared to a possible estimation based on a reasonably sized Finnish language tagged corpus.

---

[7]For an exploration of some features of translationese in EuroParl, see Koppel and Ordan (2011).

Further work could address the issues with the gold standard by creating a cross-domain manually annotated corpus, ideally based on a corpus of text originally in Finnish. A training corpus could also be created manually, but this would be a much larger task. This would however allow a better MFS baseline to be created. A less work intensive way of improving the situation with the MFS baseline would be to add one based on the supervised training data, and consider this as an extra MFS baseline, only for supervised methods.

The implementations of the techniques reimplemented for this evaluation and the scripts and configuration files for the adapted open source systems are publicly available under the Apache v2 license. To ease replicability further, the entire evaluation framework, including all the requirements, WSD systems and lexical resources are made available as a Docker image[8].

Acknowledgments

Thanks to the anonymous reviewers for their useful comments. Thanks also to my wife Miia for helping with the Finnish abstract. Finally, thanks to my supervisor Michael Cochez for his valuable advice and comments.

References

Eneko Agirre, Oier López de Lacalle, and Aitor Soroa. 2018. The risk of sub-optimal use of open source nlp software: Ukb is inadvertently state-of-the-art in knowledge-based wsd. *arXiv preprint arXiv:1805.04277* .

Eneko Agirre, Oier López de Lacalle, and Aitor Soroa. 2014. Random walks for knowledge-based word sense disambiguation. *Computational Linguistics* 40(1):57–84.

Sanjeev Arora, Yingyu Liang, and Tengyu Ma. 2017. A simple but tough-to-beat baseline for sentence embeddings .

Satanjeev Banerjee and T Pedersen. 2002. *Adapting the Lesk algorithm for word sense disambiguation to WordNet*. Master's thesis, University of Minnesota.

Pierpaolo Basile, Annalina Caputo, and Giovanni Semeraro. 2014. An enhanced lesk word sense disambiguation algorithm through a distributional semantic model. In *Proceedings of COLING 2014, the 25th International Conference on Computational Linguistics: Technical Papers*. pages 1591–1600. http://www.aclweb.org/anthology/C14-1151.

Claudio Delli Bovi, Jose Camacho-Collados, Alessandro Raganato, and Roberto Navigli. 2017. Eurosense: Automatic harvesting of multilingual sense annotations from parallel text. In *Proceedings of the 55th Annual Meeting of the Association for Computational Linguistics (Volume 2: Short Papers)*. volume 2, pages 594–600.

Alexis Conneau, Guillaume Lample, Marc'Aurelio Ranzato, Ludovic Denoyer, and Hervé Jégou. 2017. Word translation without parallel data. *arXiv preprint arXiv:1710.04087* .

---

[8]https://github.com/frankier/finn-wsd-eval

Philip Edmonds. 2002. Senseval: The evaluation of word sense disambiguation systems. volume 7. http://www2.denizyuret.com/ref/edmonds/edmonds2002-elra.pdf.

Murhaf Fares, Andrey Kutuzov, Stephan Oepen, and Erik Velldal. 2017. Word vectors, reuse, and replicability: Towards a community repository of large-text resources. In *Proceedings of the 21st Nordic Conference on Computational Linguistics, NoDaLiDa, 22-24 May 2017, Gothenburg, Sweden.* Linköping University Electronic Press, Linköpings universitet, 131, pages 271–276.

Ignacio Iacobacci, Mohammad Taher Pilehvar, and Roberto Navigli. 2016. Embeddings for word sense disambiguation: An evaluation study. In *Proceedings of the 54th Annual Meeting of the Association for Computational Linguistics (Volume 1: Long Papers).* volume 1, pages 897–907.

Neeme Kahusk, Heili Orav, and Haldur Oim. 2001. Sensiting inflectionality: Estonian task for senseval-2. In *Proceedings of SENSEVAL-2 Second International Workshop on Evaluating Word Sense Disambiguation Systems.* Association for Computational Linguistics, pages 25–28. http://www.aclweb.org/anthology/S01-1006.

Adam Kilgarriff and Joseph Rosenzweig. 2000. English senseval: Report and results. In *LREC.* volume 6, page 2.

Moshe Koppel and Noam Ordan. 2011. Translationese and its dialects. In *Proceedings of the 49th Annual Meeting of the Association for Computational Linguistics: Human Language Technologies-Volume 1.* Association for Computational Linguistics, pages 1318–1326.

Krister Lindén and Lauri Carlson. 2010. Finnwordnet–finnish wordnet by translation. *LexicoNordica–Nordic Journal of Lexicography* 17:119–140. http://www.ling.helsinki.fi/ klinden/pubs/FinnWordnetInLexicoNordica-en.pdf.

John C. Mallery. 1988. *Thinking About Foreign Policy: Finding an Appropriate Role for Artificially Intelligent Computers.* Master's thesis, Massachusetts Institute of Technology.

Oren Melamud, Jacob Goldberger, and Ido Dagan. 2016. context2vec: Learning generic context embedding with bidirectional lstm. In *Proceedings of The 20th SIGNLL Conference on Computational Natural Language Learning.* pages 51–61.

Márton Miháltz. 2010. *Semantic resources and their applications in Hungarian natural language processing.* Ph.D. thesis, Pázmány Péter Katolikus Egyetem.

George A Miller, Richard Beckwith, Christiane Fellbaum, Derek Gross, and Katherine J Miller. 1990. Introduction to wordnet: An on-line lexical database. *International journal of lexicography* 3(4):235–244.

George A Miller, Claudia Leacock, Randee Tengi, and Ross T Bunker. 1993. A semantic concordance. In *Proceedings of the workshop on Human Language Technology.* Association for Computational Linguistics, pages 303–308.

Andrea Moro, Alessandro Raganato, and Roberto Navigli. 2014. Entity Linking meets Word Sense Disambiguation: a Unified Approach. *Transactions of the Association for Computational Linguistics (TACL)* 2:231–244. http://www.aclweb.org/anthology/Q14-1019.

Roberto Navigli and Simone Paolo Ponzetto. 2012. Babelnet: The automatic construction, evaluation and application of a wide-coverage multilingual semantic network. *Artificial Intelligence* 193:217–250. https://doi.org/10.1016/j.artint.2012.07.001.

Simone Papandrea, Alessandro Raganato, and Claudio Delli Bovi. 2017. Supwsd: A flexible toolkit for supervised word sense disambiguation. In *Proceedings of the 2017 Conference on Empirical Methods in Natural Language Processing: System Demonstrations.* pages 103–108.

Tommi A Pirinen. 2015. Development and use of computational morphology of finnish in the open source and open science era: Notes on experiences with omorfi development. *SKY Journal of Linguistics* 28:381–393.

Alessandro Raganato, Jose Camacho-Collados, and Roberto Navigli. 2017. Word sense disambiguation: A unified evaluation framework and empirical comparison. In *Proceedings of EACL.* pages 99–110. https://aclanthology.info/pdf/E/E17/E17-1010.pdf.

Andreas Rücklé, Steffen Eger, Maxime Peyrard, and Iryna Gurevych. 2018. Concatenated p-mean word embeddings as universal cross-lingual sentence representations. *arXiv preprint arXiv:1803.01400* .

Miikka Silfverberg, Teemu Ruokolainen, Krister Lindén, and Mikko Kurimo. 2016. Finnpos: an open-source morphological tagging and lemmatization toolkit for finnish. *Language Resources and Evaluation* 50(4):863–878.

Robert Speer, Joshua Chin, and Catherine Havasi. 2016. ConceptNet 5.5: An Open Multilingual Graph of General Knowledge .

Robyn Speer, Joshua Chin, Andrew Lin, Sara Jewett, and Lance Nathan. 2018. Luminosoinsight/wordfreq: v2.2. https://doi.org/10.5281/zenodo.1443582.

Alan M Turing. 1950. Computing machinery and intelligence. *Mind* 59(236):433–460. https://doi.org/10.1093/mind/LIX.236.433.

Kadri Vider and Kaarel Kaljurand. 2001. Automatic wsd: Does it make sense of estonian? In *Proceedings of SENSEVAL-2 Second International Workshop on Evaluating Word Sense Disambiguation Systems.* Association for Computational Linguistics, pages 159–162. http://www.aclweb.org/anthology/S01-1039.

David Yarowsky, Silviu Cucerzan, Radu Florian, Charles Schafer, and Richard Wicentowski. 2001. The johns hopkins senseval2 system descriptions. In *The Proceedings of the Second International Workshop on Evaluating Word Sense Disambiguation Systems.* Association for Computational Linguistics, pages 163–166.

Zhi Zhong and Hwee Tou Ng. 2010. It makes sense: A wide-coverage word sense disambiguation system for free text. In *Proceedings of the ACL 2010 system demonstrations.* Association for Computational Linguistics, pages 78–83.

Elliptical Constructions in Estonian UD Treebank

Kadri Muischnek
University of Tartu
Institute of Computer Science/
Institute of Estonian and General Linguistics
Kadri.Muischnek@ut.ee

Liisi Torga
University of Tartu
Institute of Computer Science
Liisi.Torga@ut.ee

Abstract

This contribution is about the annotation of sentences with verbal predicate ellipsis in the Estonian Universal Dependencies (UD) treebank. The main aim of the UD initiative is to develop a cross-linguistically consistent treebank annotation scheme and build a multilingual treebank collection. There are more than 70 treebanks in over 100 languages in UD treebank collection version 2.2. However, the UD annotation scheme is constantly improved and amended and so the annotation of the treebanks is also changing from version to version.

Our article studies a problematic issue in representing syntactic structure – clauses with predicate verb ellipsis. UD syntactic annotation scheme is based on dependency syntax and as the dependency structure is verb-centered, predicate verb ellipsis causes more annotation problems than other types of ellipsis. We focus on such constructions (referred to in English often as gapping and stripping) in Estonian and their annotation in Estonian UD treebank versions 1 and 2.2.

Kokkuvõte

Artikkel käsitleb elliptilise öeldisega laustete märgendamist eesti keele *Universal Dependencies'* (UD) puudepangas. UD eesmärgiks on esiteks töötada välja puudepankade morfoloogilise ja sõltuvussüntaktilise märgendamise skeem, mis oleks keelest sõltumatu selles mõttes, et sobiks kõigi keelte märgendamiseks, ja teiseks luua selle märgendusskeemi järgi annoteeritud puudepankade kollektsioon. UD versioon 2.2 sisaldab enam kui 100 puudepanka rohkem kui 70 keeles. Märgendusskeemi arendatakse ja täiustatakse pidevalt ja seega tuleb UD kujul olevaid puudepanku uute versioonide tarbeks pidevalt ümber märgendada.

UD süntaktiline märgendus põhineb sõltuvussüntaksi põhimõtetel, mille järgi lause keskmeks on öeldis, tavaliselt finiitne verbivorm. Erandiks on koopulalaused (eesti keele puhul *olema*-verbiga laused), mille kõrgeimaks ülemuseks on

Proceedings of the fifth Workshop on Computational Linguistics for Uralic Languages, pages 55–65,
Tartu, Estonia, January 7 - January 8, 2019.

mitte-verbiline predikaat. Kuna UD süntaksimärgendus on oma olemuselt ver-
bikeskne, põhjustab öeldise ellips lausepuu moodustamisel rohkem probleeme
kui mõne muu lausemoodustaja väljajätt. Tavaline on öeldisverbi väljajätt koor-
dinatsiooniseoses olevates identse öeldisverbiga osalausetes, kus öeldisverb on
olemas ainult esimeses osalauses ning järgnevates on tüüpiliselt kustutatud. Artiklis ongi vaatluse all sellised öeldisverbi ellipsiga laused eesti keele UD puudepangas: nende lausete tüpoloogia, automaatne tuvastamine ning automaatne
(ümber)märgendamine eesti keele UD puudepanga versiooni 2.2 jaoks.

1   Introduction

Universal Dependencies[1] (henceworth: UD) (McDonald et al., 2013) is an initiative
aimed at developing cross-linguistically consistent treebank annotation for many languages. UD is an ongoing project, which means that the annotation guidelines and
treebank annotations are subject to constant changes. Its Version 2.2 includes more
than 100 treebanks in over than 70 languages.

Syntactic annotation in the UD framework represents dependency relations between tokens; the dependency arcs are labelled, i.e. they are typed dependencies.
Dependency description of a clause is verb-centered: the root of a dependency tree is
a finite verb form or, in copular sentences, a predicative word-form. So predicate verb
ellipsis poses more problems for building a dependency tree structure than ellipsis of
some argument or adjunct.

In Estonian, the most common cases of predicate verb ellipsis are gapping and
stripping constructions that appear in coordinated clauses. Gapping means that the
identical finite verb (together with the possible auxiliaries) is omitted in the second
coordinate clause. Extended gapping construction means that some other constituent
also has been elided together with the predicate verb. By stripping everything is elided
from the coordinate clause except one constituent and often an additive or adversative
particle is added to the single remaining constituent.

The UD version 2.2 Annotation Guidelines[2] suggest that the elliptical constructions should be annotated as follows:

1. If the elided element has no overt dependents, there is no special annotation,
i.e. the elided element remains unnoticed.

2. If the elided element has overt dependents, one of these should be promoted to
take the role of the head.

3. If the elided element is a predicate and the promoted element is one of its
arguments or adjuncts, a special relation – orphan – should be used when attaching
other non-functional dependents to the promoted head.

As Schuster et al. (2017) point out, these guidelines "put stripping in a gray zone" as
the additive/negative particle can be annotated using the relation "orphan" or simply
as an adverbial modifier.

Ellipsis has been a relatively popular research topic in UD framework. Droganova
and Zeman (2017) provide an overview of annotating gapping and stripping constructions (usage of label "orphan") in UD 2.0 treebanks. Schuster et al. (2017) analyse gapping constructions in several languages and argue in favor of the annotation scheme
of these constructions proposed in UD v2.

---

[1]`www.universaldependencies.org`
[2]`http://universaldependencies.org/u/overview/specific-syntax.html#ellipsis`

As the main aim of UD initiative is to facilitate multi-lingual parsing, there have already been a couple of papers that report on experiments on improving the parsing of elliptical constructions, e.g. Droganova et al. (2018) or Schuster et al. (2018).

The rest of the paper is organized as follows. Section 2 gives an overview of predicate ellipsis types in Estonian and Section 3 briefly describes their annotation in Estonian treebanks prior to Estonian UD v2.2. Method for detecting and re-annotating elliptical constructions in Estonian UD v2.2 is introduced in Section 4 as well as the main findings, i.e. types of predicate verb ellipsis in the treebank and their annotation.

2 Gapping, stripping and similar constructions in Estonian

Estonian word-order is relatively free, meaning that it is mostly determined by information structure and the main principle determining the word order is V2 (verb-second). However, there are also several clause types where the finite verb form is placed in the very beginning or in the very end (Lindström, 2017).

Gapping is norm in coordinated V2 clauses where the predicate verb has at least two dependents – the identical predicate verb is omitted in all other clauses except the first one. (Erelt, 2017, pp 598–599) So there are typically at least two orphans in an Estonian gapping clause, as in (1).

(1) *Mari sööb jäätist   ja Jüri 0 kommi.*
     Mari eats ice-cream-Ptv and Jüri 0 candy-Ptv

     'Mari is eating an ice-cream and Jüri a candy.'

An extended gapping construction is also quite common. If the clause starts with an adverbial, subject is placed next to the verb and the subject and verb are identical in coordinated clauses, the subject can be omitted together with the verb (2). (Erelt, 2017, p 599)

(2) *Suvel   sööb Mari jäätist   ja talvel   0 kommi.*
     Summer-Ade eats Mari ice-cream-Ptv and winter-Ade 0 candy-Ptv

     'Mari eats ice-cream during the summer and candy during the winter.'

Non-contiguous gaps are also present in Estonian: in sentence (3) the identical finite verb form *andis* 'gave' and adverbial modifier *kingituseks* 'as a gift' are omitted in the second coordinated clause.

(3) *Ta   andis mulle kingituseks   raamatu ja mina 0 talle   0 roosi.*
     S/he gave I-All present-Trans book-Gen and I   0 s/he-All 0 rose-Ptv

     'S/he gave me a book as a gift and I him/her a rose.'

The stripping construction has two subtypes: coordinating (4) and adversative (5). In both cases the elliptical clause contains only one argument plus a particle. Common additive particles in coordinating stripping constructions are *ka* 'also' and *samuti* 'also'; in negative clauses *ka mitte* 'also not' and *samuti mitte* 'also not'. In adversative constructions particle *mitte* 'not' is used.(Erelt, 2017, pp 599–601)

(4) *Jüri sööb jäätist*   *ja   Mari   0   ka.*
    Jüri eats ice-cream-Ptv and Mari 0 too

    'Jüri is eating an ice-cream and so does Mari.'

(5) *Jüri sööb jäätist,*   *aga   Mari   0   mitte.*
    Jüri eats ice-cream-Ptv but Mari 0 not

    'Jüri is eating an ice-cream but Mari is not.'

Another construction that has been annotated as an example of ellipsis in Estonian UD v 2.2 is the so-called *seda*-construction (*seda* is singular partitive case form of pronoun *see* 'it, this'), exemplified in (6).

There are two alternative ways to analyse this construction. One possibility is to consider it a clause that has undergone two successive alternations: anaphoric substitution and ellipsis. The other possibility is to interpret it as a result of one-step anaphoric substitution. In both cases, the "full" version of the sentence would look like (7). In the first alternative case, there are two alternations taking place: as the first step the whole first clause *raba pakub kordumatuid elamusi* 'marsh offers unique experiences' is substituted with anaphoric expression *teeb seda* 'does it'. As the second step, the finite verb form *teeb* 'does' is deleted. So the output of the first step – the anaphoric substitution would look like (8), which is a grammatical, well-formed Estonian sentence, and the final, elliptical version like (6).

(6) *Raba   pakub   kordumatuid   elamusi*   *ja   seda   eriti*
    Mash offers unique-Pl-Ptv experience-Pl-Ptv and it-Ptv especially
         talvel.
         winter-Ade

    'Marsh offers unique experiences, especially during the winter.'

(7) *Raba   pakub   kordumatuid   elamusi*   *ja   raba   pakub*
    Mash offers unique-Pl-Ptv experience-Pl-Ptv and marsh offers
         kordumatuid   elamusi   *eriti   talvel.*
         unique-Pl-Ptv experiences-PlPtv especially winter-Pl

(8) *Raba   pakub   kordumatuid   elamusi*   *ja   teeb   seda   eriti*
    Mash offers unique-Pl-Ptv experience-Pl-Ptv and does it-Ptv especially
         talvel.
         winter-Ade

Another way to explain the *seda*-construction is to say that the whole first clause is simply substituted with pronominal form *seda*, thus producing a verbless clause in one step.

This construction has passed unnoticed by Estonian grammar books so far, so we have no linguistic analyses to base our annotation principles on. We have decided to adopt two-step explanation (anaphora followed by ellipsis) and we treat it as an example of predicate verb ellipsis. However, this construction differs from gapping and stripping as the deleted verb is not identical with the predicate verb in the previous coordinate clause.

3   Previous treatment of ellipsis in Estonian treebanks

The Estonian UD treebank has been created by semi-automatically converting the
Estonian Dependency Treebank (EDT) (Muischnek et al., 2014) into UD format. The
EDT annotation scheme was based on Dependency Constraint Grammar (Karlsson
et al., 1995; Bick and Didriksen, 2015).

Annotations of Estonian UD treebank are produced by several semi-automatic
annotation conversions (from EDT to UD v1 and then from UD 1 to UD v2) and as
such contain errors and inconsistencies.

In the original EDT the elliptical constructions were annotated so that one of the
remaining arguments in the elliptical clause was promoted as the root of the clause
and dependents of the deleted verb-form were annotated as dependents of the promoted argument, keeping their original syntactic labels. So the attachment of dependents is in principle same as in UD v2, but no special label (orphan in UD v2) was
used to annotate the "orphaned" dependents.

In contrast, UD v1 annotation scheme used a special relation remnant to attach
dependents of the elided verb to their correlates in the coordinated clause where the
verb is present. However, this annotation principle was not followed in Estonian UD
v1, mainly due to lack of (human) resources for re-annotation. Figure 1 depicts annotation of an elliptical sentence in Estonian UD v1 treebank. The example sentence
consists of three coordinated clauses, all sharing identical predicate verb *õpib* 'studies'
that is omitted in the second and third clause. In the elliptical clauses the "orphaned"
subjects *Maarit* and *Ilmar* are annotated as the roots of the respective clauses and the
"orphaned" objects *kirjandust* 'literature' and *ajalugu* 'history' are, somewhat illogi-
cally, attached to the promoted subjects.

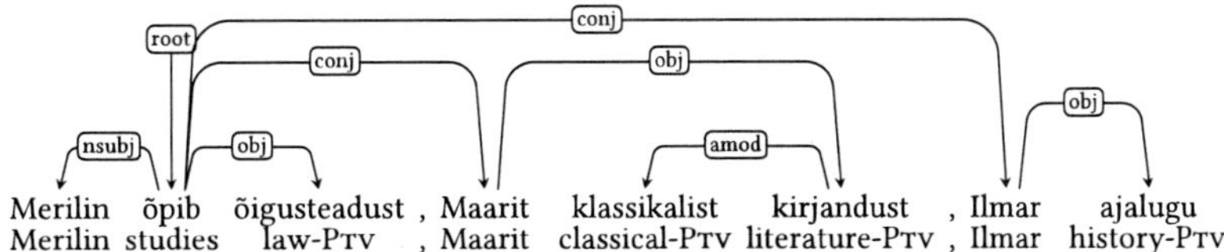

Figure 1: 'Merilin studies law, Maarit classical literature, Ilmar history' (Annotation
of an elliptical sentence in the Estonian UD v1 treebank)

4   Detecting and re-annotating clauses with predicate verb ellipsis in Estonian UD v2.2 treebank

As elliptical constructions were not explicitly annotated in the previous versions of
the Estonian UD treebank, a special effort was needed to find and re-annotate them.
A rule-based program (Python3) was created to find and re-annotate clauses with
predicate verb ellipsis. The main principle is quite simple: the program looks for a
verb that has a conjunct which is not a verb. This conjunct has to have at least one
dependent that is not a punctuation mark or a coordinating conjunction. In order
to exclude copular clauses, the conjunct also should not have a dependent labelled
as copula. It means that the created piece of software works only with the locally
(mis)customized version of UD v1 annotation.

As already mentioned, according to the UD v2 annotation scheme, in an elliptical clause one of the "orphaned" dependents of the deleted verb is promoted as the head of the clause and the other dependents of the deleted verb are attached to it using the label orphan. However, in the enhanced version[3] of UD syntactic annotation the label orphan should be replaced with the label that the token would have as a dependent of the elided (and restored as a null node) verb, which is the same label that the token had in v1 of the Estonian UD treebank. In order to be able to restore the correct label in the enhanced dependencies version, we have introduced special subtypes of the label orphan, e.g orphan:obj, orphan:advmod etc.

The program achieved 95% precision and 73% recall on a test corpus consisting of 1000 sentences. It means that 95% of the detected sentences were really elliptical sentences and that 73% of the targeted sentences were actually found by the program. For the re-annotation of orphans these figures were 81.8% and 94.4%, respectively. The relatively low recall for elliptical sentence detection is mainly due to inconsistent and erroneous annotations in the treebank.

There were 359 sentences containing predicate verb ellipsis in Estonian UD treebank. Given that the treebank has a little more than 30,000 sentences, only ca 1.2% of trees contain gapping or stripping or other similar constructions.

Table 1 gives an overview of predicate verb ellipsis types in v2.2 of Estonian UD treebank as detected by the software. In the following subsections we analyse them one by one.

Type of ellipsis	Number of sentences	% of all sentences with predicate ellipsis
Simple gapping	151	42.1
Extended gapping	23	6.4
Non-contiguous gaps	19	5.3
Stripping	23	6.4
seda-construction	14	3.8
Elided copular verb	100	28
Errors	29	8
	359	100

Table 1: Frequency of predicate verb ellipsis types in Estonian UD treebank v 2.2

4.1 Simple gapping constructions

Simple gapping construction is the most frequent type of predicate ellipsis in the Estonian UD treebank, making up 42.1% of all elliptical clauses. Figures 2 and 3 depict a typical case of gapping: the identical verb-form *juhivad* '(they) lead' has been deleted in the second coordinated clause, leaving an "orphaned" object *analüüsi* 'analysis in partitive case form'. The annotation on Figure 2 is that of v1 of Estonian UD treebank. On Figure 3 we can see the annotation that has been automatically converted into UD v2.2 format.

---

[3] http://universaldependencies.org/u/overview/enhanced-syntax.html

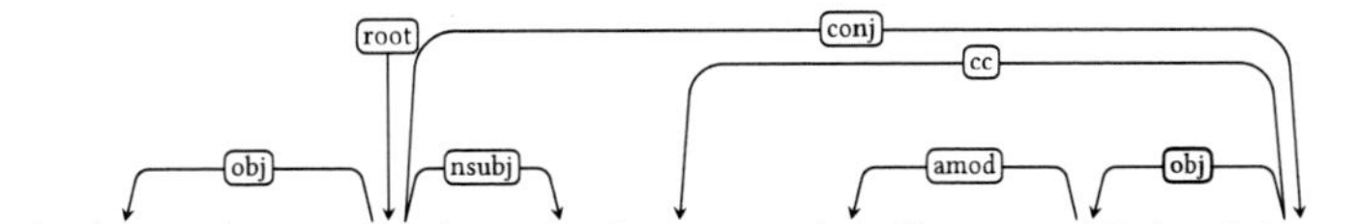

Figure 2: 'Data mining is directed by data and statistical analysis by humans' (Gapping construction in Estonian UD v1)

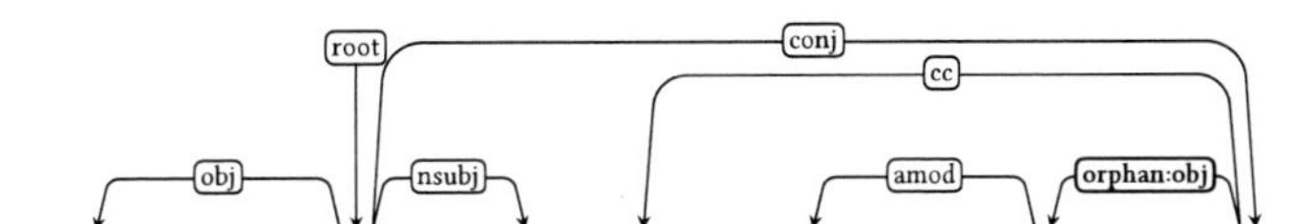

Figure 3: 'Data mining is directed by data and statistical analysis by humans' (Gapping construction in Estonian UD v2.2)

4.2   Extended gapping constructions

Extended gapping constructions make up 6.4% of all elliptical clauses. In this case, in addition to the predicate verb, also some of its dependents (subject, object, oblique dependents etc) are deleted. Figures 4 and 5 depict a typical case of extended gapping: both conjuncted clauses have the same finite verb *on hõivatud* 'are occupied' plus the same oblique dependent *kõrvaltöödega* 'with additional jobs', both are elided in the second clause. The annotation on Figure 4 is that of v1 of Estonian UD treebank, on Figure 5 that of the v2.2.

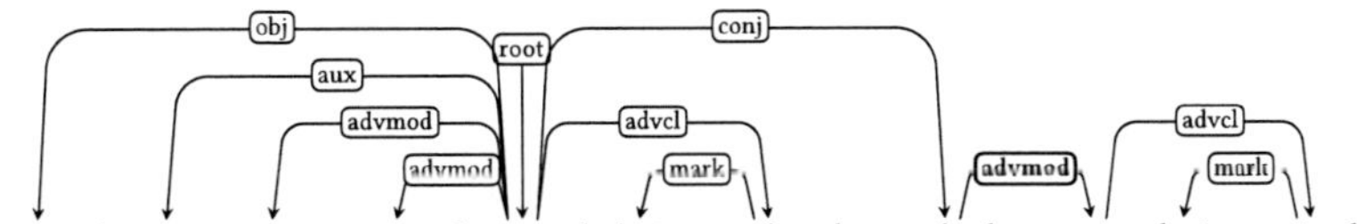

Figure 4: 'Estonians are more occupied with job that Russians, men more than women.' (Extended gapping construction in Estonian UD v1)

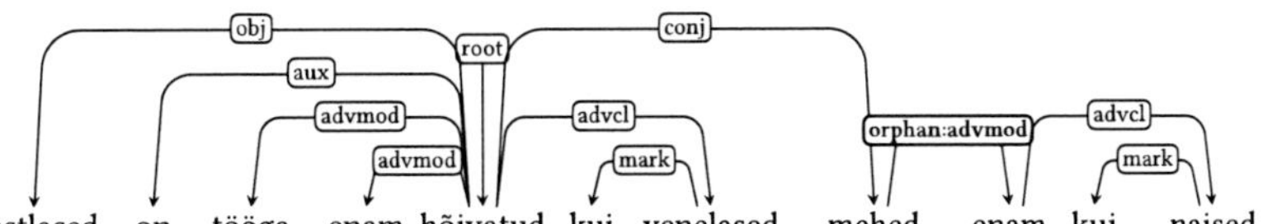

Figure 5: 'Estonians are more occupied with job that Russians, men more than women.' (Extended gapping construction in Estonian UD v2.2)

4.3 Non-contiguous gaps

Non-contiguous gaps make up 5.3% of all elliptical clauses. Among them, the most frequent pattern is that the identical verb and head of a numerical or adjectival modifier are deleted from the coordinated clause.

Figures 6 and 7 depict a typical example of non-contiguous gapping: the finite verb form *maksti* 'was paid' and the adverbial modifier *rubla* 'rouble' are deleted from the coordinated clause. Deletion of finite verb leaves behind two orphaned modifiers: adverbial modifier *tollal* 'then' and oblique modifier *410* that has been promoted to the position of the deleted oblique modifier *rubla* 'rouble'.

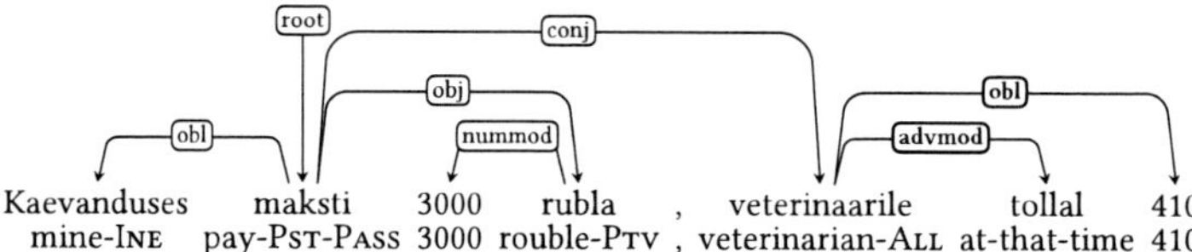

Figure 6: 'Miner was paid 3000 roubles but veterinarian 410.' (Non-contiguous gapping construction in Estonian UD v1)

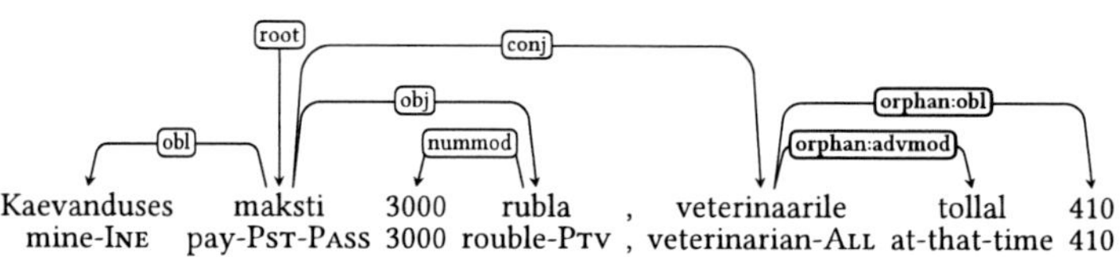

Figure 7: 'Miner was paid 3000 roubles but veterinarian 410.' (Non-contiguous gapping construction in Estonian UD v2.2)

4.4 Stripping constructions

Stripping constructions make up 6.4% of all elliptical clauses in Estonian UD treebank. As already mentioned in Section 2, by stripping everything is deleted from the coordinated clause except one argument plus an additive or adversative particle.

In the example sentences on Figure 8 and Figure 9 everything except the subject *mõned* 'some' is deleted from the coordinated clause. The adversative particle *mitte* 'not' reverses the meaning of the stripped coordinated clause. The remaining subject is annotated as the head of the clause and the adversative particle is attached to it as an adverbial modifier.

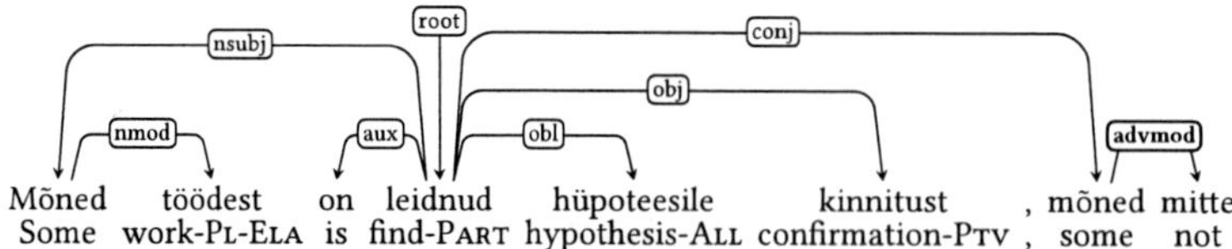

Figure 8: 'Some works have confirmed the hypothesis, some not.' (Stripping construction in Estonian UD v1)

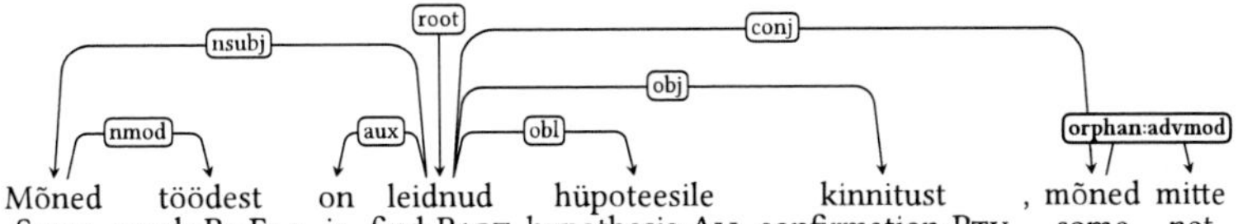

Figure 9: 'Some works have confirmed the hypothesis, some not.' (Stripping construction in Estonian UD v2.2)

4.5 *seda*-constructions

3.8% of the clauses with predicate ellipsis are the so-called *seda*-constructions (cf Section 2). Figure 10 depicts a sentence with *seda*-construction annotated in UD v1 style and Figure 11 the same sentence as in Estonian UD v2.2. The second coordinated clause consists of pronominal form *seda* 'it/that in partitive case form' plus an oblique modifier *sündmusega* 'with/by event' and its determiner *mitme* 'several in genitive case form'. seda is annotated as the head of the elliptical clause and sündmusega as its "orphaned" oblique dependent.

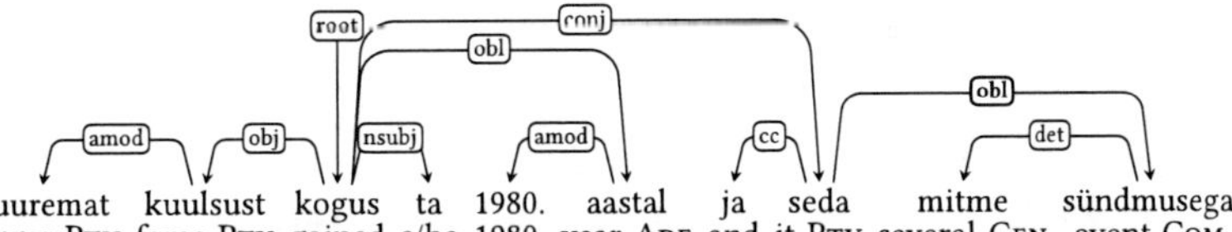

Figure 10: 'S/he gained greater fame in the 1980s, due to several events.' (*seda*-construction in Estonian UD v1)

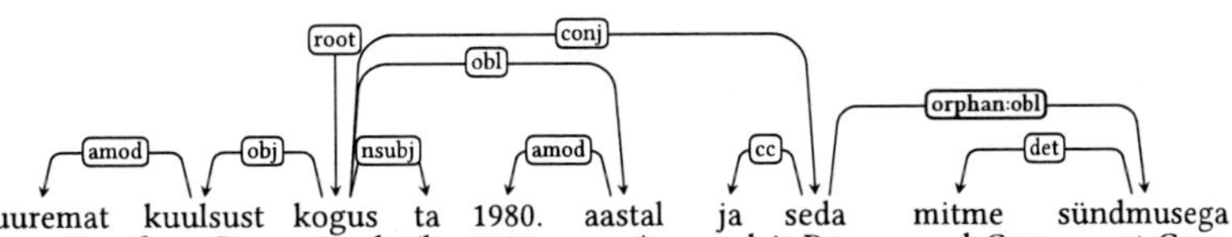

Figure 11: 'S/he gained greater fame in the 1980s, due to several events.' (*seda*-construction in Estonian UD v2.2)

4.6 Copular constructions

Clauses with missing copula verb *olema* 'be' make up 28% of all clauses with finite verb form ellipsis.

A special note on copula sentences is perhaps needed here. Our program also detects sentences with missing copular verb *olema* 'to be'. However, according to the UD Annotation Guidelines[4], the copular clauses are regarded as instances of nonverbal predication and some argument is annotated as the root of the clause whereas the copular verb is attached to this root using the syntactic relation label cop. So, the deletion of *olema* 'be' does not leave behind any "orphaned" constituents.

---

[4] http://universaldependencies.org/u/overview/simple-syntax.html#
nonverbal-clauses

It should be pointed out that in Estonian texts there seems to be no difference between deleting *olema* or any other verb, the clause patterns are more or less the same. Figure 12 depicts a sentence with two coordinated copular clauses, where the copular verb form *on* 'is' is deleted from the second clause, but that does not result in any need for special annotation as the predicatives *kitsas* 'narrow' and *tihe* 'tight, here: heavy' serve as clause roots. The annotation is the same in both version 1 and version 2.2 of the Estonian UD treebank.

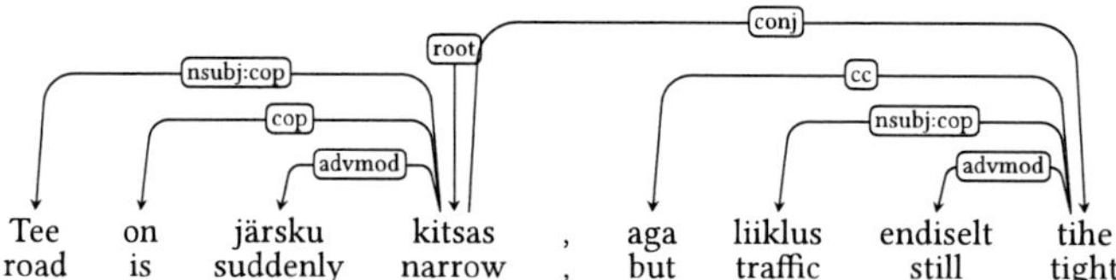

Figure 12: 'The road is suddenly narrow but traffic (is) still heavy.' (Sentence with elided copula verb in Estonian UD versions 1 and 2.2)

5   Conclusion

Predicate verb ellipsis is a difficult case for dependency syntax as the finite verb form should, as a rule, be the head of a clause. In case of its absence, dependency structure of a clause has to be constructed in some more or less artificial way.

Universal Dependencies' (UD) syntactic annotation scheme has evolved and changed over several years and so also the UD treebank annotations need to be amended and improved for the new treebank releases. Ellipsis, especially gapping and stripping, are one of those constructions that have been annotated differently in UD versions 1 and 2 and that are planned to have a special annotation (null-node insertion) in the enhanced version of UD.

This article gave an overview of predicate verb ellipsis – gapping, stripping and related constructions – in Estonian language and their frequency and annotation in the Estonian UD treebank versions 1 and 2.2.

The work described in this article has resulted in more accurate version of Estonian UD treebank. The next step would be annotating an enhanced dependencies version of the Estonian UD treebank. For elliptical constructions it means "restoring" the elided predicate verbs as null-nodes and re-attaching and re-naming its dependents.

Acknowledgments

This research has been supported by the Centre of Excellence in Estonian Studies (CEES, European Regional Development Fund) and is related to research project IUT20-56 (Estonian Research Council).

References

Eckhard Bick and Tino Didriksen. 2015. Cg-3—beyond classical constraint grammar. In *Proceedings of the 20th Nordic Conference of Computational Linguistics,*

NODALIDA 2015, May 11-13, 2015, Vilnius, Lithuania. Linköping University Electronic Press, 109, pages 31–39.

Kira Droganova, Filip Ginter, Jenna Kanerva, and Daniel Zeman. 2018. Mind the gap: Data enrichment in dependency parsing of elliptical constructions. In *Proceedings of the Second Workshop on Universal Dependencies (UDW 2018).* pages 47–54.

Kira Droganova and Daniel Zeman. 2017. Elliptic constructions: Spotting patterns in ud treebanks. In *Proceedings of the NoDaLiDa 2017 Workshop on Universal Dependencies (UDW 2017).* pages 48–57.

Mati Erelt. 2017. Ellips. *Eesti keele süntaks. Tartu: Tartu Ülikool.* pages 591–601.

Fred Karlsson, Atro Voutilainen, Juha Heikkila, and Atro Anttila. 1995. *Constraint Grammar, A Language-independent System for Parsing Unrestricted Text.* Mouton de Gruyter.

Liina Lindström. 2017. Lause infostruktuur ja sõnajärg. *Eesti keele süntaks. Tartu: Tartu Ülikooli Kirjastus* pages 537–564.

Ryan McDonald, Joakim Nivre, Yvonne Quirmbach-Brundage, Yoav Goldberg, Dipanjan Das, Kuzman Ganchev, Keith Hall, Slav Petrov, Hao Zhang, Oscar Täckström, et al. 2013. Universal dependency annotation for multilingual parsing. In *Proceedings of the 51st Annual Meeting of the Association for Computational Linguistics (Volume 2: Short Papers).* volume 2, pages 92–97.

Kadri Muischnek, Kaili Müürisep, Tiina Puolakainen, Eleri Aedmaa, Riin Kirt, and Dage Särg. 2014. Estonian dependency treebank and its annotation scheme. In *Proceedings of 13th Workshop on Treebanks and Linguistic Theories (TLT13).* pages 285–291.

Sebastian Schuster, Matthew Lamm, and Christopher D Manning. 2017. Gapping constructions in universal dependencies v2. In *Proceedings of the NoDaLiDa 2017 Workshop on Universal Dependencies (UDW 2017).* pages 123–132.

Sebastian Schuster, Joakim Nivre, and Christopher D. Manning. 2018. Sentences with gapping: Parsing and reconstructing elided predicates. In *Proceedings of the 2018 Conference of the North American Chapter of the Association for Computational Linguistics: Human Language Technologies, NAACL-HLT 2018, New Orleans, Louisiana, USA, June 1-6, 2018, Volume 1 (Long Papers).* pages 1156–1168. https://aclanthology.info/papers/N18-1105/n18-1105.

FiST – towards a Free Semantic Tagger of Modern Standard Finnish[1]

Kimmo Kettunen [0000-0003-2747-1382]

The National Library of Finland, DH Research

firstname.lastname@helsinki.fi

Abstract

This paper introduces a work in progress for implementing a free full text semantic tagger for Finnish, FiST. The tagger is based on a 46 226 lexeme semantic lexicon of Finnish that was published in 2016. The basis of the semantic lexicon was developed in the early 2000s in an EU funded project Benedict (Löfberg et al., 2005). Löfberg (2017) describes compilation of the lexicon and evaluates a proprietary version of the Finnish Semantic Tagger, the FST[2]. The FST and its lexicon were developed using the English Semantic Tagger (The EST) of University of Lancaster as a model. This semantic tagger was developed at the University Centre for Corpus Research on Language (UCREL) at Lancaster University as part of the UCREL Semantic Analysis System (USAS[3]) framework. The semantic lexicon of the USAS framework is based on the modified and enriched categories of the *Longman Lexicon of Contemporary English* (McArthur, 1981).

We have implemented a basic working version of a new full text semantic tagger for Finnish based on freely available components. The implementation uses Omorfi and FinnPos for morphological analysis of Finnish words. After the morphological recognition phase words from the 46K semantic lexicon are matched against the morphologically unambiguous base forms. In our comprehensive tests the lexical tagging coverage of the current implementation is around 82–90% with different text types. The present version needs still some enhancements, at least processing of semantic ambiguity of words and analysis of compounds, and perhaps also treatment of multiword expressions. Also a semantically marked ground truth evaluation collection should be established for evaluation of the tagger.

Tiivistelmä

Suomessa on harjoitettu kieliteknologiaa laaja-alaisesti 1980-luvun alusta, ja melkein 40 vuotta jatkunut tutkimus ja kehitystyö on tuottanut useita merkittäviä ohjelmistoja suomen kielen analyysiin. Alkuvuosikymmenien käytöltään rajoitetuista ohjelmistoista on siirrytty 2000-luvulla paljolti joko avoimen lähdekoodin ohjelmiin tai ohjelmien vapaaseen saatavuuteen. Vapaasti saatavia suomen kielen keskeisiä kieliteknologisia ohjelmia on olemassa tällä hetkellä hyvin morfologiseen ja syntaktiseen analyysiin, esimerkiksi *Omorfi, Voikko ja FinnPos* morfologiaan ja *Finnish depedency parser* lauseenjäsennykseen. FiNER-ohjelmistolla voidaan tunnistaa ja merkitä erisnimiä. Toistaiseksi ei kuitenkaan ole olemassa ainoatakaan vapaasti saatavaa suomenkielisten kokotekstien kattavaa semanttista merkintää tekevää ohjelmaa, semanttista taggeria. Voikin todeta, että suomen kielen automaattiseen semanttiseen käsittelyyn on jäänyt jos ei aivan tyhjiö, niin kuitenkin suuri aukko.

Tässä julkaisussa esitellään FiST, työn alla oleva suomen nykykielen kokotekstien semanttinen merkitsin. FiSTin ensimmäinen versio perustuu vapaasti saatavilla oleviin osiin: 46 226 sanan semanttiseen leksikkoon sekä vapaisiin morfologisen analyysin ohjelmiin Omorfiin ja FinnPosin. Ohjelma merkitsee teksteihin sanojen semanttisia luokkia noin 82–90 %:n sanastollisella kattavuudella.

---

[2] The tagger was implemented by Kielikone Ltd. It used proprietary analysis modules of Kielikone for morphological and morpho-syntactic analysis of Finnish. The software has not been publicly available and can be considered partly outdated now. Its operational design is described in Löfberg et al. (2005).

[3] http://ucrel.lancs.ac.uk/usas/

Proceedings of the fifth Workshop on Computational Linguistics for Uralic Languages, pages 66–76,
Tartu, Estonia, January 7 - January 8, 2019.

1 Introduction

Language technological resources for analysis of written modern standard Finnish can be considered reasonably good overall. However, a major aspect of automatic analysis of written Finnish is still poorly covered as there is no freely available full text semantic analyzer or tagger of Finnish. Lack of semantic resources for Finnish was already noted in the META NET white paper (Koskenniemi et al., 2012). The situation has not improved noticeably since the publication of the META NET report, although some semantic lexical resources have been published in recent years.

Computational linguistics has been practiced in Finland since the early 1980s. During the last almost four decades several important analysis software for Finnish morphology and syntax have been produced. Without going too deeply in to historical details, early implementations include e.g. the first full computational morphological model for Finnish, TWOL (Koskenniemi, 1983), and a general syntactic parsing formalism Constraint Grammar (CG, Karlsson, 1990). In the 21st century most of the major new linguistic analysis tools have become either open source or at least freely available or usable. Such programs are, e.g., free morphological analyzers Omorfi[4] (Pirinen, 2015), Voikko[5] and FinnPos[6] (Silfverberg et al., 2016). A free dependency parser for Finnish is provided by the BioNLP group at the University of Turku (Turku Neural Parser Pipeline[7]). The Language Bank of Finland[8] provides also access to these and other tools, such as a Finnish named entity tagger FiNER.

As good as these tools may be in their tasks, they serve only a quite limited function. Morphological and syntactic analyses are rarely goals in themselves in real life text analysis outside linguistics; morphological and syntactic analyses serve only as mid-level results for further processing of textual content. In information oriented parlance, these tools do not reveal anything about the content of the texts or their aboutness. Most of the time contents of the texts are interesting for research outside linguistics, not the linguistic form. Proper content analysis tools for Finnish are scarce. Out of the existing tools only FiNER has limited semantic capabilities, as it marks names and name like entities.

A few semantically oriented lexicons have also been compiled and published for Finnish, namely FinnWordnet (Lindén and Carlson, 2010; Lindén and Niemi, 2016) and FrameNet (Lindén et al., 2017). Some type of semantic analyzers for Finnish could be produced using FinnWordnet, but so far usage of FinnWordnet for semantic level analyses seems to have been non-existent. WordNets are also not comprehensive semantic lexicons for full text analysis: they contain only words belonging to four main word classes, nouns, verbs, adjectives and adverbs. Their contents seem also a bit problematic. FrameNet, on the other hand, is an even more restricted description of a set of situations, entities and relationships of the participants (lexemes) in a lexical frame. A third available lexical tool, YSO[9], General Finnish Ontology, serves mainly indexing of Finnish cultural content (Hyvönen et al., 2008). Ontologies are useful for many purposes, but they are mainly non-linguistic descriptions (Hirst, 2004) and do not even aim to cover all word classes of natural language. Thus they do not suit for full text analysis. A proper semantically oriented full text analyzer of Finnish would improve possibilities of textual content analysis vastly.[10]

---

[4] https://github.com/flammie/omorfi

[5] https://voikko.puimula.org/

[6] https://github.com/mpsilfve/FinnPos

[7] https://github.com/TurkuNLP/Turku-neural-parser-pipeline

[8] https://www.kielipankki.fi/language-bank/

[9] http://finto.fi/yso/en/?clang=fi

[10] A few other approaches can also be mentioned here. Besides YSO several smaller subject matter ontologies exist, e.g. AFO (agriculture and forestry), JUHO (Government) etc. (https://seco.cs.aalto.fi/ontologies/). Haverinen (2014) introduces semantic role labeling for Finnish. This is related to argument structure of verbs in syntactic parsing of sentences and is of limited semantic value. BabelNet (https://babelnet.org/, Navigli and Ponzetto, 2012) is a large multilingual encyclopedic database, which includes also Finnish. Its descriptions for words have been collected from multilingual Wikipedia articles using WordNet.

This paper introduces a work in progress for implementing a free full text semantic tagger for Finnish, FiST. The tagger is based on freely available morphological processors and a 46 226 lexeme semantic lexicon of Finnish that was published in 2016. We shall first discuss semantic tagging in general and design of FiST. After that we evaluate lexical coverage of the tagger with different types of available digital Finnish corpora. Finally, we discuss improvements needed for the tagger and conclude the paper.

2   Semantic Tagging

Semantic tagging is defined here as a process of identifying and labelling the meaning of words in a given text according to some semantic scheme. This process is also called semantic annotation, and in our case it uses a semantic lexicon to add labels or tags to the words. (Leech, 2003; Löfberg, 2017; Wilson and Thomas, 1997).

Semantic tagging discussed here is based on the idea of semantic (lexical) fields. Wilson and Thomas (1997, p. 54) define a semantic field as "a theoretical construct which groups together words that are related by virtue of their being connected – at some level of generality – with the same mental concept". In other words "a semantic field is a group of words which are united according to a common basic semantic component" (Dullieva, 2017, formulating Trier's insight of semantic fields; cf. also Lutzeier, 2006; Geeraerts, 2010). Semantic lexicon of USAS is divided in to 232 meaning classes or categories which belong to 21 upper level fields. Figure 1 shows one upper level semantic field, *Money & Commerce*, and its meaning classes (USAS Semantic Tag Set for Finnish). Alphanumeric abbreviations in front of the meaning classes are the actual hierarchical semantic tags used in the lexicon. According to Piao et al. (2005), the depth of the semantic hierarchical structure is limited to a maximum of three layers, since this has been found to be the most feasible approach.

I MONEY & COMMERCE	
I1	Money generally
I1.1	Money: Affluence
I1.2	Money: Debts
I1.3	Money: Price
I2	Business
I2.1	Business: Generally
I2.2	Business: Selling
I3	Work and employment
I3.1	Work and employment: Generally
I3.2	Work and employment: Professionalism
I4	Industry

Figure 1. Semantic field of Money & Commerce in the USAS Finnish semantic lexicon

The major 21 discourse fields used in the USAS are shown in Figure 2[11].

A	General & Abstract Terms
B	The Body & the Individual
C	Arts & Crafts
E	Emotional Actions, States & Processes
F	Food & Farming
G	Government & the Public Domain
H	Architecture, Building, Houses & the Home
I	Money & Commerce
K	Entertainment, Sports & Games
L	Life & Living Things
M	Movement, Location, Travel & Transport
N	Numbers & Measurement
O	Substances, Materials, Objects & Equipment
P	Education
Q	Linguistic Actions, States & Processes
S	Social Actions, States & Processes
T	Time
W	The World & Our Environment
X	Psychological Actions, States & Processes
Y	Science & Technology
Z	Names & Grammatical Words

Figure 2. Top level domains of the USAS tag set

This top level domain and its subdivisions were developed from the categories used in the Longman Lexicon of Contemporary English (LLOCE, McArthur, 1981). LLOCE uses 14 top level domains. Some of those were divided into more fine-grained classes in the USAS. Also one more class, *Names and Grammatical words*, was added (Archer et al., 2004).

3   The Finnish Semantic Lexicon

The core of this kind of approach to semantic tagging is naturally the semantically marked lexicon. Semantic lexicons using the USAS schema have so far been published in 12 languages (Multilingual USAS; Piao, 2016[12]). Out of these lexicons the Finnish lexicon is the most comprehensive and mature. It has been compiled manually, as many of the lexicons for other languages are compiled partly or wholly automatically based on the USAS English lexicon and bilingual dictionaries. In different evaluations the Finnish lexicon has been shown to be capable of dealing with most general domains which appear in modern standard Finnish texts (Löfberg, 2017; Piao et al., 2016). Furthermore, although the semantic lexical resources were originally developed for the analysis of general modern standard Finnish, evaluation results have shown that the lexical resources are also applicable to analysis of both older Finnish texts and the more informal type of writing found on the Web. The semantic lexical resources can also be tailored for various domain-specific tasks thanks to the flexible USAS category system. Lexemes can be added to the lexicon easily, as it is open and its description is fairly straightforward.

The Finnish semantic lexicon consists of 46 226 lexemes. Out of these about 58% are nouns, 7% verbs, 17% proper names, 7% adjectives and 7% adverbs (Löfberg, 2017).[13] Rest of the words belong to small fixed classes. Löfberg (2017: Table 7, 139) lists the distribution of lexical entries

---

[12] The list of the 11 other languages is: Arabic, Chinese, Czech, Dutch, Italian, Malay, Portuguese, Russian, Spanish, Urdu and Welsh. Sizes of the lexicons vary between 1 800 and 64 800 single word entries. Finnish lexicon is thus the third largest of all available after lexicons of Malay and Chinese (Piao et al., 2016). Eight of the languages have an existing semantic tagger. Those that do not have are Arabic, Malay, Urdu and Welsh.

[13] Distributions for POS categories are given in Löfberg (2017, Table 4, 135). The size of the lexicon in the thesis is slightly smaller than the size of the published lexicon.

in the top level semantic categories in the single word lexicon of the FST. The table is too large to be shown here, so we list only the five categories that have most lexemes. The largest category is Z (Names and Grammatical Words), with 9 755 lexical entries (21.31%). Second largest category is A (General & Abstract Terms) with 4 544 entries (9.93%). The third largest category is B (The Body & The Individual) with 3 734 entries (8.16%). A (Social Actions, States & Processes) and L (Life & Living Things) are the next ones with 3 401 (7.43) and 2 798 (6.11%) entries, respectively. These five categories constitute about 52 per cent of the entries in the lexicon.

4 Design of FiST

Our current implementation of FiST is simple and straightforward. It uses existing free morphological tools, Omorfi and FinnPos, for morphological analysis and disambiguation of input texts. After the morphological phase words of the input text are unambiguous and in base form, and the tagger tries to match the words to lexical entries in its semantic lexicon. If a word is found in the lexicon, it is tagged and returned with word class and the semantic label(s) found. If the word is not in the semantic lexicon, it is marked as Z99, unknown, and returned with this tag and the morphological analysis for the word, if such is available. Figure 3. shows the working process of FiST.

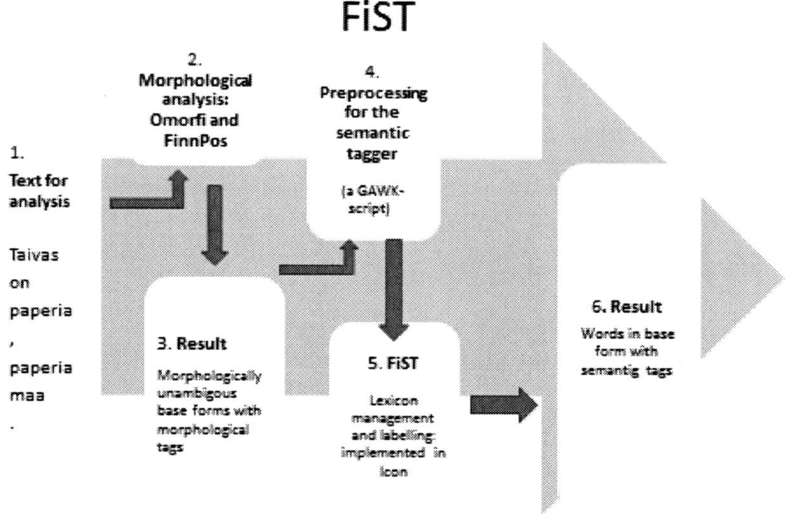

Figure 3. FiST schematically

The analysis result of the opening verse of the first poem of Pentti Saarikoski's first poetry collection in word per line form is shown in Table 1.

Input	Output of FiST	Explanation
Taivas	taivas Noun W1 S9 Z4	A noun with three semantic tags: the first one is the right one (*The Universe*).
on	olla Verb A3+ A1.1.1 M6 Z5	A verb with four semantic tags: the first one denoting to existence is the right one.
paperia	paperi Noun O1.1 Q1.2 B4 P1/Q1.2	A noun with four semantic tags: the first one denoting to solid matter, O1.1, would be the best choice.
,	PUNCT	Punctuation
paperia	paperi Noun O1.1 Q1.2 B4 P1/Q1.2	A noun with four semantic tags: the first one denoting to solid matter, O1.1, would be the best choice.
maa	Maa Noun M7	An unambiguous noun denoting to areas.
.	PUNCT	Punctuation

Table 1. FiST's analysis of the first verse of a poem by Pentti Saarikoski

5   Evaluation

As there is no semantically marked evaluation collection available, we have not been able to evaluate FiST's semantic accuracy so far. However, we have performed quite thorough testing of the current implementation's lexical coverage. Our evaluation data consists of 17 texts that range from about 42 000 words to ca. 28.6 million words, the largest corpus being the Finnish part of the Europarl corpus v6[14]. We show also morphological recognition rates for all except one of the texts with Omorfi. This gives an idea of the coverage of the semantic lexicon in comparison to the lexicon of a morphological analyzer, which is usually much larger. Omorfi's lexicon is almost ten times larger than the semantic lexicon – it consists of 424 259 words (Pirinen, 2015). Our formula for coverage of FiST is the following: *(100* (1-(missed tag/(NR-comma-number))))*. Here missed tags are those words that are tagged as Z99, unknown. Punctuation marks and numbers are subtracted from the number of records/words (NR). Input for the evaluation is one tagged word/line, with no empty lines.

Figures 4 and 5 show tagging results of our current tagger version with 17 texts. Figure 4 shows results of modern texts, and Figure 5 results of older texts.

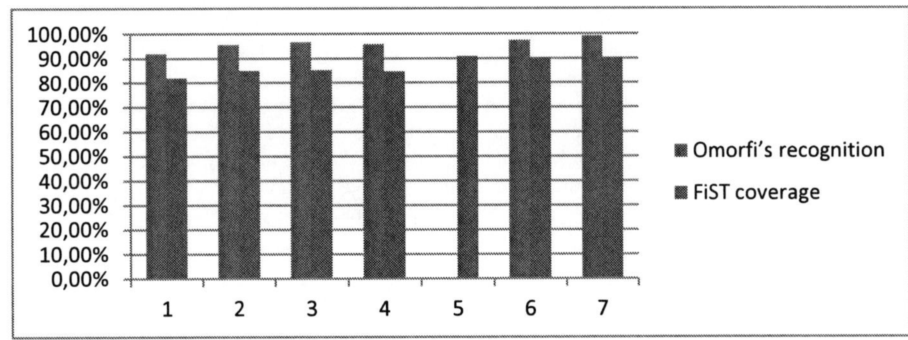

Figure 4. Coverage of semantic tagging of FiST with different modern Finnish texts (N.B. morphological recognition rate for Europarl is not available)

---

[14] http://www.statmt.org/europarl/archives.html

In Figure 4 text #1 is Suomi24[15] discussion forum data (494 000 tokens), texts #2-4 are sentences from news in the Leipzig corpus[16] (100K, 300K and 1M tokens), text #5 is Europarl v.6 text (ca. 28.6 M tokens), #6 prose of Pentti Saarikoski (172 920 tokens, not publicly available) and text #7 is sample sentences of FinnTreebank[17] (examples from a Finnish grammar, 138 949 tokens).

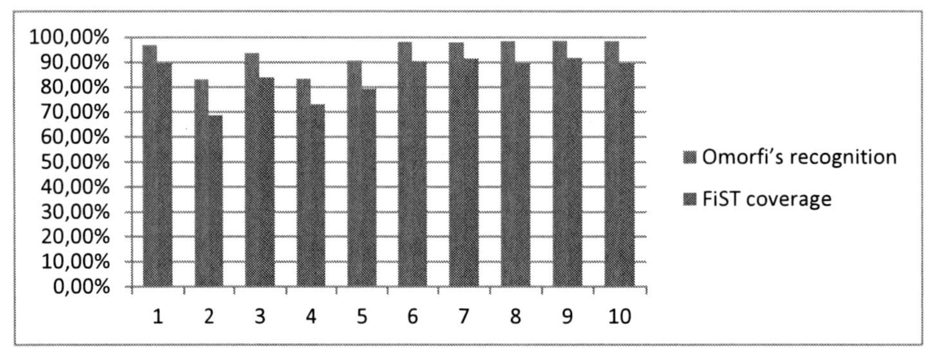

Figure 5. Coverage of semantic tagging of FiST with different older Finnish texts

In Figure 5 text number 1 is Bible translation of 1938[18] (544 474 tokens), #2 is newspaper/journal Turun Wiikkosanomat 1831 (60 390 tokens), #3 newspaper/journal Mehiläinen 1859 (154 370 tokens), #4 newspaper/journal Oulun Viikko-Sanomia 1841 (68 491 tokens), and #5 is newspaper/journal Sanansaattaja Wiipurista 1841 (49 802 tokens). All the journalistic texts are from digital collection of the Institute for the Languages of Finland [19]. Texts #6–#10[20] are literary works of Finnish authors Juhani Aho, Minna Canth, Arvid Järnefelt, Teuvo Pakkala, and Kyösti Wilkuna from late 19th and early 20th century with 42 000–334 000 tokens. They are also from the collection of the Institute for the Languages of Finland. These collections are manually edited.

Results of the analyses show that FiST is capable of annotating texts of modern standard Finnish quite well already now. With many of the texts about 90% of the words get a semantic label in FiST's analysis. This applies also to literary texts of Pentti Saarikoski, both prose and poetry. Proceedings of the European Parliament v6 (Koehn, 2005), our largest data collection, gets also a high coverage: 90.9%. Suomi24 data and data from the Leipzig corpus obtain clearly lower coverage. This is mainly due to the nature of the texts. Suomi24 contains informal discussions that may include lots of misspelled words, slang and foreign words. Texts of the Leipzig corpus have been crawled from the Web automatically and may thus contain more noise, i.e. misspellings, control characters, HTML code etc. (Quasthoff et al., 2006).

Older literary texts and the Bible translation of 1938, however, obtain a quite good coverage, round 90%, as can be seen in Figure 5. Our oldest texts are from 1831–1859, four newspapers: Turun Wiikko-Sanomia (1831), Oulun Viikko-Sanomia (1841), Sanansaattaja Wiipurista (1841) and Mehiläinen (1859). These versions are manually edited clean versions from the Institute for the Languages of Finland. Considering the age of the data, these get also quite good coverage with FiST, 68.6, 73, 79.22 and 84 per cent.

---

[15]http://metashare.csc.fi/repository/browse/the-suomi-24-corpus-2015h1/b4db73da85ce11e4912c005056be118ea699d93902fa49d69b0f4d1e692dd5f1/

[16] http://wortschatz.uni-leipzig.de/de/download

[17] http://www.ling.helsinki.fi/kieliteknologia/tutkimus/treebank/sources/

[18] http://raamattu.fi/1933,38/

[19] http://kaino.kotus.fi/korpus/1800/meta/1800_coll_rdf.xml

[20] http://kaino.kotus.fi/korpus/klassikot/meta/klassikot_coll_rdf.xml

We performed also a few small scale test runs with our text data using one available lexicon to get more insight into lexical coverage. The so called Kotus wordlist[21] which contains ca. 94 000 lexemes from a dictionary of modern Finnish, has a good coverage: it was only a few per cent units below coverage of the semantic lexicon. When we tested coverage by combining the semantic lexicon and words of the Kotus wordlist not included in the semantic lexicon, we noticed an increase of few per cent units in matching of our evaluation data. Our tests were performed with three small texts, and the tests are thus not as comprehensive as our tests with FiST's main version, but clearly indicative.

Lindén and Niemi (2016) have evaluated FinnWordnet's lexical coverage with samples. In a large newspaper corpus (of unspecified size) coverage was 57.3%. If only nouns, verbs, adjectives and adverbs were counted and proper names excluded, the coverage was 82.4%. Thus FinnWordnet's lexicon is probably not sufficient for good lexical coverage of Finnish texts as an only lexical resource. On the other hand, lexical coverage of the semantic lexicon of FiST could be increased with a few per cent units by adding lexemes to it from other available lexicons. This, of course, would also mean laborious semantic marking of the additions.

6   Discussion

The current implementation of FiST is a simplified basic version of a semantic tagger. It lacks at least two main components: word sense disambiguation (WSD) and proper handling of compounds. The semantic lexicon of Finnish marks ambiguous meanings of words by giving several meaning tags. Word *huone* ('room'), for example, is given an entry *huone Noun H2 S9*. Parts of buildings belong to class H2, and S9 is for words that have a religious or supernatural meaning. The primary meaning of *huone* is H2, but in some contexts, especially in astrology, it could be S9. Thus semantic disambiguation would be needed to be able to distinguish meanings of ambiguous words. Word sense disambiguation has gained lots of interest in computational linguistics during the past 20 years, and thus ways to disambiguate ambiguous words should be found with a reasonable effort (Edmonds, 2006). Rayson et al. (2004), e.g., describe several methods they use for WSD in the English Semantic Tagger. A few most simple ones of these should be easy to implement.

If the word is ambiguous, i.e. it has more than one sense, the different senses are listed in the lexicon arranged in perceived frequency order (Löfberg, 2017: 74). The earlier example from analysis of the poem of Pentti Saarikoski shows this: *paperi Noun O1.1 Q1.2 B4 P1/Q1.2.* In the analysis we can also see an example of so called "slash tag" (or "portmanteau tag") of the USAS framework. The slash shows that the word belongs to more than one category. *Paperi* belongs to solid matter, but also to category of education (P1) and literary documents and writing, Q1.2. A counting in the lexicon shows that 7 791 lexemes have been described as ambiguous and 10 556 have the slash tag. Out of the ambiguous lexemes 5 476 have two meanings, and 1 449 three meanings. There are almost 500 words with four meanings and almost 200 with five, but after six meanings number of lexemes having more meanings drops to tens. The more meanings the lexeme has been given, the more abstract it tends to be. Abstract nouns like *meneminen* ('going') and *tuleminen* ('coming') have 10 meanings in the lexicon. 85% of the slash category words have only one slash tag.

Another deficiency in the FiST's implementation is handling of compounds. Finnish is notoriously rich in compounds, and no lexicon can contain all of them. The Finnish semantic lexicon includes the most common compounds as such, but for those that are not included, the meaning should be composed out of the meanings of component parts. *Kivitalo* ('house made of stone/concrete'), for example, is not in the lexicon, but its parts are. *Kivi* is **Noun O1.1 B5,** and *talo **Noun H1 S5+ I3.1/M.*** In practice the semantic marking should be *kivitalo **H1/O1.1**,* as the most meaningful part of the compound is usually the last part. For this to succeed, much depends on the morphological analyzer, as it analyzes and splits the compounds for the semantic tagger.

---

[21] http://kaino.kotus.fi/sanat/nykysuomi/

It would be desirable, that the morphological analyzer returned compounds both as wholes and split, as it would make search of available compounds in the semantic lexicon easier.[22]

A third possible improvement for the FiST would be handling of multiword expressions (MWEs) that consist of two or more separate orthographic words. *Englannin kanaali, Euroopan Unioni* and *musta pörssi* are some examples of MWEs. The original FST (and the EST) has a separate lexicon of over 6000 entries for multi word expressions (Löfberg, 2017).This lexicon has not been published. A list of MWEs could be compiled with a reasonable effort, but semantic description of thousands of words would take time, especially as a substantial part of the MWEs are non-compositional idiomatic expressions (Piao et al., 2016). The Finnish Wordnet, for example, contains about 13 000 multiword nouns, but considering that the lexicon was produced as a direct translation of the English Wordnet, many of the MWES do not seem very frequent or crucial to Finnish.

7   Conclusion

We have described in this paper FiST, a first version of a full text semantic tagger for Finnish. We have provided background for the tagger's lexical semantic approach and evaluated its capabilities mainly as a semantic tagger of modern standard Finnish. The first results can be considered promising: the tagger works robustly even with large data of millions of words and achieves a good lexical coverage with many types of texts. Our evaluation of FiST confirms also that the Finnish semantic lexicon of USAS is of high quality and it covers also data from time periods that are supposedly out of its main scope.

Semantic tagging can be used in many natural language processing applications, such as terminology extraction, machine translation, bilingual and multilingual extraction of multi-word expressions, monolingual and cross-lingual information extraction, as well as in automatic generation, interpretation, and classification of language. Semantic tagging with the English Semantic Tagger of UCREL has been successfully utilized for content analysis, analysis of online language, training chatbots, ontology learning, corpus stylistics, discourse analysis, phraseology, analysis of interview transcripts, and key domain analysis (Löfberg, 2017; http://ucrel.lancs.ac.uk/usas/; http://ucrel.lancs.ac.uk/wmatrix/#apps). These kinds of applications could also be targets for FiST.

In the future we wish to improve the tagger's performance with the still missing features. If possible, we evaluate the tagger's semantic accuracy with semantically marked data. We also believe that even the current plain implementation is suitable for many textual analysis purposes, e.g. content wise topic analysis (vs. statistical, where words are only strings without meaning), lexical content surveying, semantically oriented lexical statistics etc. We have also performed some trials to use data tagged with FiST as training data for a machine learning algorithm to learn a semantic tagger for Finnish. So far our trials have not been very successful due to the rich feature set of semantic marking. Most of the standard machine learning environments we have tried run out of memory with the number of features of semantically tagged data. Probably at least some smaller scale niche semantic field analyzer could be developed with marked data provided by FiST.

Acknowledgements

We wish to thank Dr. Laura Löfberg for useful comments and providing some of her evaluation data for use. Our largest data file, Europarl v6, was analyzed in Taito cluster of the CSC - It Center For Science Ltd.

---

[22] We have been using FinnPos from the Mylly resources (https://www.kielipankki.fi/support/mylly/) of the Language Bank of Finland. Currently FinnPos does not split compounds to their parts, although it analyzes the base forms of the wholes. Omorfi splits compounds, as does Voikko, too. Voikko's splitting, however, does not seem very useful, as it separates also sub-word parts, e.g. derivational endings, in the output. Omorfi and Voikko do not disambiguate the different morphological interpretations, which makes usage of either of them as sole morphological component complicated.

References

Dawn Archer, Paul Rayson, Scott Piao, Tony McEnery. 2004. Comparing the UCREL Semantic Annotation Scheme with Lexicographical Taxonomies. In Williams G. and Vessier S. (eds.) Proceedings of the 11th EURALEX (European Association for Lexicography) International Congress (Euralex 2004), Lorient, France, 6-10 July 2004. Université de Bretagne Sud. Volume III, pp. 817-827. ISBN 2-9522-4570-3.

Karina Dullieva. 2017. Semantic Fields: Formal Modelling and Interlanguage Comparison. Journal of Quantitative Linguistics, 24:1, 1-15. DOI: 10.1080/09296174.2016.1239400

Philip Edmonds. 2006. Disambiguation. In Allan, K. (ed.), Concise Encyclopedia of Semantics, 223–239. Elsevier.

Dirk Geeraerts. 2010. Theories of Lexical Semantics. Oxford: Oxford University Press.

Katri Haverinen. 2014. Natural Language Processing Resources for Finnish Corpus Development in the General and Clinical Domains. TUCS Dissertations No 179. https://www.utupub.fi/bitstream/handle/10024/98608/TUCSD179Dissertation.pdf?sequence=2&isAllowed=y

Grame Hirst. 2004. Ontology and the lexicon. In Staab S., Studer R. (eds.) Handbook on Ontologies. International Handbooks on Information Systems. Springer, Berlin, Heidelberg

Eero Hyvönen, Kim Viljanen, Jouni Tuominen, Katri Seppälä. 2008. Building a National Semantic Web Ontology and Ontology Service Infrastructure –The FinnONTO Approach. In: Bechhofer S., Hauswirth M., Hoffmann J., Koubarakis M. (eds) The Semantic Web: Research and Applications. ESWC 2008. Lecture Notes in Computer Science, vol 5021. Springer, Berlin, Heidelberg

Fred Karlsson. 1990. Constraint Grammar as a Framework for Parsing Unrestricted Text. H. Karlgren, ed., Proceedings of the 13th International Conference of Computational Linguistics, Vol. 3. Helsinki 1990, 168–173.

Philip Koehn. 2005. Europarl: A Parallel Corpus for Statistical Machine Translation. MT Summit 2005.

Kimmo Koskenniemi. 1983. Two-level Morphology: A computational model for wordform recognition and production. Publications of the Department of General Linguistics, University of Helsinki 11. Helsinki: University of Helsinki.

Kimmo Koskenniemi et al. 2012. The Finnish Language in the Digital Age. META NET White paper series. http://www.meta-net.eu/whitepapers/e-book/finnish.pdf/view?searchterm=Finnish

Geoffrey Leech. 2004. Developing Linguistic Corpora: a Guide to Good Practice Adding Linguistic Annotation. https://ota.ox.ac.uk/documents/creating/dlc/chapter2.htm

Krister Lindén, Lauri Carlson. 2010. FinnWordNet – WordNet på finska via översättning. LexicoNordica – Nordic Journal of Lexicography, 17:119–140.

Krister Lindén, Jyrki Niemi. 2014. Is it possible to create a very large wordnet in 100 days? An evaluation. Language Resources and Evaluation, 48(2), 191–201.

Krister Lindén, Heidi Haltia, Juha Luukkonen, Antti O Laine, Henri Roivainen, Niina Väisänen. 2017. FinnFN 1.0: The Finnish frame semantic database. Nordic Journal of Linguistics, 40(3), 287-311.

Peter R Lutzeier. 2006. Lexical fields. In Allan, K. (ed.), Concise Encyclopedia of Semantics, 470–473. Elsevier.

Laura Löfberg, Scott Piao, Paul Rayson, Jukka-Pekka Juntunen, Asko Nykänen, Krista Varantola. 2005. A semantic tagger for the Finnish language. http://eprints.lancs.ac.uk/12685/1/cl2005_fst.pdf

Laura Löfberg. 2017. Creating large semantic lexical resources for the Finnish language. Lancaster University, 2017. 422 pages. http://www.research.lancs.ac.uk/portal/en/publications/creating-large-semantic-lexical-resources-for-the-finnish-language(cc08322c-f6a4-4c2b-8c43-e447f3d1201a)/export.html

Tom McArthur. 1981. Longman Lexicon of Contemporary English. Longman, London.

Multilingual USAS. https://github.com/UCREL/Multilingual-USAS

Roberto Navigli, Simone Paolo Ponzetto. 2012. BabelNet: The Automatic Construction, Evaluation and Application of a Wide-Coverage Multilingual Semantic Network. Artificial Intelligence, 193:217–250.

Scott Piao, Dawn Archer, Olga Mudraya, Paul Rayson, Roger Garside, Tom McEnery, Andrew Wilson. 2005. A Large Semantic Lexicon for Corpus Annotation. In proceedings of the Corpus Linguistics 2005 conference, July 14-17, Birmingham, UK. Proceedings from the Corpus Linguistics Conference Series on-line e-journal, Vol. 1, no. 1, ISSN 1747-9398

Scott Piao et al. 2016. Lexical Coverage Evaluation of Large-scale Multilingual Semantic Lexicons for Twelve Languages. In Proceedings of the 10th edition of the Language Resources and Evaluation Conference (LREC2016), Portoroz, Slovenia, 2614–2619.

Tommi A Pirinen. 2015. Development and Use of Computational Morphology of Finnish in the Open Source and Open Science Era: Notes on Experiences with Omorfi Development. SKY Journal of Linguistics, vol 28, 381–393. http://www.linguistics.fi/julkaisut/SKY2015/SKYJoL28_Pirinen.pdf

Uwe Quasthoff, Matthias Richter, Christian Biemann. 2006. Corpus portal for search in monolingual corpora. In Proceedings of the fifth international conference on Language Resources and Evaluation, LREC 2006, Genoa, 1799–1802.

Paul Rayson, Dawn Archer, Scott Piao, Tom McEnery. 2004. The UCREL semantic analysis system. In Proceedings of the workshop on Beyond Named Entity Recognition Semantic labelling for NLP tasks in association with 4th International Conference on Language Resources and Evaluation (LREC 2004), 25th May 2004, Lisbon, Portugal, pp. 7-12.

Miikka Silfverberg, Teemu Ruokolainen, Krister Lindén, Mikko Kurimo. 2016. FinnPos: an open-source morphological tagging and lemmatization toolkit for Finnish. Lang Resources & Evaluation 50: 863–878. https://doi.org/10.1007/s10579-015-9326-3

USAS Semantic Tag Set for Finnish. https://github.com/UCREL/Multilingual-USAS/raw/master/Finnish/USASSemanticTagset-Finnish.pdf

Andrew Wilson, Jenny Thomas. 1997. Semantic annotation. In Garside, R., Leech, G., & McEnery, T. (Eds.), Corpus annotation: Linguistic information from computer text corpora (pp. 53–65). New York: Longman.

An OCR system for the
Unified Northern Alphabet

Niko Partanen
Institute for the Languages of Finland
niko.partanen@kotus.fi

Michael Rießler
Bielefeld University
michael.riessler@uni-bielefeld.de

Abstract

This paper presents experiments done in order to build a functional OCR
model for the Unified Northern Alphabet. This writing system was used between
1931 and 1937 for 16 (Uralic and non-Uralic) minority languages spoken in the Soviet Union. The character accuracy of the developed model reaches more than 98%
and clearly shows cross-linguistic applicability. The tests described here therefore
also include general guidelines for the amount of training data needed to bootstrap an OCR system under similar conditions.

Tiivistelmä

Tutkimus esittelee Yhteiselle pohjoiselle aakkostolle kehitettävään tekstin-
tunnistusmalliin tähtääviä kokeita. Kyseistä aakkostoa käytettiin 16 Neuvostolii-
ton pohjoiselle kielelle noin vuosina 1931–1937. Kehitetty malli saavuttaa merkki-
tasolla parhaimmillaan yli 98% tunnistustarkkuuden, ja se kykenee tunnistamaan
samalla kirjoitusjärjestelmällä kirjoitettuja eri kieliä. Tehtyjen kokeiden perusteella tehdään arvioita siitä, kuinka suuria aineistomääriä tarvitaan uuden teks-
tintunnistusjärjestelmän toteuttamiseen.

1 Introduction

This article describes the tests conducted recently as part of the Kone Foundation-
funded IKDP-2 project on developing an OCR system for the Unified Northern Alphabet, a writing system used during a period of time for several languages spoken
in Northern areas of the Soviet Union. Part of the work has been conducted in the
Institute for the Languages of Finland in relation to the OCR and HTR experiments
recently carried out at the institute. The study uses openly available materials so that
the resources created and evaluated here can be used further in downstream NLP
tasks. The trained models and the scripts used to create them, alongside the evaluation scripts, are all published alongside the paper as an independent data package

Proceedings of the fifth Workshop on Computational Linguistics for Uralic Languages, pages 77–89,
Tartu, Estonia, January 7 - January 8, 2019.

(Partanen and Rießler, 2018a)[1], which allows them to be fine tuned and used directly
for text written in this writing system.

OCR systems are known to be well suited for specific writing systems and fonts
rather than specific languages. Adding more sophisticated language models to known
OCR systems has proven challenging, especially for agglutinative languages. For instance, trying to integrate a morphological analyser into the Tesseract system produced much worse results than using simple wordlists (Silfverberg and Rueter, 2014).
The extent to which OCR systems require linguistic information is unclear, which
raises question of how language-independent they even are. The research question in
our study emerges from this issue, and we evaluate whether an OCR system developed
using multiple languages performs better or worse than a system that has seen data
from only one specific language. The remaining errors will be analyzed separately in
order to shed more light on the current bottlenecks in the model.

Another important question is to what extent it is possible to bootstrap an OCR
system for new, rare or idiosyncratic writing systems. In the course of their histories,
Uralic languages have seen a very large variety of such writing systems, and many
writing conventions are used only in a small number of publications. It is therefore
important to have a general understanding of the amount of resources needed to reach
results that are comparable to the current state of the art in OCR applications. Only
with this information is it possible to decide on which tasks further work should focus
on. The goal of this kind of work is not necessarily to develop an OCR system that
works for one language in a wider set of situations, but simply to extract the texts of
individual publications so that they can be used for linguistic research purposes, in
addition to other applications.

Reul et al. (2018) describe how the various OCR systems have shifted to use recurrent neural networks, which results in typical character error rates (CER) below 1% for
books published using modern typographic conventions. Early printed books show
more variation and may often require book-specific training to reach CERs below 1–
2%. Since the Soviet publications from the 1930s presumably qualify as non-modern
prints, these figures also provide a baseline for our study.

2 History of the Unified Northern Alphabet

The Unified Northern Alphabet (UNA) was developed for 16 minority languages of
Northern Russia in the late 1920s and taken into use in 1930. It is connected to the
Latinization process in the Soviet Union, which started during the early 1920s and
was first introduced to Islamic populations that had previously used the Arabic script
(Grenoble, 2003, 49). In the 1930s, the alphabet was extended to cover more languages,
including several very small languages for which UNA became the first common writing standard in 1932. In principle, UNA is similar to other Latin alphabets created during the same period. For the smaller northern languages, UNA represented the first
effort to create an alphabet, whereas for other languages the Latin scripts replaced
the systems that had previously been in use.

UNA works on the principle that all languages use the same base forms of characters, which are modified with diacritics depending from the phonological requirements of individual languages. The system seems to have been used in a phonologically consistent manner, so that the characters chosen for each language represent
the phonetic realization of phoneme in the given language.

---

[1] https://github.com/langdoc/iwclul2019

The languages for which UNA was used are listed below (cf. (Siegl and Rießler, 2015, 203)), with ISO 639-3 codes in parentheses:

- Aleut (ale)
- Central Siberian Yupik (ess)
- Chukchi (ckt)
- Even (eve)
- Evenki (evn)
- Itelmen (itl)
- Ket (ket)
- Kildin Saami (sjd)
- Koryak (kpy)
- Nanai (gld)
- Nivkh (niv)
- Northern Khanty (kca)
- Northern Mansi (mns)
- Northern Selkup (sel)
- Tundra Nenets (yrk)
- Udege (ude)

In connection with this process, a large number of textbooks and dictionaries were published (Grenoble, 2003, 164). Since these books were printed in St. Petersburg and clearly designed using common materials, they are very close to one another in their content and style. The fact that these materials were intended to be used in creating literacy among these peoples explains why there are no translations of the same books in larger languages of the Soviet Union, which also had their own widely translated titles.

UNA was abandoned in 1937 in favour of individual Cyrillic writing systems. In practice, this change halted the written use of these languages for decades to come, and the next written standards did not arise until the 1950s, or much later in the case of certain languages (Siegl and Rießler, 2015, 204–205).

It is unknown to us how many books were ever published in UNA, but based on searches in various library catalogues, the number is probably some dozens per language. This is not an enormously large corpus, but it is still enough that for languages that have extremely narrow resources at the moment, the digital accessibility of these resources can be of utmost importance. The fact that these books are starting to be old enough to be released as Public Domain even further increases their value. Already the fact that these books can be used for any purposes without licensing issues should speak on behalf of their wider inclusion in different corpora.

Texts published in UNA are also very important for the current documentation efforts, since they represent the language as it was used almost a century ago. It is clear these texts have their drawbacks and represent only a limited range of genres, but still they certainly complement the other types of resources very well and are worth further research.

3 Materials used

A large number of books written in UNA is available in the Public Domain as part of the Fenno-Ugrica collection (The National Library of Finland, 2018).[2] In addition to this, individual texts can be found in the collections of other libraries.

P. N. Žulev's primer was translated to several languages using UNA, and the Kildin Saami (Zuļov, 1934), Northern Mansi (Zuļov, 1933a), Northern Selkup (Zuļov, 1934) and Tundra Nenets (Zuļov, 1933b) versions are available in Fenno-Ugrica. In addition

---

[2]`https://fennougrica.kansalliskirjasto.fi/`

(a) Kildin Saami   (b) Northern Mansi

(c) Northern Selkup   (d) Tundra Nenets

Figure 1: Examples from P. N. Žulev's primer in various languages

to this, the E-resource repository of the University of Latvia offers an Evenki version of the primer (Zulew, 1933).

The first Ground Truth package for UNA was recently published (Partanen and Rießler, 2018b) by the authors of this paper. This is essentially a collection of manually corrected lines in the different languages. Our study uses a sample from the version 1.1 of the package, which is available in GitHub.[3]

Figure 1 illustrates the way the alphabet was used, showing matching excerpts from P. N. Žulev's primer. The texts are not completely identical translations in each language. The content differs to some degree, for instance for various culture-specific backgrounds. The translations have also been published separately in Russian, which indicates that the differences may be more significant. For example, there is a Russian translation of the Mansi primer[4], and similar Russian editions exist for other languages too. This is a clear sign that they are not only translations from one source. To our knowledge, no analysis of these differences has been conducted.

The Figure 2 displays the cover image and page 5 of the Evenki version of the book. The font is the same as before, but obviously the language is different, with some

---

[3] https://github.com/langdoc/unified-northern-alphabet-ocr
[4] http://urn.fi/URN:NBN:fi-fe2014060526307

(a) Cover

Ʒəlgərə, əkəl damgatira.

Ʒəlgərə əcə əwiʒərə. Ʒəlgərə onŋandu damgatiʒaran.

Ʒalunca gunən:

— Əkəl damgatira. Ənunkə oʒaŋas. Oktaʙrcikar, tatigawʒəril kuŋakar əwkil damgatira.

Kuŋakar gunə:

— Ʒəlgərə, nodakəl mogdiwi. Əməkəl, əwilgət.

Bərkəwul tawicimni.

Ʒalunca Bərkəwultiki gunən:

— Ołdoksowo təsikəl. Bagdamawa dukuŋkiwa nəkəl. Taduk kuŋakardu duku-wurwatin, dukuŋkilwatin ʙukəl. Əsi-tirga si tawicimni ʙisinni. Mit upkat amarulta tawitcarap.

Ajicimni.

Ajicimni tatki-ttula əmərən. Nu-ŋan kuŋakar ŋa-ləlwətin minərən. Ɫurʒawul ŋələl-lən. Tuksamurən. Ajicimni gunən:

(b) Page 5, cf. figure 1

Figure 2: Cover and page 5 of P. N. Žulev's Evenki primer

KIE ḶAJ LENIN.

Figure 3: Kildin Saami title in capital letters

new characters. The usual font in the books is shown in figures 1 and 2. The books
also contain some headlines that are in very unusual all-caps typeface that is only
sporadically covered in the train and test data. Figure 3 illustrates this. Since these
lines are very rare, they are not used in our experiments at all. The Ground Truth
package metadata is used to distinguish these lines. Since they occur only in very
specific portion of the book, the Ground Truth package does not contain examples of
this in all four languages.

However, the texts still exhibit some variation. For example, some elements are
in bold font, and these are kept as they are. They are not separately tagged in the
Ground Truth data either, although one could suggest this as an improvement so the
effect of the presence of different font types in the training and testing sets as well as
the accuracy rate for these font types could be better evaluated.

To contextualize further what kind of data this is, these books contains on average 100 words per page, the number of characters being on average 600–700 per
page. The lines, of which there are usually 20 per page, have around 30 characters on
average. One page contains approximately 100 words, with great variation depending on image locations and spacing around titles. These numbers are not exact since
they represent only the Ground Truth data, which does not contain the whole content
of the books. Still, the figures are similar across the translations and can be seen as
highly representative.

4   Experiment design

The model training is done with Ocropy (Breuel, 2008)[5], as it offers a very convenient
set of tools for various OCR-related tasks. Other options would have been Tesseract
and Transkribus, and repeating the tests with various systems should be carried out
in further research.

Ocropy, as with other modern OCR systems, is given training data as pairs of line
images and corresponding text. The text recognition is distinct from Layout Analysis,
which refers to element detection and line segmentation, with the goal of finding
the lines in their correct order. It is important to note that when we speak of OCR
accuracy we mean the accuracy for already correctly segmented lines. The model is
given line-based material, which Ocropy keeps learning iteratively, saving the model
at regular intervals. The number of iterations controls the time the model is given to
train. The model learns the correspondence of line images and texts, and it does not
need any specific font or character style information. If a character does not exist in
Unicode, as is the case with several letters used in UNA, a mapping has been done in
Ground Truth to visually similar but factually incorrect letters. This is done simply to
aid visual inspection of the results, as mapping could have been done for any unique
characters.

The primary languages involved in the study are Kildin Saami, Northern Selkup,
Tundra Nenets and Northern Mansi. These were used in the Ground Truth package,
and the large amount of Kildin Saami material made it possible to design our study so

---

[5]`https://github.com/tmbdev/ocropy`

that Kildin Saami could be compared to a setting in which all four languages are mixed together in the same OCR system. The third Evenki experiment is also explained below.

The Ground Truth package was sampled and processed for our experiments with a script that prepares the working environment for the experiments. It is provided with other documentation in an additional data packagePartanen and Rießler (2018a) stored in a GitHub repository associated with the paper. The repository also contains detailed examples of how to reproduce all plots and figures presented in this study.

In the first experiment, the idea was to test the amount resources needed to bootstrap an OCR system in this kind of situation. We tested the training of a model on different amounts of lines, divided equally into subsets that are equivalent to pages (an addition of 20 lines counted as an increase of one page). Twenty experiments were carried out, for an incrementally growing amount of training material. The Ocropy system was trained for 10,000 iterations per model.

In the next experiment, two different OCR models were trained using a larger, apparently sufficiently sized, body of training material. One model was trained on all four languages in equal proportions, and the other with only data from Kildin Saami. In this experiment, the model was trained for 50,000 iterations and the number of training lines was also larger, 200 lines per language, for a total of 800 lines. Similarly, the Kildin Saami monolingual model was trained for an equal number of iterations and with 800 lines.

The test sets common for both experiments contained 100 lines per language, or altogether 400 lines. A test set that is half the size of the training set may seem too large, but this seemed reasonable since otherwise the number of lines in individual languages would have been so small that it would have been uncertain whether the different characters were at all equally present. Similarly, one of our primary topics of investigation was whether a practical OCR system could be built with these resources and training scenarios, which makes extensive testing reasonable.

Since we aim to provide an OCR system for the Unified Northern Alphabet, it would be important to test the system on a language that is not at all included in the current models. This would truly reveal whether the OCR system actually generalizes toward the whole writing system. With this in mind, the Evenki dataset described in section 3 was used as an additional test experiment. The scores on the Evenki dataset were reported and analysed in context, but this data was not used in training in any of the models.

Section 6 contains an error analysis. In this section, the error output of Ocropy is evaluated in order to identify the language-specific bottlenecks that keep the error rate high in some test scenarios.

5   Results

5.1   Gradual page increase test

Figure 4 shows the gradual improvement in the accuracy of the Kildin Saami model as the number of training pages is increased. The figure shows that the model improves very quickly when more pages are added for training. With 8 pages, the model reaches an error rate approaching 2%, and falls below that if the number of pages is increased to 11. The remaining mistakes are analysed further in section 6. By increasing the training time per model and adjusting other parameters, this accuracy could

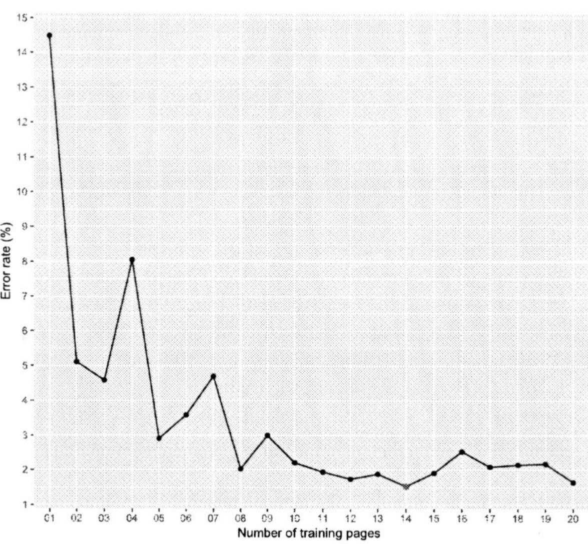

Figure 4: Test scores for Kildin Saami OCR model. Best score with error rate of 1.527% with 14 pages marked with red

maybe have been reached even earlier, but the increase in the amount of training data clearly brings continuous improvements in accuracy. In itself this is not surprising, and nothing else could have been expected from this experiment.

However, the test does offer some very valuable insight. After 5 pages, the error rate had already fallen into 2.91%. This is perhaps not yet a state-of-the-art level, but a character accuracy of 97% is already rather effortless and quick to proofread. Individual percentages can be squeezed out by increasing the number of pages, but in order to OCR an entirely new book, five pages, or approximately 100 lines, seems to be enough to bootstrap a useful OCR system that, although not necessarily ready for production, can at least be used to produce the needed increase in the number of pages more quickly and easily.

5.2 Comparable monolingual–multilingual test

This test aims to compare the performance of OCR models trained using monolingual and multilingual materials on different language specific-test sets. Figure 5 follows the pattern observed in the earlier test, as the Kildin Saami reached the same accuracy below 2% that it had also exhibited before. For the sake of clarity, the character sizes and accuracy of the test sets are presented in detail in table 5 and visualized in figure 5.

The Kildin Saami model does not perform equally well on other language tests, which makes sense, since the Kildin Saami model alone has never seen some of the special characters used in these languages. The result with Northern Mansi is the closest, and indeed the difference between the Northern Mansi character set and that of Kildin Saami is also the smallest. The errors are more thoroughly discussed in section 6.

The mixed test does not outperform the monolingual Kildin Saami model, which,

model	test	errors	characters	error percent
mixed	mns	45	3428	1.313
mixed	sel	31	3772	0.822
mixed	sjd	61	3405	1.791
mixed	yrk	60	3564	1.684
sjd	mns	110	3428	3.209
sjd	sel	421	3772	11.161
sjd	sjd	54	3405	1.586
sjd	yrk	442	3564	12.402

Table 1: Mixed and monolingual OCR models compared

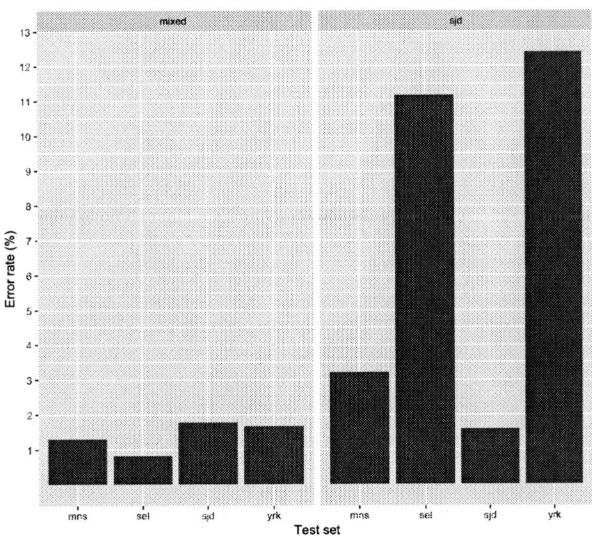

Figure 5: Mixed and monolingual OCR models compared

indeed, has had only one fourth of the exposure to the Kildin Saami special characters
that the monolingual Kildin Saami model received. Nevertheless, the results are very
close. Even more importantly, the mixed model achieves above 98% accuracy for all
of the four languages, and above 99% accuracy for Northern Selkup. The experiment
demonstrates that from the point of view of one language, it does not make a very big
difference whether the 800 lines used in training are from the same language or from
four different languages, as long as the character set is shared.

5.3   Additional Evenki test

The Evenki test was conducted using the same model as in the previous test presented
in section 5.2. The error rate was 5.073 % using the mixed model and 12.832 % using
the Kildin Saami model. This falls well below the accuracy of the previous tests but is
in line with the early phases of the gradual page increase test. Important conclusions
can also be drawn from the fact that the Kildin Saami result is close to the Kildin Saami
results on Selkup and Tundra Nenets – Evenki is equally foreign to the Kildin model
as these languages are, as would be expected.

6   Analysis and error evaluation

Some of the characters recognized poorly belong to a group of characters that generally resemble one another quite a lot; especially pairs such as I : l, e : ε, s : ѕ, z : ʐ
are confused occasionally even with the best-performing models. A more common type of remaining mistake comes from uppercase letters. However, since
the training has been done in a low-resource scenario with a smaller amount
of training data than would be common, the prevalence of capital letters in
the errors seems easily explainable. Uppercase letters are used rarely in most
of the texts, making up only slightly more than 5% of all letter characters in
the training data. From this point of view, it seems obvious that the accuracy
of uppercase letters will trail behind the rest until the entire training set has
reached a relatively large size.

The Kildin Saami model performed relatively poorly on Selkup and Tundra Nenets. The previous error analysis in this section showed that this was
related to the lack of recognition accuracy in those letters that are present in
those languages but not in Kildin Saami. The fact that the Kildin Saami model
performed rather well on Northern Mansi must be related to the somewhat
small character inventory used in Mansi and to the fact that it largely overlaps
with the inventory of Kildin Saami. The only character present in Northern
Mansi but missing in Kildin Saami, at least in this dataset, is ӈ.

The additional Evenki test further and more profoundly illustrates the problems seen in section 5.2 when testing different language combinations. For
example, the Evenki letters that were not recognized by the mixed model were
з and ӭ, both of which are rare or non-existent in the current training data.
Kildin Saami has four instances of з in entire Ground Truth package in word
internal positions, whereas in Evenki this is a highly common character. The
Kildin model has a more narrow character set in use than the mixed model,
which is illustrated by the very common error that occurs when using Kildin
Saami model for Evenki: w : vv. Kildin Saami does not use w in UNA, whereas
Evenki does not use v. These differences, when added up, provide a good ex-

planation for the accuracy rates seen in the experiment. They also illustrate how a cross-linguistic writing system such as UNA benefits specifically from mixed language training, as the model has the opportunity to see characters across the languages.

A further type of error comes from numerals, which are very rare in the Ground Truth package. They occur a few times in running text, but at the moment the models simply do not recognize them at all.

7 Conclusions

The error rates using mixed model for all languages were below 2%, for Northern Selkup even below 1%. In section 3, we mentioned that one page had on average 600-700 characters. These error rates would translate into 6–12 errors per page on average. The error analysis in section 6 demonstrated that the errors are rather concentrated to specific character pairs.

One observation that arises from our work is that training an OCR model for a new writing system, even with incomplete Unicode support, can be done very easily with the current technology. Arbitrary mapping of line texts and images is, as explained in section 4, in principle independent from whether the characters recognized actually correspond to those that are printed. A fast iterative process where the first model is trained using a very small dataset, which is then used to create a somewhat larger dataset with which the same procedure is repeated, appears to be a very effective and effortless method. Based on our incremental page test, five pages (100 lines) was enough to bring the accuracy up to more than 97% percent, suggesting that the initial model should already be trained with a very small amount of training data, if the situation is indeed such that the training has to be started from scratch. This rate of accuracy results in around 20 corrections per page, which is arguably a bearable task. Our study also indicates that in a situation where there is training material available for some languages, we can use that to train an OCR system that also works sufficiently well on other unseen languages, at least if the entire character set of the target language is covered in the training materials.

The accuracy problems were clearly connected to characters missing from the training data but encountered in test languages, and this is an area where cross-lingual OCR will inevitably experience problems. Uppercase characters were also recognized at a poorer rate than others throughout the tests, and this is obviously connected to their sparsity in the training data. It is difficult to imagine a way around this problem, which is a major bottleneck in low-resource scenarios. One suggestion could be to make sure that even the rarer letters are at least sporadically present in the training data, perhaps by picking out lines in the available materials that contain these characters in initial position. The initial character issue brings even more problems in multilingual scenarios, as there are many language-specific phonotactic limitations on which characters can occur in initial position and will thus be present in uppercase form. Naturally they can still occur occasionally in lines that are entirely capitalized, an instance of which was presented in figure 3. Further research should evaluate whether lines in all capitals improve the accuracy of word-initial capital letters as well.

The use of various languages to train one OCR system provides a potential answer to the question on the degree to which OCR models are language specific and how much they actually generalize across languages. We do not claim that our experiments would have yet shed much light on this question, but further experiments with Unified Northern Alphabet are a good avenue for studying this topic further. For sake of comparison, some scenarios that are similar to OCR recognition of UNA include recognizing texts written in UPA, IPA or Americanist Phonetic Notation. In all these cases, a writing system that is in principle uniform is used across different languages.

Moving forward, full parallel texts should be extracted from these books using the OCR models provided. This data should also be converted into the contemporary orthographies, after which it could be used for a variety of purposes. For example, creating new treebanks within the Universal Dependencies project could be a very interesting way to improve the digital infrastructure of these languages rather visibly. Similarly, language documentation projects working with the endangered northern Eurasian languages should certainly be interested in resources such as texts written in UNA. Since these materials are largely in the Public Domain, there are exceptionally few limitations to what could be done.

Acknowledgments

The authors collaborate within the project "Language Documentation meets Language Technology: the Next Step in the Description of Komi" funded by Kone Foundation. Thanks to Alexandra Kellner for proofreading this article.

References

Thomas M Breuel. 2008. The OCRopus open source OCR system. In *Document Recognition and Retrieval XV*. International Society for Optics and Photonics, volume 6815, page 68150F.

Lenore A. Grenoble. 2003. *Language policy in the Soviet Union*. Kluwer Academic Publishers.

Niko Partanen and Michael Rießler. 2018a. An OCR system for the Unified Northern Alphabet – data package https://doi.org/10.5281/zenodo.2506880.

Niko Partanen and Michael Rießler. 2018b. Unified Northern Alphabet OCR Ground Truth v1.1 https://doi.org/10.5281/zenodo.2443922.

Christian Reul, Uwe Springmann, Christoph Wick, and Frank Puppe. 2018. State of the art optical character recognition of 19th century fraktur scripts using open source engines. *arXiv preprint arXiv:1810.03436* .

Florian Siegl and Michael Rießler. 2015. Uneven steps to literacy. In Heiko F. Marten, Michael Rießler, Janne Saarikivi, and Reetta Toivanen, editors, *Cultural and linguistic minorities in the Russian Federation and the European*

Union, Springer, number 13 in Multilingual Education, pages 189–229. https://doi.org/10.1007/978-3-319-10455-3$_8$.

Miikka Silfverberg and Jack Rueter. 2014. Can morphological analyzers improve the quality of optical character recognition? In *Proceedings of 1st International Workshop in Computational Linguistics for Uralic Languages*. http://dx.doi.org/10.7557/5.3467.

The National Library of Finland. 2018. Fenno-ugrica. https://fennougrica. kansalliskirjasto.fi/. Accessed: 2018-12-21.

P. N. Zulew. 1933. Taŋin ʒarin dukuwun: nonopti hanin, nonopti anŋani alagun ʒarin. *E-resource repository of the University of Latvia. Prof. Pētera Šmita kolekcija* https://dspace.lu.lv/dspace/handle/7/28252.

P. N. Žuḷov. 1933a. Lovintan maβьs lovintanut: oul lomt :oul haniš tan tal maβьs. *Fenno-Ugrica collection. The National Library of Finland* http://urn.fi/URN:NBN:fi-fe2014060426213.

P. N. Žuḷov. 1933b. Tolaŋgowa jeβemṇa tolaŋgobçβ: ṇurtej peḷa: ṇurtej toholambawa po jeβemṇa padawъ. *Fenno-Ugrica collection. The National Library of Finland* http://urn.fi/URN:NBN:fi-fe2014061629286.

P. N. Žuḷov. 1934. Kniga logkəm guejka: vəsmus pieḷ vəsmus egest opnuvmus. *Fenno-Ugrica collection. The National Library of Finland* http://urn.fi/URN:NBN:fi-fe2016051212324.

ELAN as a search engine
for hierarchically structured, tagged corpora

Joshua Wilbur

Albert-Ludwigs-Universität Freiburg
Department of Scandinavian Studies
Freiburg Research Group in Saami Studies
joshua.wilbur@skandinavistik.uni-freiburg.de

2018-12-20

Abstract

The main goal of this paper is to outline and explore the usefulness of the corpus search functionalities provided in the ELAN annotation application when annotations are provided in hierarchically organized tiers. A general overview of ELAN's search functions is provided first, highlighting the program's usefulness as a corpus search engine for corpus and computational linguists. To illustrate this, the updated hierarchical tier structure for ELAN developed by the Freiburg Research Group in Saami Studies for the group's projects on both Saamic and Komi languages is presented as an example template. The suitability of hierarchical structures for annotations and the ELAN search interfaces for doing corpus linguistics is explored critically, including the description of a fundamental flaw in the "Multiple Layer Search" mode which likely prevents ELAN from being used as a search engine for complex corpus studies.

Kokkuvõte

Artikli peamine eesmärk on kirjeldada ning uurida, millised on programmi ELAN korpusepäringu võimalused, kui materjal on annoteeritud hierarhiliste kihtidena. Selleks antakse kõigepealt ülevaade programmi otsimootori üldistest võimalustest, tuues välja selle kasulikud omadused korpus- ja arvutilingvistide jaoks. Näitena tutvustatakse ELAN-i uuendatud hierarhilist kihistruktuuri, mille on välja arendanud Freiburg Research Group in Saami Studies töötades nii saami keelte kui ka komi keele teadusprojektidega. Artiklis arutletakse selle üle, kuivõrd hierarhiline kihistruktuur ja ELAN-i otsinguliides sobivad korpuslingvistilise uurimistöö jaoks. Ilmneb, et ELAN-i otsimootor võimaldab teha lihtsamaid päringuid, kuid keerulisemad otsingud on raskendatud. Programmi „Multiple Layer Search" töörežiimis esineb fundamentaalne puudus, mistõttu komplekssete korpusuuringute jaoks seda tõenäoliselt kasutada ei saa.

Proceedings of the fifth Workshop on Computational Linguistics for Uralic Languages, pages 90–103,
Tartu, Estonia, January 7 - January 8, 2019.

1   Overview of ELAN search functionalities

ELAN is a multimedia language annotation program which enables textual annotation of audio and/or video media files within a single application. It is free software developed by the Technical Group of the Max Planck Institute for Psycholinguistics, and can be downloaded from `https://tla.mpi.nl/tools/tla-tools/elan`. ELAN was created with linguists who work with non-text-based linguistic data as the main target user group, and continues to be developed with them in mind. ELAN annotation files are plain text files in xml format with the file extension `.eaf`. They are fully compatible with the unicode standard. Because they are in xml format, they can be accessed using other protocols, and even automatically generated.

The general functionality of ELAN is described in detail in the ELAN manual (available from the ELAN website), in various training materials for documentary and corpus linguistics, and in a few scientific publications; for instance, see § 4 in Gerstenberger et al. (2016) for a general description, and Nagy and Meyerhoff (2015) for a detailed example of an ELAN implementation for sociolinguistic research. With these publications in mind, the present discussion will be limited to those aspects of ELAN which are directly relevant to its use as a corpus search engine.

Annotations in ELAN are time-aligned with a media file or files, and are organized into layers called "tiers" which can be defined on an individual basis; typically, each tier corresponds to the specific type of information it contains (e.g., orthographic transcription, meta-language translation, etc.). The information provided in the annotations must be represented as a string of characters, but ELAN provides neither restrictions nor suggestions concerning the type of content annotations contain; as a result, every user or project must come up with a set of relevant tiers. Tiers can be structured hierarchically, such that one tier is subordinate to another tier, e.g., a Russian translation may be under a tier containing a target language transcription. The hierarchical relationship between superordinate and subordinate tiers is governed by "Tier Types"[1] which essentially define how tiers are organized with respect to the timeline and within the hierarchy. Having hierarchically structured tiers allows ELAN searches to be more targeted, and thus more powerful, than when no tier hierarchy is present because it is therefore possible to limit the scope of a search to specific inter-tier relationships; this is illustrated below in section 3.3. Note that a typical ELAN annotation file is structured so that each participant in the annotated linguistic event has his/her own set of tiers using the same hierarchy. This makes it possible for ELAN to deal with overlapping speech, a typical characteristic of spoken language.

In the following section (section 2), I briefly present a specific implementation of ELAN as a corpus collection tool in order to later illustrate how ELAN searches can be performed. After that, the various search functions built into ELAN are summarized in section 3, including examples for how these can be used to search hierarchical tier structures (as illustrated by the Freiburg template). Finally, in section 4, I describe a significant problem concerning how to limit the scope of search criteria found in the "Multiple Layer Search" function, and discuss why this likely prevents ELAN from

---

[1]In older versions of ELAN, these were referred to as 'Linguistic Types'.

ultimately being used as corpus search engine for complex queries. A summary and conclusions are found in section 5.

2   An example tier structure

Although tiers do not necessarily have to be organized hierarchically in ELAN, searches in ELAN can be more powerful if a meaningful tier hierarchy is present. In order to understand how ELAN can be used as a search tool, it is useful to provide an example for how ELAN annotation tiers can be organized hierarchically. In this section, I provide an overview of the ELAN tier hierarchy standard as developed and implemented in various projects on Saami languages and Komi variants carried out within the auspices of the Freiburg Research Group in Saami Studies. Note that this structure is only one possible template, and is provided here simply as an illustration; indeed, ELAN allows users to define any kind of hierarchy structure (including a flat structure).

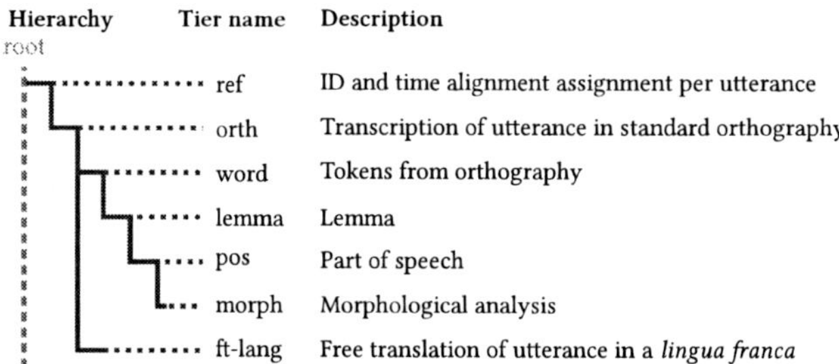

Figure 1: The minimal ELAN annotation tier hierarchy template used in the Freiburg Research Group in Saami Studies' corpora

ELAN annotation tiers used in the Freiburg projects are organized hierarchically using the minimal template shown in Figure 1 for each individual participant in a text.[2] Time-alignment relative to the original media file (usually at least a .wav-file, often with accompanying video) is set in the root node tier named ref, which also serves to assign the utterance a unique number within the text; this is the only tier in the hierarchy which is linked directly to the time line (as opposed to being symbolically linked via another tier). The orth tier contains an orthographic representation of the utterance at hand; there is one and only one orth tier for each ref tier, and, due to its tier type, it time-aligns exactly with its superordinate ref tier. The word tier contains individual annotations for each token in the orth tier. Each token in the word tier is assigned a lemma in the subordinate lemma tier. The part of speech for each lemma is presented in the pos tier. When applicable, relevant morphological values for the specific wordform found in the token are presented in the morph tier, which completes

---

[2] A more thorough, dynamic description of the Freiburg tier structure can be found at `https://github.com/langdoc/FRechdoc/wiki/ELAN-tiers`, including an inventory of the tier types used. An older version of the hierarchy is presented in Gerstenberger et al. (2016, 37-38).

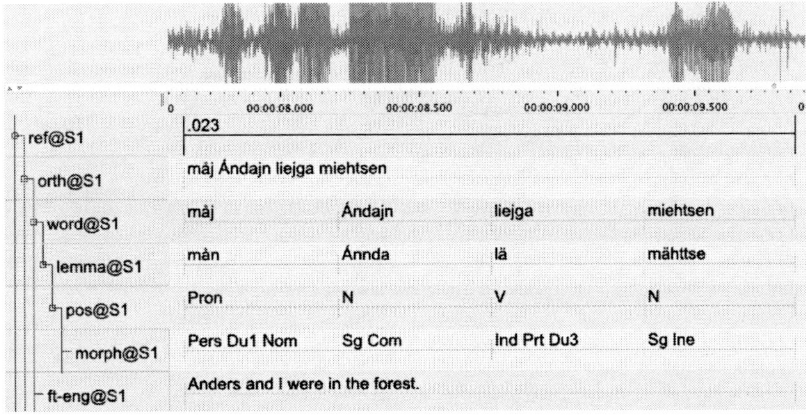

Figure 2: A screenshot presenting an implementation of the hierarchical tier structure for an utterance annotated in ELAN

the grammatical annotations. Finally, the ft-lang tier provides a free translation of the utterance in a specific *lingua franca* (here, the iso-639 code is used in place of 'lang', e.g., the tier ft-eng is for a free English translation).

A screenshot is provided in figure 2 to show what the implementation of this actually looks like in an ELAN annotation file. Here, the hierarchical tier structure is on the left, and the wave file is at the top; the utterance itself, here numbered ".023", and the corresponding annotations are shown in the rest of the image. Each participant has the same set of tiers, but each tier name is extended by a "domain" name identifying the speaker (formatted much like an email address); in the example in figure 2, the first speaker is simply identified as "S1", and thus all of this speaker's tiers are modified with the extension "@S1", as in ref@S1, orth@S1, word@S1, etc. Aside from being a clear way to mark the speaker for a specific annotation, naming tiers this way allows ELAN search queries to also be limited to a specific tier for a specific speaker, but across the corpus.

Other, project- or text-specific tiers may also exist, and these are located at the relevant level of the hierarchy.[3] In the Freiburg corpora, all annotations from the word tier through the morph tier are created automatically (using a python script) from the output that results from feeding the orthographic representation in the orth tier through Finite State Transducer and Constraint Grammar implementations.[4]

---

[3] Examples of other tiers found in some of the Freiburg corpora include an orth-orig tier containing older orthographic transcriptions of a text and subordinate to the ref tier, or a gloss tier presenting rough translations of each lemma and subordinate to the pos tier.

[4] See Blokland et al. (2015); Gerstenberger et al. (2016, 2017b,a) for discussions of various aspects of this approach, including how ambiguous analyses are handled.

3 ELAN as a corpus search engine

Typically, a single ELAN file contains annotations for a single recorded linguistic event, and corresponds to one or more audio or video files.[5] An ELAN corpus thus consists of all ELAN annotation files corresponding to the texts considered to be part of the corpus.

The ability to search within a single ELAN file when it is currently open is impressively powerful, and includes the ability to limit the search to specific tiers, to use regular expressions, to replace all hits with a different string, and to recursively perform searches limited to the results of a previous search. However, since this discussion is interested in ELAN as a *corpus* search engine, this functionality will not be discussed here in any further detail. Instead, search functions that can be applied simultaneously to multiple ELAN files (i.e., an ELAN corpus) will be described and reviewed below.

In order to perform a corpus search, one first has to choose the set of ELAN files to be considered.[6] These can be selected either one by one, or users can choose all the ELAN files in a certain path, or a domain can be constructed of ELAN files sharing specific metadata characteristics (the last option requires having metadata for each file in IMDI[7] format). Once the files have been selected to comprise the corpus, searching can commence.

3.1 Basic search modes

The results of searches using either of the menu items "Search Multiple eaf" or "FAST-Search" are listed in concordance format, including information such as file name, tier name, etc., and with the preceding and following annotations shown to provide immediate context. Regular expressions[8] can be used in this interface, case-sensitivity can be set, and the results can be exported into tab delimited format. However, that is the extent of the functionality of this type of search; as such, it is useful to get a quick, impressionistic result set, but it is not sufficient for more complex, specific corpus searches, and thus is rather insignificant for corpus linguistics and computational linguistics, and will not be discussed further here.

Choosing the menu item "Structured Search Multiple eaf" opens a search interface window with three types of searches which increase in complexity from left to right. A "Substring Search" is similar to the "Search Multiple eaf" functionality outlined in the previous paragraph, but without even the regular expression or case-sensitivity options. However, search results in this mode can be presented in multiple ways: as a concordance, as a list of frequencies, or as found in the individual ELAN files, including time-alignment, file name, tier name and tier type; these types of results can be saved in tab separated value format. As with "Search Multiple eaf", this search

---

[5]Note that it is not obligatory to have a media file; it is thus also possible to use ELAN to annotate exclusively written sources, such as heritage texts.

[6]In the ELAN interface, this set of files is referred to as the "domain".

[7]Cf. `https://tla.mpi.nl/imdi-metadata/`.

[8]These are based on regular expressions in java, cf. `https://docs.oracle.com/javase/7/docs/api/java/util/regex/Pattern.html`.

is quite superficial for essentially the same reasons, and it is not clear why these two types of search exist as separate entities.

3.2 Complex corpus search modes

The other two search modes are called "Single Layer Search" and "Multiple Layer Search". These are significantly more powerful concerning many aspects of the search criteria accepted, from mere convenience features to significantly increased query precision. The existence of these modes is what allows the ELAN search functionality to even be considered a potentially useful corpus search engine. The difference between these two search modes is found in the complexity of queries concerning the features of tiers which can be referenced; this will be further examined below. But to begin with, their common functionalities will be specified.

Search queries in these two modes can be saved and loaded again later, which allows for increased ease of reproducibility. There are < and > buttons for conveniently 'browsing' between previously entered search queries (essentially like those found in internet browsers). In the basic annotation mode, one can further specify a query for character matches (either substrings or white-space separated units (the latter are known as "exact matches" in ELAN)), or one using regular expressions. Furthermore, the search scope can be set to all extant tiers in the corpus, to a subset defined either by a specific tier name, or all tiers with a common tier type, or finally, to all tiers corresponding to a specific participant. However, these searches are limited to a single tier name, a single tier type or a single participant; no complex subset of various tier names, or multiple participants, etc. is possible. Therefore, any more specific restriction on the structural scope of a search query (i.e., filtering any type of information not directly included in the actual annotations, e.g., speaker gender, age, etc.) must be done in either pre-processing (by defining the corpus for the ELAN search), or in post-processing results outside of ELAN.

Search results for both modes can be displayed as a concordance, as a frequency table, or as individual annotations.[9] Results from each of these ways of organizing hits can be stored as a tab-separated value file. This allows search results to be exported for further processing elsewhere, if desired.

Generally speaking, a "Single Layer Search" is useful because of the characteristics detailed above, but defining the scope of the search is limited (as the name implies). With this in mind, the "Multiple Layer Search" mode is the focus of the rest of this discussion because it presents the only opportunity to perform complex search queries across the corpus while taking advantage of the hierarchical structure of tiers. Figure 3 provides a screen shot of a relatively simple multiple layer search query which restricts the search scope to the hierarchical limitations of a single column. This image serves to illustrate the basic idea behind multiple layer searches in ELAN. Note that users need to be thoroughly familiar with the tier hierarchy of the ELAN files in the search domain to use and take full advantage of the Multiple Layer Search.

Here, a case-sensitive regular expression search looking vertically through the

---

[9]These are discussed in more detail below, and illustrated there by screenshots in figures 4, 5 and 6, respectively.

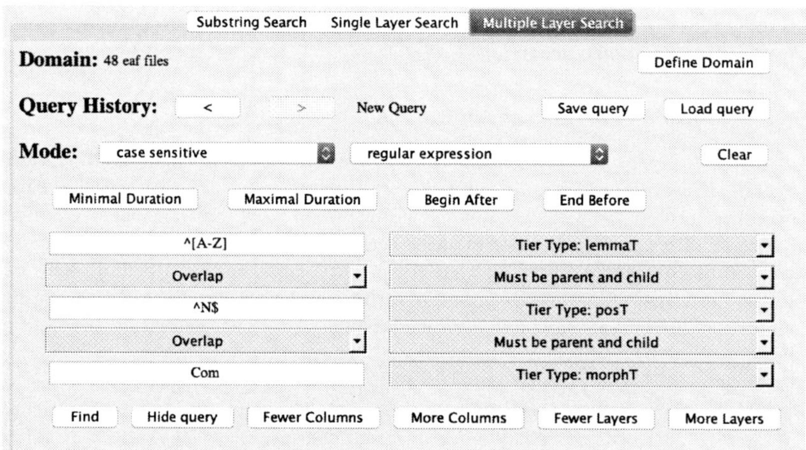

Figure 3: An example of a "Multiple Layer Search" with a search query for a single column, looking for proper names in comitative case

hierarchy is defined.[10] In the column on the left, the search criteria themselves are entered in the white fields, while the temporal relationship between the layers are set in the green drop-down menu boxes. In the column on the right, the search criteria setting the scope of search for each of the white search-criteria boxes is defined, as is a further hierarchical relationship between the layers to be searched. In this example, the search is intended to find all hits of proper names in comitative case.

The uppermost layer is set on the right to look only at tiers with the type lemmaT, which in the Freiburg hierarchy[11] selects only lemma tiers, and on the left to look for lemma annotations that begin with a capital letter using the regular expression ^[A–Z].

The middle layer is set on the right to look only at tiers with the type posT, which in the Freiburg hierarchy selects only pos tiers, and only when a specific annotation is in a "parent and child" hierarchical relationship to the uppermost level; in other words, ELAN is set to only find hits on the pos tier which are directly subordinate to a lemma tier. Similarly, the middle layer is set on the left side to look for annotations that consist solely of the character N (used to signify 'noun') using the regular expression ^N$.

Finally, the lowest layer is set on the right to look only at tiers with the type morphT, which in the Freiburg hierarchy selects only morph tiers, and only when a specific annotation is in a "parent and child" hierarchical relationship to the middle

---

[10]Time restrictions on the duration or location within the recording can be set using the "Minimal Duration", "Maximal Duration", "Begin After" and "End Before" buttons, but are not used in this example. Indeed, for the type of searches looking for lexical or grammatical structures that the author uses, these are not relevant at all.

[11]Cf. section 3.3.

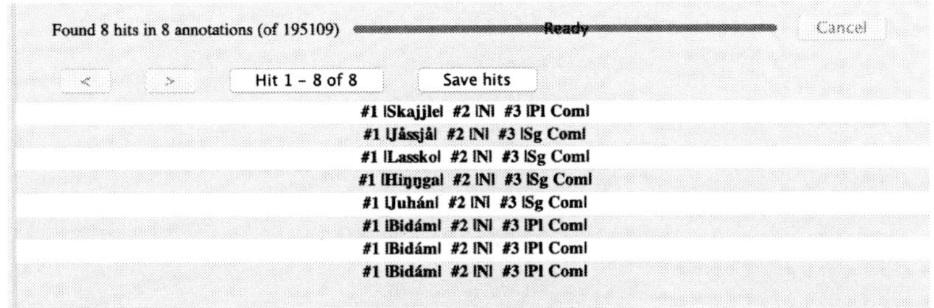

Figure 4: An example of search results presented in "Concordance view"

Figure 5: An example of search results presented in "Frequency view"

level; in other words, here ELAN limits hits to those on the morph tier which are directly subordinate to a pos tier. Similarly, the lowest layer is set on the left side to look for annotations that contain the character string Com (used to tag wordforms in comitative case).

Resulting hits can be viewed in three ways: 1) as a concordance (cf. figure 4); 2) listed by frequency, and further arrangeable by frequency (from most to least) or alphabetically by annotation (cf. figure 5); as well as in 3) "Alignment view" showing each hit as found in the respective set of annotations and time-aligned (cf. figure 6). Clicking on a hit automatically opens the corresponding ELAN file to the specific place where the hit is found. This makes it very easy to go to a specific spot in the corpus to further inspect a hit in its actual context.

In addition to being able to search vertically within a tier hierarchy, the "Multiple Layer Search" also allows one to search horizontally by specifying search criteria that look at annotations to the left or right on a specific tier. This is done by adding additional columns in the search interface, as illustrated by the screenshot in figure 7.[12] This idea is essentially the same as with the single column search presented above (cf. figure 3), but here, the horizontal distance between annotations which fulfill the

---

[12]Note that columns and layers can be added or taken away, depending on the specific search query, using the "Fewer Columns" and "More Columns" or "Fewer Layers" and "More Layers" buttons; a maximum of eight columns and eight layers can be used.

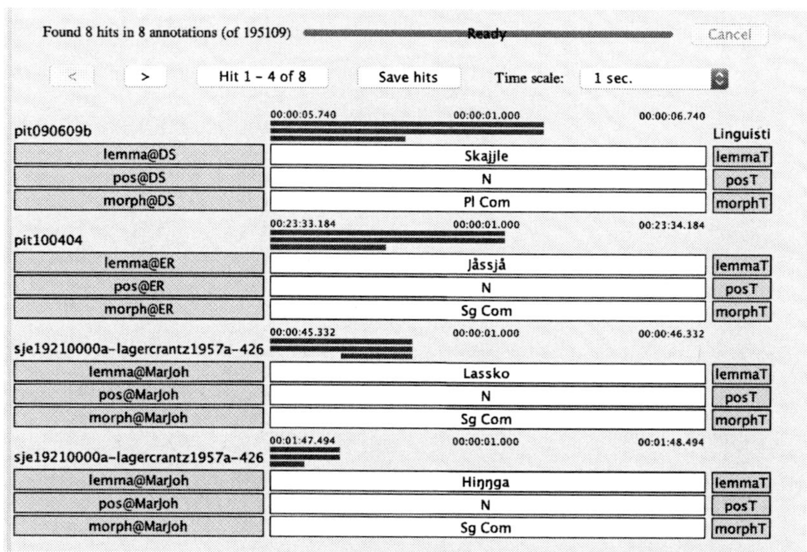

Figure 6: An example of search results presented in "Alignment view"

Figure 7: An example of a "Multiple Layer Search" with a search query for two columns, looking for proper names in comitative case immediately preceded by a pronoun

search criteria can be set, and is measured either in the number of intervening annotations or in milliseconds. The minimum setting is zero, i.e., no annotations or no milliseconds between neighboring annotations with hits. Note, however, that this entails that any given hit *must* consist of at least two separate annotations throughout the respective hierarchies which return the hits; thus any given search result *is not able* to refer to the same individual annotation in more than one part of the respective sub-hit's vertical hierarchy. This is a significant weakness of ELAN searches using hierarchical tier structures that is discussed at the end of section 3.3 below. Aside from this additional horizontal operation, the search interface is the same as presented above for the "Single Layer Search".

3.3   Searching Freiburg-style ELAN corpora

It is hopefully obvious from the description in section 2 above that the hierarchical tier structure developed for corpora in the language documentation projects carried out by the Freiburg Research Group in Saami Studies is intended to take advantage of two functionalities of ELAN searches. First, we distinguish structurally between different types of information by restricting tiers to contain only specific types of information. Thus, the orthographic representation is saved in the orth tier, an English translation is in the ft-eng tier, etc. For linguistic annotations, individual tokens[13] are in the word tier, the corresponding lemma is in the lemma tier, the part of speech in the pos tier, and relevant values of morphological categories are in the morph tier. Second, these types of information are symbolically linked to each other by structuring the tiers into a hierarchy. In this way, any given annotation in the ref tier is the root node and time-aligned to the master media file; annotations on this tier consist only of a unique and symbolic identifier (a number), while all other relevant annotations are subordinate to this main, time-aligned annotation. Tokens from the orth tier are found as individual annotations in the word tier, the corresponding lemma is subordinate to each token, the part of speech is subordinate to the lemma, and morphological information is subordinate to the part of speech (cf. figures 1 and 2).

In addition to being a transparent, well structured presentation format, the idea behind structuring annotations in this way is to increase efficiency in searching. As is probably obvious, grouping types of information separately allows one to more easily limit search results to a specific type, or filter out unwanted hits; a simple example for this would be restricting the result set to only include nouns by looking only for hits with 'N' in the pos tier. By combining this type of specific searches restricting results to specific hits on more than one tier in the search interface, searches in ELAN can, theoretically, be quite specific, without having exceptionally complicated regular expression statements that would otherwise be required in a flat tier structure. An example of this is provided above in figure 3), where proper nouns in comitative case are the target of the search criteria; here, detailed search criteria on three levels of the tier hierarchy are specified.

---

[13]As it is consistent with the Giellatekno preprocessing scripts, we treat punctuation as tokens. However, note that particularly spoken language corpora are not consistently annotated using punctuation to mark the end of utterances, so punctuation characters are not a reliable tool to find utterance boundaries.

4   A fundamental problem of scope restriction

Because the information which the Freiburg-style annotations contain are of a lexico-grammatical nature, as well as due to the hierarchical tier structure, the Freiburg corpora are intended to be particularly useful for searching for morphosyntactic, syntactic or discourse syntactic patterns. However, the ELAN multiple layer search interface has a significant flaw that prevents it from being the powerful corpus search engine it appears to be on the surface, both for Freiburg-style tier hierarchies and likely for any hierarchically structured ELAN file. This flaw stems from the fact that it is impossible to restrict search criteria in two or more columns lower in the hierarchy to fall within one and the same higher-level parent (or grandparent, great-grandparent, etc.) tier.[14]

This is best illustrated with an example. Say for instance you want to find all utterances which have a dual pronoun followed by a singular noun in comitative case (for example in searching for instances of comitative coordination (cf. Morottaja et al., 2017)). For the left column, the morphological search criteria (in the morph tier) would be Du to find hits marked for dual, and for the right column Sg Com to find hits for "comitative singular". For the pos tier, the left column would be set for Pron for "pronoun", and the right column for ^N$ for nouns.[15] But there is no way to restrict hits to be *within* a single superordinate tier (such as the orth tier), and thus even hits which cross annotations boundaries on the orth tier will be included in the result set. It is possible to set the search to be limited to directly neighboring annotations (i.e., two annotations which do not have other annotations in between; in the ELAN search interface, this corresponds to "= 0 ann."), but even this does not exclude hits with an intervening annotation boundary in a superordinate tier. Thus the Pite Saami example in (1) would correctly produce the hit *måjå Ándajn*. However, if the examples in (2) and (3) are neighboring annotations, they would *also* produce the hit *måjå Ándajn*, even though these are two *separate* utterances.[16]

(1)   *måjå*   *Ándajn*   *lijmen*   *miehtsen*
        PERS.1DU.NOM Anders-COM.SG be-1DU.PRT forest-INESS.SG

'Anders and I were in the woods'

(2)   *dä*   *buhtin*   *måjå*
        then come-1DU.PRS PERS.1DU.NOM

'Then we (two) came'

---

[14]Note that ELAN has a search mode in the "Multiple Layer Search" interface which one could potentially expect to be able to deal with this: the "variable match" mode. However, variables cannot be self-referential, so the higher-level matches must be separate, unique annotations which are identical in form, so this would not work. On top of that, regular expressions are not allowed in this mode, so it would not be particularly powerful or useful in any case.

[15]This regular expression is necessary because the set of abbreviations for parts of speech includes "Num" for numerals, and a search simply for N would include numerals as well.

[16]Note that particularly spoken language corpora are not consistently annotated using punctuation to mark the end of utterances, so punctuation is not a reliable tool to be used for ruling out such hits as in the second half of this example.

(3) *Ándajn*   *lä*   *állkep*
     Anders-COM.SG be\3SG.PRS easy-COMP.NOM.SG

     'It's easier with Anders'

Note that one could think that a search which looks for directly neighboring hits
(such as in the examples above, which look for a dual pronoun directly followed by a
singular noun in comitative case) could get around this flaw by setting the constraint
concerning number of annotations allowed to intervene between hits to "0". However,
this still does not avoid getting hits such as the one arising from examples 2 and 3,
as illustrated above, since the scope still cannot be set to take higher-level annotation
boundaries into account. Furthermore, in the current state of the Freiburg workflow
and infrastructure, this sort of restriction is useless as well because each ambiguity
which is not removed by constraint grammar rules is automatically added as a unique
annotation to an ELAN file in random order. Thus, it is feasible that another possible
analysis (arising from ambiguous morphological surface forms) may occur between
the correct form itself and a following annotation, but such actual hits would not be
output to the search results if the intervening number of annotations is set to "0". For
instance, since Pite Saami comitative singular and inessive plural forms are always
homophonous, if the constraint grammar rules are not able to disambiguate, both
possible analyses will be written as annotations in the ELAN file, as in the double
gloss for *Ándajn* in example 4 below. If no annotations are allowed to occur between
the hits, then this entirely relevant hit will not be found.

(4) *måjå*   *Ándajn*   *lijmen*   *miehtsen*
     PERS.1DU.NOM Anders-INESS.PL/COM.SG be-1DU.PRT forest-INESS.SG

     'Anders and I were in the woods'

On the other hand, if no constraint is set, then *any* and *every* possible co-occurance
of the two criteria throughout the entirety of any given ELAN file will be found. In
other words, given an ELAN file with a hundred utterance annotations, an instance
of *måjå* in the first annotation and an instance of *Ándajn* in the hundredth annotation
will also be returned as a hit.

It could potentially be claimed that this is not a flaw in the ELAN interface, but
instead an unsuitable hierarchical tier structure developed by the Freiburg group. Perhaps a different tier structure would allow for better searching, but the fundamental
problem that a higher-level annotation cannot be set as the scope of a search query
still exists. This calls into question whether a hierarchical tier structure consisting of
annotations with lexico-grammatical information is even a useful construction, aside
from its clear benefits of being a functional storage format and an elegant presentation format. Indeed, one current work-around for doing complex searches in ELAN
which are limited in scope to looking within – and not across – higher-level annotation boundaries (specifically those of the orth tier) involves a flat structure consisting
of the utterance-level annotations each containing an utterance's entire FST/CG[17] out-

---

[17]Finite State Transducer and Constraint Grammar

put. For such search queries, it is sufficient to use complex regular expressions in the
"Single Layer Search" mode of the ELAN search interface.[18]

5   Conclusion

In summary, ELAN presents a complex way of handling linguistic annotations, including the ability to differentiate between types of information by using an annotation-
tier hierarchy. With this in mind, the Freiburg Research Group in Saami Studies
has developed such a hierarchy for annotating lexico-grammatical features such as
lemma, part of speech and morphological information for the group's various, mainly
spoken-language corpora for endangered Uralic languages. It is clear that, as an annotation and presentation tool, ELAN is very useful; this paper has attempted to explore
the functionality of ELAN as a corpus search engine using the complex hierarchical
tier structure developed by the Freiburg group to illustrate this.

ELAN offers various levels of complexity in its search capabilities. The most complex of these, the "Multiple Layer Search", includes the ability to stipulate search criteria both vertically within the hierarchy on a tier-by-tier level, and horizontally across
annotations. Despite this complex-looking search interface, it has a significant weakness which makes it insufficient for complex corpus queries looking for morphosyntactic or syntactic patterns. Specifically, it is not possible to limit the scope of a search
to take utterance-level boundaries into account. Thus, even false hits which contain
one or more utterance-level boundaries will always be returned. With this weakness
in mind, ELAN is not an ideal corpus search tool. Fortunately, ELAN search results
can be exported to other open formats such as tab separated files, which can then be
further refined using other utilities.

References

Rogier Blokland, Ciprian Gerstenberger, Marina Fedina, Niko Partanen, Michael
Rießler, and Joshua Wilbur. 2015. Language documentation meets language tech-
nology. In Tommi A. Pirinen, Francis M. Tyers, and Trond Trosterud, editors, *First
International Workshop on Computational Linguistics for Uralic Languages, 16th Jan-
uary, 2015, Tromsø, Norway*, The University Library of Tromsø, number 2015:2 in
Septentrio Conference Series, pages 8–18.

Ciprian Gerstenberger, Niko Partanen, and Michael Rießler. 2017a. Instant annotations in ELAN corpora of spoken and written Komi, an endangered language of
the Barents Sea region. In Antti Arppe, Jeff Good, Mans Hulden, Jordan Lachler,
Alexis Palmer, and Lane Schwartz, editors, *Proceedings of the 2nd Workshop on the
Use of Computational Methods in the Study of Endangered Languages*, Association
for Computational Linguistics, ACL Anthology, pages 57–66.

---

[18]To be fair, it should be noted that if the data set is small enough, search results can be gone through by
hand, eliminating those which should not in fact be included. But from a computational linguistics point
of view, this is obviously not a tenable solution, especially when dealing with massive data sets ('big data').

Ciprian Gerstenberger, Niko Partanen, Michael Rießler, and Joshua Wilbur. 2016. Utilizing language technology in the documentation of endangered Uralic languages 4:29–47.

Ciprian Gerstenberger, Niko Partanen, Michael Rießler, and Joshua Wilbur. 2017b. Instant annotations. Association for Computational Linguistics, ACL Anthology, pages 25–36.

Petter Morottaja, Raj Singh, and Ida Toivonen. 2017. Comitative coordination in inari saami. Presentation at the 3rd Saami Linguistics Symposium, Albrecht-Ludwigs-Universität Freiburg, 19-20 October 2017.

Naomi Nagy and Miriam Meyerhoff. 2015. Extending ELAN into variationist sociolinguistics. *Linguistics Vanguard* 1(1):271–281.

Neural and rule-based Finnish NLP models—expectations, experiments and experiences

Tommi A Pirinen
Universität Hamburg
Hamburger Zentrum für Sprachkorpora
Max-Brauer-Allee 60, D-22765 Hamburg
`tommi.antero.pirinen@uni-hamburg.de`

Abstract

In this article I take a critical look at some recent results in the field of neural language modeling of Finnish in terms of popular shared tasks. One novel point of view I present is comparing the neural methods' results to traditional rule-based systems for the given tasks, since most of the shared tasks have concentrated on the supervised learning concept. The shared task results I re-evaluate, are morphological regeneration by SIGMORPHON 2016, universal dependency parsing by CONLL-2018 and a machine translation application that imitates WMT 2018 for German instead of English. The Uralic language used throughout is Finnish. I use out of the box, best performing neural systems and rule-based systems and evaluate their results.

Tiivistelmä

Tässä artikkelissa tarkastelemme joitain hiljattaisia tuloksia niinkutsutuissa shared task -kilpailuissa suomen kielen hemroverkkomallien osalta. Yksi tämän artikkelin kontribuutioista on hermoverkkomallien tuottamien tulosten vertailu perinteisiin sääntöpohjaisiin kielimallituloksiin, sillä shared task -kisailut pääosin keskittyvät täysin tai osittain hallitsemattomien mallien oppimisen konseptiin. Shared taskit joita tässä artikkelissa tarkastelemme ovat SIGMORPHONin 2016 morfologisen uudelleengeneroinnin kisa, CONLL:n 2018 jäsennyskilpailu sekä WMT 2018:n konekäännöskilpailu uudelleensovellettuna saksan kielelle. Uralilainen kieli jota käytämme kaikissa kokeissa on suomi. Järjestelmät joita käytetään ovat avoimen lähdekoodin järjestelmiä jotka ovat olleet parhaita näissä kilpailuissa.

1   Introduction

The popularity of the neural networks in natural language processing is at the moment climbing very rapidly to the extent that we commonly get to hear that non-neural

Proceedings of the fifth Workshop on Computational Linguistics for Uralic Languages, pages 104–114,
Tartu, Estonia, January 7 - January 8, 2019.

methods should be abandoned. While naturally the majority of this hype is based on English-centric or mostly European NLP, there are some reports of good successes within the less resourced and more morphological languages, including Uralic languages. In this paper I compare directly the state-of-the-art methods between the neural and rule-based language processing for Finnish. I specifically devised experiments based on the following shared tasks and popular systems:

- Generating morphology: Sigmorphon 2016 results (Cotterell et al., 2016) vs. omorfi (Pirinen, 2015a)

- Parsing of morphosyntax: Turku neural parser (Kanerva et al., 2018) vs. omorfi (Pirinen, 2015a)

- Machine translation between Finnish and German: OpenNMT (Klein et al., 2017) vs. apertium-fin-deu (Pirinen, 2018)

Comparing a few different tasks gives us a good overview of the state of the art in the neural processing of Finnish. Parsing tasks give an idea of the potential usability of the language models in various linguistic tasks, such as corpus annotation, whereas the machine translation task provides an important view on the full capacity of the models for a more wide-ranging language understanding task.

One of the contributions of this paper is to gain more insight of the similarities and differences of the traditional rule-based systems for the given tasks, since the shared tasks are virtually always earmarked for more or less supervised language learning, any evaluations between the neural and the rule-based systems are not so commonly found in the literature.

The rest of article is organised as follows: in Section 2, I introduce the shared tasks and rule-based systems at large, in Section 3, I describe the systems used for the experiments, in Section 4, I describe the system setup, in Section 5, I go through the experiments and results, in Section 6, I perform the error analysis, in Section 7, I relate the results to current state of the art as well as practical usage and development of the systems and finally in Section 8, I summarise the findings.

2 Background

In recent years the neural network-based systems, especially so-called deep neural systems, have been brought forward as a solution to all natural language processing problems. Some results have also been provided for Uralic languages. In the case of morphology, there was a popular task of morphological generation as a shared task of the ACL 2016 SIGMORPHON workshop (Cotterell et al., 2016), which included the Finnish generation, and showed some very promising results. In the context of the machine translation, the shared task of the WMT conference has had a Finnish task since 2015, and since 2017 the participants have predominantly been the neural systems (e.g. for 2018 c.f Bojar et al. (2018)). For the morphosyntax, the popular shared task to test a parser with, is the CONLL task on the dependency parsing (Zeman et al., 2018). What is common with these shared tasks, is that they are aimed for supervised learning of such language models, while in the Uralic NLP the predominant methodology is rule-based, expert-written systems (Moshagen et al., 2014). In this article, I take a practical comparison of building and using the systems for the given tasks as well as a tool in actual linguistic research.

Dictionary	Words	Rules
Omorfi	445,453	58
Apertium-fin-deu	13,119	93

Table 1: Size of the dictionaries in rule-based systems.

3 Methods and Datasets

Omorfi[1] is a lexical database of Finnish, that can be compiled into a finite-state automaton for efficient parsing. Omorfi has wide support for morphological analysis and generation (matching the SIGMORPHON task of morphological regeneration) and parsing (matching the CONLL task for parsing). Apertium-fin-deu[2] is a hand-crafted rule-based machine translation system based on omorfi, with an addition of a bilingual dictionary and some sets of bilingual rules. This can be used with the apertium tools to translate between German and Finnish.

The default mode of operation in a rule-based system is often based on the concept of *all possible hypotheses*, this is in contrast to shared tasks, which are based on 1-best parsing instead; measuring the results is based on only a single hypothesis per token. To bridge this gap between rule-based morphology and shared tasks, I have used a combination of popular strategies implemented with python scripting language.[3] These strategies build in principle on both constraint grammar (Karlsson, 1990; Pirinen, 2015b) and my previous experiences with unigram models in rule-based morphologies (Lindén and Pirinen, 2009), it may, however, be noteworthy that at the time of the writing the solution described is very much a work in progress, so it should not be understood as having any specific advances over the above-referred previous experiments yet. Furthermore, to perform the SIGMORPHON and CONLL tasks I have written small python scripts to analyse and map the analyses between omorfi's formats and theirs. For machine translation I use the `apertium` command and discard the debugging symbols. Examples of the output mangling we perform can be seen in listing 1. As can be seen in the example, the token 7 (*2017*) has no rule-based dependency analysis, since it is not covered by the very basic dependency labeling script we use.

Some statistics of the rule-based dictionaries can be seen in the table 1.

The *Turku neural parsing pipeline* (refered from now on to as TNPP)[4] is a recent, popular parser for a language-independent parsing of the dependency structures. They ranked highly in the 2018 CONLL shared task. For the experiments of this paper, I have downloaded the system following the instructions and have not changed any hyperparametres. The model used is `fi_tdt`.

OpenNMT[5] is one of the many popular neural systems for machine translation. For these experiments I chose it because it provides usable python bindings and it seemed most robust in our early experiments.

The training was performed based on the instructions in the OpenNMT README[6]

---

[1] `https://flammie.github.io/omorfi/`
[2] `https://apertium.github.io/apertium-fin-deu`
[3] `https://github.com/flammie/omorfi/tree/develop/src/python`
[4] `https://turkunlp.github.io/Turku-neural-parser-pipeline/`
[5] `https://github.com/OpenNMT`
[6] `https://github.com/OpenNMT/OpenNMT-py#quickstart`

```
$ omorfi-analyse-text.sh -X test/test.text
Juankosken    WORD_ID=Juankoski UPOS=PROPN PROPER=GEO NUM=SG CASE=GEN
Juankosken    WORD_ID=juan UPOS=NOUN SEM=CURRENCY NUM=SG CASE=NOM
         BOUNDARY=COMPOUND WORD_ID=koski UPOS=NOUN NUM=SG CASE=GEN

kaupunki    WORD_ID=kaupunki UPOS=NOUN NUM=SG CASE=NOM

liittyy    WORD_ID=liittyä UPOS=VERB VOICE=ACT MOOD=INDV TENSE=PRESENT PERS=SG0

liittyy    WORD_ID=liittyä UPOS=VERB VOICE=ACT MOOD=INDV TENSE=PRESENT PERS=SG3


Kuopion    WORD_ID=Kuopio UPOS=PROPN PROPER=GEO NUM=SG CASE=GEN
Kuopion    WORD_ID=kuopia UPOS=VERB VOICE=ACT MOOD=OPT PERS=SG1 STYLE=ARCHAIC

kaupunkiin    WORD_ID=kaupunki UPOS=NOUN NUM=SG CASE=ILL

vuoden    WORD_ID=vuoden UPOS=ADV
vuoden    WORD_ID=vuosi UPOS=NOUN NUM=SG CASE=GEN

2017    WORD_ID=2017 UPOS=NUM SUBCAT=DIGIT NUMTYPE=CARD
2017    WORD_ID=2017 UPOS=NUM SUBCAT=DIGIT NUMTYPE=CARD NUM=SG CASE=NOM

alussa    WORD_ID=alku UPOS=NOUN NUM=SG CASE=INE
alussa    WORD_ID=alunen UPOS=NOUN NUM=SG CASE=ESS STYLE=ARCHAIC
alussa    WORD_ID=alussa UPOS=ADP ADPTYPE=POST
alussa    WORD_ID=alussa_2 UPOS=ADV

.    WORD_ID=. UPOS=PUNCT BOUNDARY=SENTENCE

$ omorfi-tokenise.py -a src/generated/omorfi.describe.hfst -O conllu -i
      test/test.text |
      omorfi-conllu.py -a src/generated/omorfi.describe.hfst
      --not-rules src/disamparsulation/omorfi.xml

# new doc id= test/test.text
# sent_id = 1
# text = Juankosken kaupunki liittyy Kuopion kaupunkiin vuoden 2017 alussa.
1   Juankosken   Juankoski   PROPN   N   Case=Gen|Number=Sing   2   nmod:poss
      _   Weight=0.01
2   kaupunki   kaupunki   NOUN   N   Case=Nom|Number=Sing   3   nsubj   _
      Weight=0.005
3   liittyy   liittyä   VERB   V
      Mood=Ind|Number=Sing|Person=3|Tense=Pres|VerbForm=Fin|Voice=Act   0
      root   _   Weight=0.21000000000000002
4   Kuopion   Kuopio   PROPN   N   Case=Gen|Number=Sing   5   nmod:poss   _
      Weight=0.01
5   kaupunkiin   kaupunki   NOUN   N   Case=Ill|Number=Sing   3   obl   _
      Weight=0.01
6   vuoden   vuosi   NOUN   N   Case=Gen|Number=Sing   3   obj   _   Weight=0.015
7   2017   2017   NUM   Num   NumType=Card   _   _   _   Weight=500.0
8   alussa   alku   NOUN   N   Case=Ine|Number=Sing   3   obl   _   Weight=0.025
9   .   .   PUNCT   Punct   _   3   punct   _   Weight=0.03
```

Same output is directly generated by TNPP:

```
$ cat ~/github/flammie/omorfi/test/test.text |
      python3 full_pipeline_stream.py --conf models_fi_tdt/pipelines.yaml --pipeline parse_plaintext
# newdoc
# newpar
# sent_id = 1
# text = Juankosken kaupunki liittyy Kuopion kaupunkiin vuoden 2017 alussa.
1   Juankosken   Juankoski   PROPN   N   Case=Gen|Number=Sing   2   nmod:poss _
      _
2   kaupunki   kaupunki   NOUN   N   Case=Nom|Number=Sing   3   nsubj   _   _
3   liittyy   liittyä   VERB   V
      Mood=Ind|Number=Sing|Person=3|Tense=Pres|VerbForm=Fin|Voice=Act   0
      root   _   _
4   Kuopion   Kuopio   PROPN   N   Case=Gen|Number=Sing   5   nmod:poss   _   _
5   kaupunkiin   kaupunki   NOUN   N   Case=Ill|Number=Sing   3   obl   _   _
6   vuoden   vuosi   NOUN   N   Case=Gen|Number=Sing   8   nmod:poss   _   _
7   2017   2017   NUM   Num   NumType=Card   6   nummod   _   _
8   alussa   alku   NOUN   N   Case=Ine|Derivation=U|Number=Sing   3   obl   _
      SpaceAfter=No
9   .   .   PUNCT   Punct   _   3   punct   _   SpacesAfter=\n
```

Figure 1: Example of omorfi's outputs and the shared-task equivalents converted.

Corpus	Sentences
Europarl train	1,768,817
dev	1620
test	1620

Table 2: Size of the corpora in sentences

and no additional hyperparametre-tuning was performed. The training was based on europarl version 7 (Koehn, 2005), pre-processed as suggested on their website[7]. The resulting corpus is summarised in Table 2.

4 Experimental setup

An interesting part of this experiment is the setup, since one of the aspects we present in this paper is usability testing of the neural vs. traditional methods for use of an average Computational Uralist, I also want to get a feel of the *user experience* (UX).

The system setup for all the systems is quite similar, all the free and open software used in these experiments are hosted by github. After cloning, the traditional rule-based systems rely on classical command-line installations, this means that user is expected to install dependencies the best they see and then run compilation of the data using `configure` and `make` scripts, and neural systems use python equivalents. In terms of dependencies, all systems are basically well covered with some easy way to install necessary dependencies with single command, such as `pip` or `apt-get`. A bit like rule-based systems, the neural systems need to "compile" i.e. learn neural network binaries from large data, in practice the experience for the end user is the same, except for the wait time, which is slightly longer for the neural-based systems. For Finnish analysers an option is provided to download readily compiled models, while for translation models there is no option. This is equally true for both neural and rule-based models. To parse or translate I have run the systems with default / suggested settings.

To get an idea of intended mode of use (instant, batch processing over the weekend) of the systems and steps, I have collected some of our usage times in the table 3. The real bottleneck for our experiments was the neural machine translation training time, the multi-day training period is problematic in itself, but it is also fragile enough that minor impurities in parallel corpus may ruin the whole model which means that on typical use case user may need to train the model multiple times before reaching to a functional one.

To know how much time to create a system takes from scratch it is also useful to know the amount of data is needed to build it; for rule-based systems this is the size of dictionary, and rule-sets, for neural system it is the training data set size. Both of these factors are especially interesting for Uralistic usage, since the availability of free and open data is rather scarce. The dictionaries are summarised in Table 1 and the corpora in Table 2

For my OpenNMT setup I have created an autotools-based model builder / test runner, that is available in github for repeatability purposes[8].

---

[7]`https://statmt.org/europarl/`
[8]`https://github.com/flammie/autostuff-moses-smt/`

Phase, System	omorfi	TNPP	apertium	OpenNMT
Compiling	15 minutes	—	40 seconds	>5 days
(Downloading)	yes	yes	no	no
Parsing / translating	5 minutes	10 minutes	5 seconds	30 minutes
(Speed)	5 sents/s	3 sents/s	324 sents/s	0.9 sents/s
Model size	25 MiB	770 MiB	33 MiB	7420 MiB

Table 3: Usage times of rule-based and neural systems, time-units are indicated in the table. For TNPP I have found no documentation on how to repeat model building or what time it has taken. Sents/s stands for average sentences per second. Model sizes gives you the total size of binaries on disk in binary-prefixed bytes (by `ls -h`).

Test set	Baseline	Winning system	Omorfi
Task 1	64.45	97.30	93.92
Task 2	59.59	97.40	93.20
Task 3	56.95	96.56	92.18

Table 4: 1-Best precisions for SIGMORPHON shared task 2016 in Finnish, the winning Neural system and omorfi scores.

5   Evaluation

I present an evaluation of the systems using the standard metrics from the shared tasks.

For morphological generation, the shared task was evaluated by measuring average precisions over all languages, for this experiment I compare the results for Finnish on 1-best predictions only, as I am interested in specific comparison relevant for a single Uralic language. The results are summarized in table 4.

For morphosyntactic analysis the standard evaluations would be based on attachment scores, however, the rule-based system only creates partial dependency graphs with potentially ambiguous roots; this does not work with the official evaluation scripts, so I provide instead a raw 1-best precision result for the specific fields in the CONLL-U format. The results are shown in table 5; The *lemma* row corresponds 3rd CONLL-U column, *UPOS* 4th, *Ufeats* 6th, *XPOS* 5th, *Dephead* 7th, and *Deplabel* 8th. The match is made on strict equality on the string comparison of the whole content, i.e. no re-arranging or approximate matching is performed.

For machine translation the standard shared task evaluation method is to use well-known metrics that compare translations to reference, specifically BLEU. In table 6 I measure the BLEU scores for europarl translations.

6   Error Analysis

As a general trend I see that the precision of the neural systems as well as the BLEU score of the neural machine translation are above of the rule-based systems. I also wanted to know if there is any systematicity to the errors, that the different approaches make. Interesting way forward would be to gain some insight on how the errors for each system could be fixed if at all. One of the commonly mentioned advan-

Column	Turku Neural parsing pipeline	Omorfi
Lemma	95.54	82.63
UPOS	96.91	83.88
Ufeats	94.61	73.95
XPOS	97.89	89.58
Dephead	90.89	33.13
Deplabel	92.61	49.01

Table 5: 1-best precisions of Turku neural parsing system and omorfi. The numbers were measured with our script since the official test script does not handle partial dependency graphs or multiple roots.

Language pair	OpenNMT	Apertium
German to Finnish	7.09	0.6
Finnish to German	7.12	0.3

Table 6: Automatic translation evaluations, metrics from WMT shared tasks 2018 and corpora from europarl evaluation section. BLEU scores have been measured with the tool `mteval-14.perl`.

tages of a rule-based system is that it is predictable and easy to fix or extend; whether a missing form in generation or analysis is caused by a missing word in lexicon, a missing word-form in paradigm or ordering of the alternative forms, the solution is easy to see. With a neural system the possibilities are limited to adding more data or modifying hyperparametres.

When looking at the errors in the morphological regeneration test for rule-based system, I can see several categories emerge: *True OOV* for lexemes missing from the database (e.g. *ovovivivipaarisuus*), *Wrong paradigm* for wordforms that are generated but with some errors, such as wrong vowel harmony or consonant gradation (e.g. *manuskripteiltä* pro *manuskripteilta* (from manuscripts)) and *Real allomorph / homograph* for cases where the correct form is recalled but not at best-1 due to ambiguous lexeme or free allomorphy (for example, I generate *köykistämäisillänsä* pro *köykistämäisillään* (about to defeat), but both are equally acceptable). In the leftover category I found among others, actual bugs in the generation functionality. For example, I was unable to generate the forms of *aliluutnantti* (sub-lieutenant) since the generation function failed to take into account extra semantic tags it contains.[9] I sampled a total of 65 errors and the results can be seen in the table 7.

In the dependency parsing task one of the most common errors in the rule-based system seems to be the Person=0 feature with 766 occurrences in the test set, as it is systematically ambiguous with Person=3 for all singulars, it is probably a true ambiguity in that there are not many context clues to disambiguate it. Another systematic source of errors seems to be the systematic ambiguity between auxiliary and common verbs, which also shows up in the parsing of copula structures and in the morphological features. Similarly, a common problem of rule-based systems in parsing tasks is the etymological systematic ambiguity created by derivation and lexicalisation, that

---

[9]a bug has been since fixed but I include the original error analysis in the article for an interesting reference

Type	Count	Percentage
OOVs	23	36 %
Wrong paradigm	20	31 %
Allomorphs	9	15 %
Others	13	20 %
Total	65	100%

Table 7: Rule-based morphology generation errors classified. .

affects participle above anything, but also less productive features. It would appear that OOV's do not contribute here greatly to the error mass, despite consisting total of 460 appearances the baseline guess of singular nominative nominal for the OOV's is surprisingly often sufficient.

Looking at both rule-based and neural systems for MT, it is easy to tell that for example the OOV's constitute a large part of errors, and exist in most sentences. Judging the actual translation quality by sampling the sentences also reveals a quality that is overall not sufficient for computer aided translation or gisting, to the extent that I believe further analysis may not be fruitful without further development of the underlying models first.

7 Discussion

One of the goals in this experiment was to find out how usable the neural and traditional models are for a computational linguist who might want to pick a state-of-the-art parser off-the-shelf and use it for text analysis or translation related tasks. Based on my initial impression, I would probably recommend making use of the neural parsers for languages where enough training data is available, and aiming to make training data where it is not. However, for a low resource language, it might often be easier to create a sufficiently large dictionary with rule-based model than to curate realistic corpus and annotate it, and given that the results of a rule-based system are not such far from the state-of-the-art in neural systems for the given metrics, they should be well sufficient for parsing. On top of that, the resources created with a rule-based system are a part of necessary NLP system for language survival (writer's tools, electronic dictionaries) that neural systems do not offer it does not make sense to put all eggs in one neural network.

One thing that has been left out of the experiment is what is required for developing a new system: dictionaries and grammars for rule-based systems, treebanks or parallel texts for the neural systems. These are available at the moment for the main Uralic languages: Finnish, Hungarian and Estonian, and to smaller extent also for Northern Sámi, Erzya. The question then remains, is it easier for a minority Uralic language to develop a treebank and a parallel corpus, or dictionaries and grammar, or both.

One noteworthy point to the method of developing resources, as well as to our evaluation, is, that the original Turku dependency treebank was in fact developed based on the analyses provided by an old version of omorfi Haverinen et al. (2014),[10] and that was used as a basis for building the UD-Finnish-TDT treebank, that is used

---

[10] we thank the anonymous reviewer for bringing point up

as a model for the TNPP analyser. So a traditional way to build resources for neural parsers still requires an existing high-quality rule-based parser as well as a lot of native human annotation work on the one hand, on the other hand, the combination of rule-based parses and human annotation does result in a parser that is more precise at predicting in basic setup.

One thing that might be a common expectation is, is that a rule-based systems that have been developed for a long time, should score very highly in basic tasks like morphological generation and parsing, since apart from real OOV's and bugs, correctly made morphology should virtually be able to generate 100 % of the word-forms in its dictionary. For the precision of 1-best analyses however, there can be small portion of word-forms that either exhibit unexpected (in terms that writer of rule-based parser had expected form to be ungrammatical) or free variation. For recall, which is typically the first goal for rule-based analyser, the value is nearer to the virtual 100 % (Pirinen, 2015a).

One surprising thing I found out, that when testing the machine translations on a non-English pair, the out-of-the-box results for both approaches are very modest, suggesting that more work is needed to for a usable MT as a tool for Uralist than just picking off-the-shelf product at the moment. While our test was still based on non-Uralic language partly due to resource and time constraints, I believe the results will still give a good indication of the current state-of-the-art. Notably, it is not unlikely for a research group in Uralistics to need machine translations of German or for example Russian as well.

So far, I have only used the precision and BLEU measures to evaluate the systems, it is likely that different metrics would show more favourable results for a rule-based systems that typically maximise recall or coverage first.

One of the surprising finds that I had when fitting the rule-based systems to non-rule-based shared tasks is, is that I could repurpose the task as a new automatic continuous integration test set for the lexical database, and the tests have already proved useful for recognition several types of easily fixable errors in the database. I note that, in the rule-based system fixing the OOV-type errors and the paradigm type errors is typically a trivial fix of one line of code taking less than a minute, however, improving the allomorph selection or homograph disambiguation is an open research question.

For future work I will study both the neural and rule-based systems further with hopefully intra-Uralic pairing as well, to find if it's plausible for actual use.

8 Conclusion

I performed some experiments to find out what is the current state-of-the-art status between neural and rule-based methods for Finnish, I have found out that the neural methods perform admirably for all parsing approaches for the given test sets that they were designed for, but rule-based methods are also still within acceptable distance. For non-parsing task such as machine translation in Uralic languages the methods are probably not yet sufficient to be efficiently used as a tool for research, but further research and development is needed.

Acknowledgments

The author was employed by CLARIN-D during the writing of the article.

References

Ondřej Bojar, Christian Federmann, Mark Fishel, Yvette Graham, Barry Haddow, Philipp Koehn, and Christof Monz. 2018. Findings of the 2018 conference on machine translation (wmt18). In *Proceedings of the Third Conference on Machine Translation: Shared Task Papers*. Association for Computational Linguistics, pages 272–303. http://aclweb.org/anthology/W18-6401.

Ryan Cotterell, Christo Kirov, John Sylak-Glassman, David Yarowsky, Jason Eisner, and Mans Hulden. 2016. The sigmorphon 2016 shared task—morphological reinflection. In *Proceedings of the 14th SIGMORPHON Workshop on Computational Research in Phonetics, Phonology, and Morphology*. Association for Computational Linguistics, pages 10–22. https://doi.org/10.18653/v1/W16-2002.

Katri Haverinen, Jenna Nyblom, Timo Viljanen, Veronika Laippala, Samuel Kohonen, Anna Missilä, Stina Ojala, Tapio Salakoski, and Filip Ginter. 2014. Building the essential resources for finnish: the turku dependency treebank. *Language Resources and Evaluation* 48(3):493–531.

Jenna Kanerva, Filip Ginter, Niko Miekka, Akseli Leino, and Tapio Salakoski. 2018. Turku neural parser pipeline: An end-to-end system for the conll 2018 shared task. In *Proceedings of the CoNLL 2018 Shared Task: Multilingual Parsing from Raw Text to Universal Dependencies*. Association for Computational Linguistics.

Fred Karlsson. 1990. Constraint grammar as a framework for parsing unrestricted text. In H. Karlgren, editor, *Proceedings of the 13th International Conference of Computational Linguistics*. Helsinki, volume 3, pages 168–173.

Guillaume Klein, Yoon Kim, Yuntian Deng, Jean Senellart, and Alexander M. Rush. 2017. OpenNMT: Open-source toolkit for neural machine translation. In *Proc. ACL*. https://doi.org/10.18653/v1/P17-4012.

Philipp Koehn. 2005. Europarl: A parallel corpus for statistical machine translation. In *MT summit*. volume 5, pages 79–86.

Krister Lindén and Tommi Pirinen. 2009. Weighting finite-state morphological analyzers using HFST tools. In Bruce Watson, Derrick Courie, Loek Cleophas, and Pierre Rautenbach, editors, *FSMNLP 2009*. http://www.ling.helsinki.fi/klinden/pubs/fsmnlp2009weighting.pdf.

Sjur Moshagen, Jack Rueter, Tommi Pirinen, Trond Trosterud, and Francis M Tyers. 2014. Open-source infrastructures for collaborative work on under-resourced languages. In *Proceedings ofTh e Ninth International Conference on Language Resources and Evaluation, LREC*. pages 71–77.

Tommi A Pirinen. 2015a. Development and use of computational morphology of finnish in the open source and open science era: Notes on experiences with omorfi development. *SKY Journal of Linguistics* 28.

Tommi A Pirinen. 2015b. Using weighted finite state morphology with visl cg-3-some experiments with free open source finnish resources. In *Proceedings of the Workshop on "Constraint Grammar-methods, tools and applications" at NODALIDA 2015, May 11-13, 2015, Institute of the Lithuanian Language, Vilnius, Lithuania*. Linköping University Electronic Press, 113, pages 29–33.

Tommi A Pirinen. 2018. Rule-based machine-translation between finnish and german.

Daniel Zeman, Jan Haji{č}, Martin Popel, Martin Potthast, Milan Straka, Filip Ginter, Joakim Nivre, and Slav Petrov. 2018. Conll 2018 shared task: Multilingual parsing from raw text to universal dependencies. In *Proceedings of the CoNLL 2018 Shared Task: Multilingual Parsing from Raw Text to Universal Dependencies*. Association for Computational Linguistics, pages 1–21. http://aclweb.org/anthology/K18-2001.

Uralic multimedia corpora: ISO/TEI corpus data in the project INEL

Timofey Arkhangelskiy
Universität Hamburg / Alexander von Humboldt Foundation
timarkh@gmail.com

Anne Ferger
Universität Hamburg
anne.ferger@uni-hamburg.de

Hanna Hedeland
Universität Hamburg
hanna.hedeland@uni-hamburg.de

Abstract

In this paper, we describe a data processing pipeline used for annotated spoken corpora of Uralic languages created in the INEL (Indigenous Northern Eurasian Languages) project. With this processing pipeline we convert the data into a lossless standard format (ISO/TEI) for long-term preservation while simultaneously enabling a powerful search in this version of the data. For each corpus, the input we are working with is a set of files in EXMARaLDA XML format, which contain transcriptions, multimedia alignment, morpheme segmentation and other kinds of annotation. The first step of processing is the conversion of the data into a certain subset of TEI following the ISO standard 'Transcription of spoken language' with the help of an XSL transformation. The primary purpose of this step is to obtain a representation of our data in a standard format, which will ensure its long-term accessibility. The second step is the conversion of the ISO/TEI files to a JSON format used by the "Tsakorpus" search platform. This step allows us to make the corpora available through a web-based search interface. As an addition, the existence of such a converter allows other spoken corpora with ISO/TEI annotation to be made accessible online in the future.

Tiivistelmä

Tässä paperissa kuvataan aineistonnprosessointimenetelmä joka on käytössä uralilaisten puhuttujen korpusten luonnissa kieltedokumentointiprojekti INELissä. Prosessointimenetelmää käytetään konvertoimaan dataa häviöttömään ISO/TEI- standardiformaattiin pitkän aikavälin säilytystä varten sekä samanaikaisesti tehokkaisiin hakutoimintoihin tälle akineistoversiolle. Jokaisen korpuksen lähtöaineistona on joukko tiedostoja EXMARaLDAn XML-formaatissa, joka sisältää transkriptejä,multimediaa kohdennuksineen, morfeemijäsennyksiä ja muita annotaatiota. Ensimmäinen käsittelyaskel on aineiston konvertointi TEI:n osajouk-

Proceedings of the fifth Workshop on Computational Linguistics for Uralic Languages, pages 115–124,
Tartu, Estonia, January 7 - January 8, 2019.

koon, joka muodostaa ISO-standardin puhutun kielen transkripteille, XSL- trans-
formaatioita käyttäen. Tämän askelen ensisijainen tarkoitus on saada aineisto sel-
laiseen standardimuotoon joka kelpaa pitkäaikaissäilytykseen. Seuraava oaskel
on ISO/TEI-tiedostojen konversio JSON-formaattiin, jota "Tsakorpus"-hakualusta
käyttää. Tämän avulla saadaan korpus käytettäväksi internethakuliittymälle. Li-
säksi, konversio mahdollistaa muiden ISO/TEI-yhteensopivien korpusten anno-
taatioiden tuomisen saataville tulevaisuudessa.

1 Introduction

The primary target of our processing pipeline are the corpora that are or will be de-
veloped within the framework of the INEL project (Indigenous Northern Eurasian
Languages)[1] (Arkhipov and Däbritz, 2018). The main goal of the project is to develop
annotated spoken corpora for a number of minority languages spoken in Northern
Eurasia, most of them Uralic[2]. At the moment, corpora of Selkup (Uralic > Samoyedic),
Kamas (Uralic > Samoyedic; extinct) and Dolgan (Turkic) are under development.

The long-term project INEL, scheduled to run until 2033, bases its technical development on the infrastructure, tools and workflows for curation and publication of
digital resources available at the Hamburg Centre for Language Corpora[3], a research
data centre within the CLARIN[4] infrastructure with a main thematic focus on spoken
and multilingual data. The available technical solutions were however not developed
for the specific data types created within the INEL project, in particular glossed and
richly annotated transcripts. While the HZSK Repository used for corpus publication allows for transcript visualization and download, until now there is no advanced
web-based search functionality. The INEL project thus needs to extend not only the
existing workflows, but also the distribution channels to provide their corpora to a
research community requiring easily accessible and highly complex search mechanisms.

Creating corpora from language data that are intended for long-term usage and accessibility holds various challenges for the used data formats. For each of the different
phases the corpora undergo during their creation, different tools and therefore different data formats are needed. Because of the long-term character and the emphasis on
accessibility of the INEL project, standard compliance and openness of the formats
as well as making implicit information explicit also need to be taken into account.
We will describe how we dealt with these challenges using a special data processing
pipeline and using the ISO/TEI Standard Transcription of spoken language[5] (ISO/TC
37/SC 4, 2016) with only explicit information for short-term archiving, publishing,
and as the base format for a searching interface.

Through the use of a standard format, the pipeline described in this paper can also
be applied to similar (Uralic) corpora developed in other projects, e.g. the Nganasan
Spoken Language Corpus (Wagner-Nagy et al., 2018).

---

[1] https://inel.corpora.uni-hamburg.de/

[2] https://inel.corpora.uni-hamburg.de/?page_id=593

[3] https://corpora.uni-hamburg.de/

[4] https://www.clarin.eu/

[5] http://www.iso.org/iso/catalogue_detail.htm?csnumber=37338

2   Corpus Data

All corpora in question consist of audio/video files and/or pdf scans of (hand-)written data, accompanied by the transcription files. The annotation was carried out manually. It includes morpheme segmentation, glossing, part-of-speech tagging, syntactic functions, code switching, and other linguistically relevant information. When available, sound or video are aligned with the transcription. The files also contain parallel translations into Russian, English and German. While the transcription data is initially created with FLEx[6] and/or ELAN[7], the corpora within the INEL project are created with the EXMARaLDA[8] (Schmidt and Wörner, 2014) desktop software suite comprising a transcription and annotation editor (Partitur-Editor), a corpus and metadata manager (Coma) and a search and analysis tool (EXAKT). The transcriptions are stored in the EXMARaLDA Basic Transcription XML format (EXB) and have time-based references to the media files and multiple annotation tiers. Apart from the documentation on the creation of the corpus, detailed metadata regarding the raw data, the transcriptions and the corresponding speakers is stored in an additional file in the EXMARaLDA Coma XML format (COMA). All corpora in question have a similar design and similar annotation levels, which makes it possible to create a single set of converters capable of processing any of the existing corpora, as well as those that will be created in the course of the project. The EXMARaLDA software suite was chosen by the project because of the important advantages it offers for the corpus creation process. The metadata and corpus manager Coma and the desktop search and analysis tool EXAKT can both be used to manage and continuously assess the growing data set and also to search and analyze the corpus or any defined subcorpora. While the EXMARaLDA software might facilitate corpus creation, the time-based EXMARaLDA transcription data model is rather simple and not really suited for precise and explicit modelling of the INEL transcription data. The glossing comprises annotations which are clearly based on linguistic segments and such segment relations are not a part of the time-based EXMARaLDA transcription data model. The Basic Transcription format is not in any way tokenized and thus only allows for time-based annotations, aligned to start and end points shared with a transcription tier on which the annotation is based. In the INEL data, these start and end points coincide with token boundaries, though this is not explicitly modelled by the time-based approach. In Figure 1, you can see an example of a Selkup text annotated in the way described above.

The transcription files are generated either from (hand-)written text artifacts or from audio or video recordings. In case of transcriptions accompanied by audio or video, the EXMARaLDA transcriptions are aligned with these files by linking to time intervals in the media files. Some of those texts are dialogues. Since they are produced by multiple speakers, they contain several sets of tiers described above, one for each speaker. Finally, each corpus has very detailed metadata, which covers sociolinguistic background of the speakers and linguistic properties of the texts.

---

[6] https://software.sil.org/fieldworks/
[7] https://tla.mpi.nl/tools/tla-tools/elan/
[8] https://exmaralda.org/de/

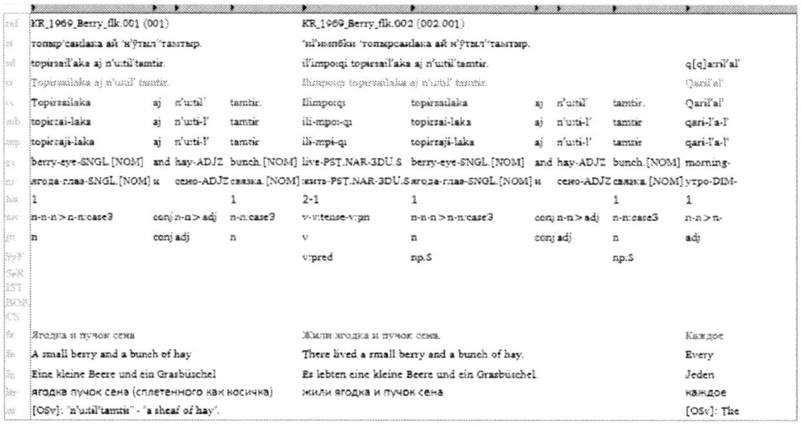

Figure 1: An example of a Selkup text annotated in EXMARaLDA

3   Conversion to ISO/TEI XML

While converters from the EXMARaLDA Basic Transcription format to the ISO/TEI
standard are included in the EXMARaLDA software for several transcription conventions, these all assume that transcriptions were created with the time-based interpretation of EXMARaLDA and thus only create time-based annotations. With the
ISO/TEI standard it is however possible to model segment based annotations, e.g.
when further enriching the transcription data using tools such as parsers or taggers.
For the INEL data, we decided to make the implicit information of the EXMARaLDA
transcriptions, i.e. the segments and relations relevant to the annotation, explicit
through corresponding modelling using ISO/TEI. The first objective was to convert
the corpora into a loss-less standard format while turning implicit information into
explicit information, which is especially important for long-term projects. Explicit
data also means to make searching in various tools and converting into different data
formats less error-prone. To achieve this we used the ISO standard "Transcription of
Spoken Language"[9], which is based on the TEI guidelines[10]. To account for the specific requirements in the INEL project and similar structured projects (like Nganasan
Spoken Language Corpus) we needed to use a defined subset of TEI that is segment-
based and allows for segmentation into sentence, word and morpheme units while
following the ISO standard. EXMARaLDA XML models transcription, description and
annotation tiers as time-based information, linking these segments to the timeline of
the linked media files. In the special case of the INEL corpora, there are also corpus
files created in the EXMARaLDA format that don't reference any audio or video information because they are generated from (hand-)written text artifacts. The timeline in
EXMARaLDA only needs to define events and not necessarily real time information,
so in the text-based files references to those segments are used.

   While this time-based format is needed for the transcription tier or "baseline", the
annotations in INEL currently are exclusively segment-based, because they refer directly to the segments transcribed in the baseline tier and not the temporal events of

[9]http://www.iso.org/iso/catalogue_detail.htm?csnumber=37338
[10]http://www.tei-c.org/guidelines/p5/

the linked audio/video files. While still leaving the possibility for time-based annotations open in future work, we decided to convert the time-based annotations (that we knew to be segment-based) into segment-based annotations during the conversion into the standard ISO/TEI format, thus turning the implicit information we had into explicit information. The alignment of annotation segments to transcription tier segments can be deduced from a relation between the annotation and one transcription tier and their relation to events in the timeline. In the ISO/TEI conversion the annotations are linked directly to the segments of the baseline without additional time information. Depending on the scope of the annotations, annotation segments in the INEL TEI subset are linked to either sentence, word or morpheme units. Since these base units are linked to speakers (in EXMARaLDA as well as in the new ISO/TEI export), the annotation can be assigned to the respective speakers too.

The special subset of the ISO/TEI standard that we used contains automatically segmented <seg> elements (sentences) that consist of <w> elements (words) and punctuation elements <pc>. The annotations are structured into <span> elements. One special annotation tier additionally contains the morpheme segmentation, modelled by spans that have special ids. While there is an <m> element available in the ISO/TEI standard, we couldn't use it for our purposes, since <m> elements need to construct the words, while we need words additionally in a different tier than morphemes (which is needed for dealing with e.g. null morphemes of which we find many in our data). The start and end points of the spans can refer to the <seg> elements (sentences/utterances in the baseline), word elements or other spans (in our case: the morpheme spans). An sample fragment of a Selkup file in ISO/TEI can be seen in the Figure 2.

To account for the metadata, a metadata enriched search is planned in the future. To realize it, the metadata from the Coma XML file concerning the transcriptions and speakers will be exported in the ISO/TEI files during the conversion additionally, using the <tei:teiHeader>.

4   Conversion from ISO/TEI to Tsakorpus

Our second objective was to give the linguists access to the corpora through a user-friendly web-based interface. We use the "Tsakorpus" corpus platform for this. In this platform, linguistic data is indexed in a document-based Elasticsearch database. The main index contains sentences (or sentence-like sequences of tokens), each sentence being a single document. Tsakorpus accepts files in a certain JSON-based format as its input. Each file corresponds to one corpus text (i.e. one EXMARaLDA transcription file in our case) and contains a list of sentences. A sentence contains a list of tokens, which are also represented as JSON objects, and additional information such as sentence-level metadata, audio/video alignment and parallel alignment.

In order to index our corpora in Tsakorpus, we wrote a Python script that transforms ISO/TEI files to the JSON files required by the corpus platform. Since all information potentially relevant for the search is already explicit in the TEI files, the conversion basically means simply recombining the existing data without recovering the information stored implicitly (such as grammatical values expressed by null morphemes). The TEI files have a tier-based structure. This means that for each property (such as part of speech, morpheme segmentation etc.), its values are listed for every word within an XML node representing that property, and nodes representing different properties follow one another. In Tsakorpus JSON, properties of each token are all stored together in the JSON object representing that token. An example featuring a fragment of a source file and the resulting JSON tokens can be seen in 3 and 4. Several tier names commonly used by linguistic annotation software (FLEX or Toolbox) are translated into names reserved for certain annotation types in Tsakorpus. E.g. the information from the ps tier, which represents part of speech, goes to the gr.pos tier in the JSON. All unrecognized tier names, such as SyF in the example (syntactic function) are left unchanged.

There are three processing steps that go beyond simple restructuring described above.

First, information about the alignment with the media file should be included in each sentence. In the ISO/TEI files, the alignment is indicated through time point labels such as T3, which come directly from the EXMARaLDA files. In the beginning of the ISO/TEI document, all these labels are listed with their time offset values in seconds. The name of the media file (one per transcription) associated with the recording is stored in the sourceDesc node of the ISO/TEI file.

The time point labels at sentence boundaries are replaced with the actual time offsets in the JSON. Additionally, the source media file is split into overlapping pieces of small length (60 seconds by default) using ffmpeg. Instead of being associated with the entire media file, each sentence in the JSON file is associated with one of these parts. The part for each sentence is chosen in such a way that the middle of the sentence segment is as close as possible to the middle of the media segment. The time offsets are changed accordingly. Such an approach allows the user to listen to the segment they found together with some context, while at the same time avoiding the need to download the entire media file, which could be quite large.

Second, there is a number of tiers with sentence-level alignment in the source files. These are alternative transcriptions and translations into Russian, English and German. To enable this sort of alignment in Tsakorpus, we are using a scheme intended for parallel corpora. The aligned segments are stored in the JSON file as separate sentences. Sentences originating in different tiers have different values of the lang parameter. The sentences that should be aligned with one another receive the same "parallel ID", a value stored in each of them.

Finally, the translations are automatically lemmatized and morphologically analyzed using the analyzers available for Russian, English and German. As of now, we have tested the analysis of the Russian tier with mystem (Segalovich, 2003). This may seem a significant departure from the principle of having all relevant information explicitly present in the ISO/TEI files. However, we treat this added annotation as an auxiliary information that is not part of the original annotated corpus and should not be stored in it. Its only purpose is facilitating the search in the data that already exists in the corpus. The queries that involve this annotation are not intended to be replicable. Therefore, this annotation is not checked manually and can be superseded by annotation produced by other morphological analyzers in the future.

After the JSON files are indexed, the corpus becomes available through a web interface. Single-word queries may contain constraints on values in any annotation tier or their combinations, possibly with regular expression or Boolean functions. Multi-word queries can additionally include constraints on the distance between the words. Each search hit is aligned with a multimedia segment, which can be played by clicking on the sentence.

5 Conclusion

By developing the EXMARaLDA > ISO/TEI and ISO/TEI > Tsakorpus JSON converters we have achieved two goals. First, the corpora annotated within the framework of INEL and similar projects can now be exported to a format suitable for long-term preservation. The version of the ISO/TEI we are using is fit for that purpose because it is based on an ISO standard and because all potentially relevant information is made explicit in it. This means that the corpora in question could be reused in the future without recourse to the software currently employed in the project or to implicit knowledge of its participants. Second, this chain of converters makes it possible to release the corpora to the public through a user-friendly web interface. This way of publishing the corpora has an advantage over simply releasing the EXMARaLDA files in that it does not require the users to install and become acquainted with any special software.

The ISO/TEI > Tsakorpus JSON converter is open source, which means that any corpus stored in a similar ISO/TEI form could be easily published online. Projects that use ISO/TEI for storing annotated spoken corpora exist, e.g. in IRCOM infrastructure (Liégeois et al., 2015), but are not numerous. The ISO/TEI format is aimed at creating enhanced interoperability for spoken data through a standardized format. Apart from the proof of concept work done by integrating transcription data from various tool formats into an ISO/TEI corpus that can be searched in its entirety, support for various other scenarios, such as linguistic web services and web-based annotation tools are in development.

Importantly, the availability of our converter could encourage researchers working in language documentation projects to export their data to ISO/TEI, which would be beneficial for their long-term availability.

Acknowledgments

This publication has been produced in the context of the projects CLARIN-D, funded by the German Ministry for Education and Research (BMBF) under grant number 01UG1620G, and INEL, within the joint research funding of the German Federal Government and Federal States in the Academies' Programme, with funding from the Federal Ministry of Education and Research and the Free and Hanseatic City of Hamburg. The Academies' Programme is coordinated by the Union of the German Academies of Sciences and Humanities.

References

Alexander Arkhipov and Chris Lasse Däbritz. 2018. Hamburg corpora for indigenous Northern Eurasian languages. *Tomsk Journal of Linguistics and Anthropology* (3):9–18. https://doi.org/10.23951/2307-6119-2018-3-9-18.

ISO/TC 37/SC 4. 2016. Language resource management – Transcription of spoken language. Standard ISO 2462:2016, International Organization for Standardization, Geneva, CH. http://www.iso.org/iso/catalogue$_d$etail.htm?csnumber = 37338.

Loïc Liégeois, Carole Etienne, Christophe Parisse, Christophe Benzitoun, and Christian Chanard. 2015. Using the TEI as a pivot format for oral and multimodal language corpora. Paper presented at Text Encoding Initiative Conference, Lyon, October 28–31, 2015.

Thomas Schmidt and Kai Wörner. 2014. EXMARaLDA. In Jacques Durand, Ulrike Gut, and Gjert Kristoffersen, editors, *Handbook on Corpus Phonology*, Oxford University Press, pages 402–419. http://ukcatalogue.oup.com/product/9780199571932.do.

Ilya Segalovich. 2003. A fast morphological algorithm with unknown word guessing induced by a dictionary for a web search engine. In *MLMTA-2003*. Las Vegas.

Beáta Wagner-Nagy, Sándor Szeverényi, and Valentin Gusev. 2018. User's Guide to Nganasan Spoken Language Corpus. *Working Papers in Corpus Linguistics and Digital Technologies: Analyses and Methodology* 1.

```
<seg subtype="declarative" xml:id="seg1">
    <w xml:id="w1">Qwärχa</w>
    <anchor synch="T1" />
    <w xml:id="w2">t'üumbädi</w>
    <anchor synch="T2" />
    <w xml:id="w3">surɨm</w>
</seg>
...
<spanGrp type="st">
    <span from="seg1" to="seg1">´kwäpχa ´
    т´ӱмбӓди ´сурым.</span>
...
</spanGrp>
<spanGrp type="mb">
    <span from="w1" to="w1">
            <span xml:id="m1">qwarχa</span>
    </span>
    <span from="w2" to="w2">
            <span xml:id="m2">t'üu</span>
            <span xml:id="m3">mbädi</span>
    </span>
...
</spanGrp>
<spanGrp type="ge">
    <span from="w1" to="w1">
            <span from="m1" to="m1">bear</span>
            <span>NOM</span>
    </span>
    <span from="w2" to="w2">
            <span from="m2" to="m2">get.angry</span>
            <span from="m3" to="m3">PTCP.PST</span>
    </span>
...
</spanGrp>
...
<spanGrp type="ps">
    <span from="w1" to="w1">n</span>
        ...
</spanGrp>
```

Figure 2: Segment-based morpheme-segmented Subset of ISO/TEI

```
<seg subtype="declarative" type="utterance" xml:id="seg1">
    <w xml:id="w4">It'e</w>
    <w xml:id="w5">pal'd'ukus</w>
</seg>
...
<spanGrp type="ps">
    <span from="w4" to="w4">nprop</span>
    <span from="w5" to="w5">n</span>
</spanGrp>
<spanGrp type="SyF">
    <span from="w4" to="w4">np.h:S</span>
    <span from="w5" to="w5">v:pred</span>
</spanGrp>
```

Figure 3: Tier-based data representation in ISO/TEI


```
{
 "wf": "It'e",
 "wtype": "word",
 "ana": [
  {
   "gr.pos": "nprop",
   "SyF": "np.h:S"
  }
 ],
 "off_start": 0,
 "off_end": 4
},
{
 "wf": "pal'd'ukus",
 "wtype": "word",
 "ana": [
  {
   "gr.pos": "n",
   "SyF": "v:pred"
  }
 ],
 "off_start": 5,
 "off_end": 15
}
```

Figure 4: Token-based data representation in Tsakorpus JSON

Corpora of social media in minority Uralic languages

Timofey Arkhangelskiy
Universität Hamburg / Alexander von Humboldt Foundation
timarkh@gmail.com

Abstract

This paper presents an ongoing project aimed at creation of corpora for minority Uralic languages that contain texts posted on social media. Corpora for Udmurt and Erzya are fully functional; Moksha and Komi-Zyrian are expected to become available in late 2018; Komi-Permyak and Meadow and Hill Mari will be ready in 2019. The paper has a twofold focus. First, I describe the pipeline used to develop the corpora. Second, I explore the linguistic properties of the corpora and how they could be used in certain types of linguistic research. Apart from being generally "noisier" than edited texts in any language (e.g. in terms of higher number of out-of-vocabulary items), social media texts in these languages present additional challenges compared to similar corpora of major languages. One of them is language identification, which is impeded by frequent code switching and borrowing instances. Another is identification of sources, which cannot be performed by entirely automatic crawling. Both problems require some degree of manual intervention. Nevertheless, the resulting corpora are worth the effort. First, the language of the texts is close to the spoken register. This contrasts to most newspapers and fiction, which tend to use partially artificial standardized varieties. Second, a lot of dialectal variation is observed in these corpora, which makes them suitable for dialectological research. Finally, the social media corpora are comparable in size to the collections of other texts available in the digital form for these languages. This makes them a valuable addition to the existing resources for these languages.

Аннотация

Статьяын урал кылъёсын социальной сетьёсысь материалъя корпус лэсьтон сярысь вераськон мынэ. Удмурт но эрзя кылъёсын корпусъёс дасесь ини; мокша но коми-зырян кылъёсын корпусъёс 2018-ти арлэн пумаз ужаны кутскозы; нош коми-пермяк но мари корпусъёс 2019-ти арын дась луозы. Та статьяын кык ужпум жутэмын. Нырысь ик, мон валэктйсько, кызьы корпус лэсьтон уж радъямын. Собере корпусъёслэсь кылтйрлык аспöртэмлыксэс эскерисько но возьматйсько, кызьы корпусэз пöртэм пумо тодосужын луэ уже кутыны. Социальной сетьёсысь текстъёс котькуд кылын «пожгес» луо, литературной текстъёсын ӵошатыса (шуом, морфологической разбортэк кылем кылъёсты лыдъяно ке). Пичи кылъёсын корпусъёсты трос поллы секытгес лэсьтыны, бадӟым кылъёсын ӵошатыса. Нырысь ик, шуг валаны, кыӵе кылын гожтэмын текст, малы ке шуоно, текстлэн кылыз ӵем вошъяське но текстын трос асэстэм кыл кутйське. Мукетыз шуг-секыт —

Proceedings of the fifth Workshop on Computational Linguistics for Uralic Languages, pages 125–140,
Tartu, Estonia, January 7 - January 8, 2019.

текстъёсты уг луы автоматической кроулинг амалэн шедьтыны. Та шуг-
секытъёсын йырин трос ужез «киын» лэсьтоно луэ. Озьы ке но, та ужлэн
пайдаез вань. Нырысь ик, корпусысь кыл вераськон кыллы матын луэ.
Озьы со газетын но литератураын кутӥськись кыллэсь пӧртэм луэ; отын
литературной кыл ӵемысь искусственной кыллы укша. Кыкетйез, корпус-
ын пӧртэм диалектъёс пумисько; соин ик та материалэз диалектъёсты эске-
рон ужын кутыны луэ. Йылпумъяса вераны кулэ, куд-ог урал кылъёсын
электронной текст люкамъёс вань ини; социальной сетьёсысь материалэн
корпусъёс мукет текстъёсын корпусъёслэсь ӧжыт пичигес ке но, быдӟала-
зыя трослы пӧртэм ӧвӧл. Озьыен, таӵе корпусъёс ӧжыт лыдъем калыкъёс-
лэсь кылтодоссэс узырмыто.

Аннотация

В статье представлен текущий проект по созданию корпусов соцсетей
на малых уральских языках. В настоящий момент готовы корпуса удмурт-
ского и эрзянского языков; мокшанский и коми-зырянский планируется
запустить в конце 2018 г., а коми-пермяцкий и марийские — в 2019 г. В
работе освещены две темы. Во-первых, я описываю процедуру разработ-
ки корпусов. Во-вторых, я рассматриваю лингвистические свойства этих
корпусов и то, как их можно использовать в разных видах исследований.
Тексты соцсетей на любом языке в принципе более «грязные», чем стан-
дартные (например, в смысле количества слов без морфологического раз-
бора), однако тексты на рассматриваемых языках представляют дополни-
тельные сложности по сравнению с аналогичными текстами на крупных
языках. Одна из них — это определение языка текста, которое затрудняет-
ся многочисленными переключениями кодов и заимствованиями. Другая
— это поиск таких текстов, который невозможно произвести с помощью
полностью автоматического кроулинга. Обе проблемы требуют некоторо-
го количества ручной работы. Тем не менее, полученные результаты стоят
приложенных усилий. Во-первых, язык в этих корпусах близок к разговор-
ному регистру. Этим он отличается от языка газет и литературы, где часто
используется до некоторой степени искусственный стандартный вариант.
Во-вторых, в корпусах наблюдается диалектная вариативность, что делает
их пригодными для диалектологических исследований. Наконец, по раз-
меру корпуса соцсетей сопоставимы с коллекциями других текстов, суще-
ствующих для соответствующих языков в электронном виде. Это делает их
ценным дополнением к существующим языковым ресурсам.

1   Introduction

There are seven minority Uralic languages in the Volga-Kama area and adjacent regions of Russia[1]: Komi (Zyrian, Permyak), Udmurt, Mari (Meadow, Hill), Erzya and
Moksha. All these languages fall in the middle of the Uralic spectrum in terms of the
number of speakers. Similarly, they all belong to the middle level of digital vitality:
based on the amount of digital resources available for them, Kornai (2016) calls them
digitally "borderline" languages. Their sociolinguistic situation is also rather similar;
see Blokland and Hasselblatt (2003) for an overview. All of them have had intensive
contact with the dominant Russian language; almost all their speakers are bilingual
in Russian; the number of speakers is on the decline. Despite the fact that all of these

---

[1] Seven literary standards, to be more precise.

languages have some official status in the respective regions, their use in the public sphere and education is very limited.

Social media have been a target for both NLP and linguistic research for a long time now. However, the overwhelming majority of papers deal with social media texts in English or one of several other major languages. Smaller languages are severely underrepresented in this domain. There are corpora of social media texts in large Uralic languages, e.g. the Suomi24 forum corpus for Finnish (Aller Media Oy, 2014), and investigations based on them, e.g. Venekoski et al. (2016). All minority Uralic languages spoken in Russia lack such corpora.

Collecting social media corpora for the seven languages listed above is the central part of my ongoing project. There are notable differences between social media in these languages and those in major languages, which pose certain challenges for corpus development. First, they are smaller in size by several orders of magnitude. While, for example, the Edinburgh Twitter Corpus contains 2.26 billion tokens of tweets in English collected within a 2.5-month span (Petrović et al., 2010), all corpora I am dealing with do not exceed 3 million tokens despite representing an 11-year period. This scarcity of data makes every single post valuable. Another difference is ubiquitous code switching instances and Russian borrowings, which makes reliable language tagging a necessity. Yet another challenge comes from the fact that many social media users are not well acquainted with, or consciously avoid, the literary norm. On the one hand, this means that dialectal variation can be studied in Uralic social media corpora, but on the other, it makes morphological annotation more difficult.

The paper is organized as follows. In Section 2, I describe how I find, harvest and process the social media texts. In Section 3, I consider the linguistic and sociolinguistic properties of collected texts and discuss how that could be beneficial for certain kinds of research. In Section 4, I briefly describe the web interface through which the corpora are available.

2 Processing the data

2.1 Identifying and harvesting texts

A common approach to harvesting various kinds of texts from the web is to apply some kind of automatic crawling, which takes a small set of URLs as a seed and then follows the hyperlinks to find more content. Unfortunately, it is almost impossible to use this approach without adjustments for languages with small digital presence. Most links that appear in pages written in such languages lead to texts written in the dominant language (Russian in this case), and sifting through all of them to find relevant pages or fragments would require too much computational power.

In order to make text harvesting more efficient and less time-consuming, I try to make the seed as close to the comprehensive URL list as possible. Only after processing all pages from that list do I apply limited crawling. When identifying the pages for the seed list, I build upon a strategy proposed and used by Orekhov et al. (2016) for collecting and researching minority languages of Russia on the Internet, as well as on the results obtained by them. A slightly different version of the same strategy was previously used by Scannell (2007) in the Crúbadán project for similar purposes. This approach involves searching for relevant pages with a conventional search engine, using a manually compiled small set of tokens which are frequent in the relevant language, but do not exist or are very infrequent in any other language. This contrasts to the strategy employed by the "Finno-Ugric Languages and the Internet" project (Jauhiainen et al., 2015), which relied on large-scale crawling and subsequent fully automatic filtering by language.

Out of a dozen social media services with presence in Russia, I currently limit my search to *vkontakte*[2], which is by far the most popular of them both in relevant regions and in Russia as a whole. My preliminary research shows that in major Western social media, such as Facebook or Twitter, texts in minority Uralic languages are almost non-existent. However, there is at least one other Russian resource, *odnoklassniki*[3], which seems to contain texts in these languages in quantities that may justify the effort needed to process them. *Odnoklassniki* is more popular with the older generation and apparently has varying popularity across regions. For example, it seems that there are more texts in Erzya there than in Udmurt. Nevertheless, relevant texts in *vkontakte* clearly outnumber those in *odnoklassniki*. Additionally, I download forums not associated with any social media service, if their primary language is one of those I am interested in. So far, I have only found forums of such kind for Erzya.

Although there are also blogs available in these languages, I did not include them in the social media corpora. Baldwin et al. (2013) show that the language of blogs could be placed somewhere between edited formal texts and social media by a number of parameters. This is true for most (although not all) blogs in minority Uralic languages, which on average contain less code-switching than social media and where the language variety seems closer to the literary standard. Nevertheless, blogs are undoubtedly a valuable source for linguistic research, which is why I downloaded them as well and included them in the "support corpora" (see below).

As a starting point, I take the URL lists of *vkontakte* pages collected by Orekhov et al. (2016).[4] I manually check all of them and remove those that were misattributed (which sometimes happens because the lists were compiled in an unsupervised fashion). An example of an erroneously marked page is a Russian group dedicated to Korean pop music where the users share the lyrics in Cyrillic transcription. Apparently, a transcribed Korean word coincided with one of frequent Udmurt tokens, which is why it ended up tagged as Udmurt.

As a second step, I perform manual search in Yandex search engine with an additional check in Google, using the same strategy as Orekhov et al. (2016). This allows me to enhance the original lists with URLs that were missed or did not exist in 2015, when the lists were compiled.

When the initial list of URLs is ready, I download the texts (posts and comments) and the metadata using the *vkontakte* API. The amount of data is small enough for it to be downloadable through a free public API with a limitation of 3 queries per second within several days. The texts with some of the metadata are stored in simple JSON files. User metadata is cached and stored in another JSON file to avoid the need of downloading it multiple times for the same user. Obviously, only texts and metadata open to the general public can be downloaded this way.

The final stage of the harvesting process involves limited crawling. The messages written by individual users are automatically language-tagged. For each user, I count the number of messages in the relevant language authored by them. All users that have at least 2 messages are added to the URL list and their "walls" (personal pages with texts and comments written by them or addressed to them) are downloaded as

---

[2]`https://vk.com/`
[3]`https://ok.ru/`
[4]The lists are available at `http://web-corpora.net/wsgi3/minorlangs/download`

well. The threshold of 2 messages was chosen to cut off instances of erroneous language tagging, which happen especially often with short messages. Besides, users with small message counts tend to have no texts in the relevant languages on their walls anyway.

2.2   Language tagging

The social media texts in minority Uralic languages are interspersed with Russian, so language tagging is of crucial importance to the project. There are standard techniques for language tagging, the most popular probably being the one based on character n-gram frequencies (Canvar and Trenkle, 1994). It is impossible, however, to achieve sufficient quality on minority Uralic social media data with these methods. The first problem is that the texts that have to be classified are too short. Mixing languages within one message is extremely common, which is why at least sentence-level tagging is needed in this case. In an overview of several n-gram-based methods, Vinosh Babu and Baskaran (2005) note that, although generally it is easy to achieve 95% or higher precision with such methods, "for most of the wrongly identified cases the size of the test data was less than 500 bytes, which is too small". This is always the case with the sentences, which most of the time contain less than 10 words. What's more, sentences in the relevant languages contain lots of Russian borrowings and place names, which would shift their n-gram-based counts closer to those of Russian. Classifying short segments with additional issues like that is still problematic with the methods commonly used at present (Jauhiainen et al., 2018, 60–61).

Instead of a character-based classification, I use a process which is mostly dictionary-based and deals with words rather than character n-grams as basic counting units. In a nutshell, it involves tokenization of the sentence, dictionary lookup for each word and tagging the sentence with the language most words can be attributed to. The classification is three-way: each sentence is tagged as either Uralic, or Russian, or "unknown". The last category is inevitable, although the corresponding bin is much smaller than the first two. It contains sentences written in another language (English, Tatar, Finnish and Hungarian are among the most common), sentences that comprise only emoji, links and/or hashtags, and those that are too difficult to classify due to intrasentential code switching. In the paragraphs below, I describe the algorithm in greater detail.

Before processing, certain frequent named entities, such as names of local newspapers and organizations, are cut out with a manually prepared regex. This is important because such names, despite being written in a Uralic language, often appear in Russian sentences unchanged. After that, the sentence is split into tokens by whitespaces and punctuation-detecting regular expressions. Only word tokens without any non-Cyrillic characters or digits were considered.

There are three counters: number of unambiguously Russian tokens (cntR), number of unambiguously Uralic tokens (cntU), and number of tokens that could belong to either language (cntBoth). Each word is compared to the Russian and Uralic frequency lists, which were compiled earlier. If it only appears on one of them without any remarks, the corresponding counter is incremented. If it appears only in the Uralic list, but is tagged as either a Russian borrowing or a place name without any inflectional morphology, cntBoth is incremented. The same happens if the word is on both lists, unless it is much more frequent, or its 6-character suffix is more common (in terms of type frequency), in one than in the other. (Exact thresholds here and in the paragraph below are adjusted manually and are slightly different for different languages of the sample.) In the latter case, the corresponding counter, cntR or cntU, is incremented.

After all words have been processed, rule-based classification is performed. If one of the counters is greater than the others and most tokens in the sentence have been attributed to one of the languages, the sentence is tagged according to the winning counter. If there are many ambivalent words and either no Uralic words or some clearly Russian words in the sentence, it is classified as Russian. Finally, if counter-based rules fail, the sentence is checked against manually prepared regexes that look for certain specific character n-grams characteristic for one language and rare in the other. If this test also does not produce a definitive answer, the sentence is classified as "unknown".

There is a certain kind of texts in social media in minority languages that poses a serious challenge to this approach. In all languages I have worked with, there are groups designed for learning the language. They often contain lists of sentences or individual words with Russian translations. A simplistic approach to sentence segmentation places most of such translation pairs inside one sentence, which is then impossible to classify as belonging to one of the languages. To alleviate this problem, the language classifier tries splitting sentences by hyphens, slashes or other sequences commonly used to separate the original from the translation. If both parts can be classified with greater certainty than the entire fragment, and they have different language tags, the sentence remains split.

During the initial language tagging, "borderline" sentences, i.e. those whose cntR and cntU counters had close values, were written to a separate file. I manually checked some of them and corrected the classification if it was wrong. During second run of tagging, each sentence was first compared to this list of pre-tagged sentences. The tagging procedure described above was only applied to sentences that were not on that list. Finally, an extended context was taken into account. If a sentence classified as "unknown" was surrounded by at least 3 sentences with the same language tag (at least one before and at least one after it), its class was switched to that of the neighboring sentences.

The resulting accuracy is high enough for practical purposes and definitely higher than an n-gram-based approach would achieve. Tables 1 and 2 show the figures for Udmurt and Erzya. The evaluation is based on a random sample that contained 200 sentences for each of the languages. Actual cases of misclassification comprise only about 2% of sentences classified as Uralic. An additional 3% accounts for problematic cases, e.g. code switching with no clear main/matrix language. The share of sentences classified as "unknown" is 2.5% for Udmurt/Russian pair and 1.3% for Erzya/Russian; most of them are indeed not classifiable. Note that the figures below refer to sentences rather than tokens. Given that wrong classification overwhelmingly occurs in short sentences (1–4 words), precision measured in tokens would be much higher.

	correct sentences	wrong language	mix / other
Udmurt	95.5%	1.5%	3%
Russian	100%	0%	0%

Table 1: Accuracy of language tagging for Udmurt.

The described approach requires much more training data and annotation than the n-gram-based classification. Specifically, it relies on word lists for the respective lan-

	correct sentences	wrong language	mix / other
Erzya	94.5%	2.5%	3%
Russian	97%	1%	2%

Table 2: Accuracy of language tagging for Erzya.

guages that are long enough, contain some morphological annotation, annotation for Russian loanwords and place names, and frequency information. Such lists are readily available for Russian; I used a frequency list that is based on the Russian National Corpus and contains about 1 million types. However, it is much more problematic to obtain such lists for the Uralic languages. In order to do so, I had to collect a "support corpus" with clean texts and no Russian insertions for each of the languages first. Fortunately, this is achievable because there are enough non-social-media digital texts in them on the web. First and foremost, for each language there are one or several newspapers that publish articles in it. Apart from that, there are translations of the Bible, blogs (surprisingly, unlike social media, most of them do not contain chaotic code switching) and fiction. By contrast, Wikipedia, which is often a primary source of training data for major languages, is of little use for this purpose because Wikipedias in these languages mostly contain low-quality and/or automatically generated articles (Orekhov and Reshetnikov, 2014). The resulting lists contain around 230,000 types for Udmurt and around 100,000 types for Erzya, Moksha and Komi-Zyrian.

Although I am primarily interested in the Uralic data, all Russian and unclassified sentences are also included in the corpus. Omitting them in mixed posts would obviously be detrimental for research because it would be impossible to restore the context of Uralic sentences and therefore, in many cases, fully understand their meaning. However posts written entirely in Russian are also not removed if their authors or the groups where they appear have Uralic posts as well. This effectively makes my corpora bilingual, although not in a sense traditionally associated with this term (Barrière, 2016). One reason why this is done is facilitating sociolinguistic investigations of language choice in communication. Another is enabling research of contact-induced phenomena in Russian spoken by native speakers of the Uralic languages. A number of corpus-based papers has been published recently about regional contact- or substrate-influenced varieties of Russian, e.g. by Daniel et al. (2010) about Daghestan or Stoynova (2018) about Siberia and Russian Far East. The availability of corpora that contain Russian produced by Uralic speakers could lead to similar research being carried out on Uralic material.

2.3 Filtering and anonymization

After the language tagging, the texts undergo filtering, which includes spam removal, deduplication and anonymization.

Since the actual content is not that important for linguistic research, there is nothing inherently wrong with having spam sentences in the corpus, as long as they are written in a relevant language. However, the main problem with spam is that it is repetitive, which biases the statistics. In order to limit this effect, I manually checked sentences that appeared more than N times in the corpus (with N varying from 2 to 5, depending on the size of the corpus). Those that could be classified as being part of automatically generated messages or messages intended for large-scale multiple posting, were put to the list of spam sentences. If they contained variable parts, such as usernames, those were replaced with regex equivalents of a wildcard. Such variable parts make template sentences resistant to ordinary duplicate search, which justifies treating them separately. Most of such sentences come from online games, digital postcards or chain letters. The resulting list contains about 800 sentences and sentence templates. Sentences in texts that match one of the templates are replaced with a <SPAM> placeholder. Posts where more than half of sentences were marked as spam are removed.

Text duplication is a serious problem for social media texts, which are designed for easily sharing and propagating messages. Posts published through the "share" button are marked as copies in the JSON returned by *vkontakte* API. If multiple copies of the same post appear in different files, they are identified by their post ID. Only one copy is left in place, and all others are replaced by the <REPOST> placeholder. However, this procedure does not solve the problem entirely. Many posts are copies of texts that originate outside of *vkontakte*, and some copies of *vkontakte* posts are made by copy-pasting (and possible editing) rather than with the "share" function. As an additional measure, posts that are longer than 90 characters are compared to each other in lowercase and with whitespaces deleted. If several identical posts are found, all but one are replaced with the placeholder. However, there are still many duplicates or half-duplicates left, which becomes clear when working with the corpora. Some of the duplicates, despite obviously coming from the same source, have slight differences in punctuation, spelling or even grammar, which means they were edited. It is a non-trivial question whether such half-copies should be removed. In any case, this remains a serious problem for the corpora in question. By my informal estimate, as much as 15% of the tokens found in the corpora could actually belong to near-duplicates. Before applying more advanced approach in the future, e.g. shingle-based (Broder, 2000), the near-duplicates have to be carefully analyzed to determine what has to be removed and what has to stay.

Final step of the filtering is anonymization. The purpose of anonymization is to avoid the possibility of identifying the users by removing their personal data. User-names and IDs of the users are replaced with identifiers such as F_312. The numbers in the labels are random, but consistent throughout each corpus. This way, the corpus users still can identify texts written by the same person (which could be important for dialectological or sociolinguistic research) without knowing their name. The names of the groups are not removed because there is no one-to-one correspondence be-tween groups and users. Similarly, user mentions in texts are removed. Just like in other major social media platforms, user mentions in *vkontakte* are automatically en-hanced with the links to the user pages and therefore are easily recognizable. All such mentions are replaced with a <USER> placeholder. All hyperlinks are replaced with a <LINK> placeholder. Finally, user metadata is aggregated (see Subsection 2.4). Only the anonymized corpus files are uploaded to the publicly accessible server.

2.4   Metadata and annotation

Each post together with its comments is conceptualized as a separate document in the corpus. There are post-level and sentence-level metadata. Both include information about the authors: the owner of the page (post-level) and the actual author of the post or comment (sentence-level), which may or may not coincide. Additionally, sentence-level metadata includes type of message (post/repost/comment), year of creation, and language of the sentence.

Author-related metadata primarily comes from the user profiles. It includes sex (which is an obligatory field) and, if the user indicated it, also their age, place of birth and current location. Simply copying the values for the latter three parameters would make it possible to identify the authors. However, these values are extremely important for any kind of sociolinguistic or dialectological research, so they have to be accessible in some way. As a compromise, these values are presented only in aggregated form. Exact year of birth is replaced with a 5-year span (1990–1995, 1995–2000, etc.) in all corpora. The solution for the geographical values has only been applied to the Udmurt corpus so far. The exact locations there are replaced with areas: districts (*район*) for Udmurtia and neighboring regions with significant Udmurt minorities; regions (*область/республика/край*) for other places in Russia; and countries otherwise. The correspondence between the exact values and areal values was established manually and stored in a CSV table, which at the moment has around 800 rows for Udmurt. Since there are a lot of ways to spell a place name (including using Udmurt names, which do not coincide with the official Russian ones), this is a time-consuming process[5], which is why I have not done that for the other corpora yet.

In order to make sure the birth places the users indicate are real at least most of the time, I read posts written by a sample of users. It is common for speakers in this region to live in cities and towns, but maintain ties with their original villages and describe them in their posts. In such descriptions, the speakers often explicitly indicate that they were born in that village. Additionally, place of origin is an important part of identity. This is why opening sections of most interviews in local press contain the information about the village the interviewee was born, along with their name and occupation. All this makes birth place information easily verifiable. In most cases, the place name indicated by the users was corroborated by the information I found in the texts. There were several cases, however, when instead of naming the exact place, the users wrote the district center closest to the real place of birth. This paradoxically makes the aggregated version of geographical data more accurate than the exact one.

The token-level annotation in the corpora includes lemmatization, part-of-speech and full morphological annotation, morpheme segmentation and glossing. This annotation is carried out automatically using rule-based analyzers, with the details (coverage, presence of disambiguation, etc.) varying from language to language. Additionally, the dictionaries used for morphological analysis were manually annotated for Russian borrowings, place names and other proper names, which is required for high-quality language tagging. Russian sentences were annotated with the *mystem 3* analyzer (Segalovich, 2003).

Social media texts in any language tend to be more "noisy" and difficult for straightforward NLP processing, having higher out-of-vocabulary rates (Baldwin et al., 2013). There are both standard and language-specific problems in this respect in the Uralic social media. The former include typos, deliberate distortions and lack of diacritics. An example of the latter is significant dialectal variation, which was to a certain extent accounted for in the morphological analyzers. The variation is explained by the facts that these languages were standardized only in the 1930s and that many people are not sufficiently well acquainted with the literary standards (or choose not to adhere to them).

---

[5]This process could be partially automatized, of course, e.g. using databases with geographical information such as DBpedia and distortion-detecting techniques such as Levenshtein distance. I would prefer this approach if I had to process tens of thousands or more place names. However, I believe that for my data, developing an automatic processing tool together with subsequent manual verification would take more time than completely manual processing.

The most frequent typos were included in the dictionaries. Some kinds of distortions, such as repeating a character multiple times, were removed before a token was morphologically analyzed (but not in the texts). Lack of diacritics is a common problem in Udmurt, Komi and Mari texts, as alphabets of these languages contain Cyrillic letters with diacritics that are absent from a standard Russian keyboard. They can be either omitted or represented in a roundabout way. Interestingly, the same letters are represented differently in different languages. In Udmurt, double dots above a letter are commonly represented by a colon or (less frequently) a double quote following it, e.g. *ö* = *o:* / *o"*. In Komi, the letter *o* in this context is most often capitalized or replaced with the zero digit. In all languages, similarly looking characters from Latin-based character sets can be inserted instead of Cyrillic ones. Alphabets of Erzya and Moksha coincide with that of Russian. Nevertheless, double dots above *ë* are often omitted, following the pattern used in Russian texts (where their use is optional). All these irregularities are taken care of during automatic processing.

3   Properties of the texts

3.1   Size and distribution of metadata values

After the language tagging, the corpus files were filtered to exclude users who wrote exclusively or almost exclusively in Russian. For each user wall, number of sentences classified as Russian, Uralic or Unknown was calculated. The file was excluded from the corpus either if it contained at most 3 Uralic sentences constituting less than 10% of all sentences, or if it contained at most 10 Uralic sentences constituting less than 1% of all sentences. If the number of sentences classified as "unknown" was suspiciously high, the file was checked manually.

The sizes of the corpora after filtering are listed in Table 3. The two columns on the right give sizes of Uralic and Russian parts of each corpus in tokens. It has to be borne in mind that some of the tokens belong to near-duplicates (see Subsection 2.2), so the actual sizes after proper deduplication may be lower. The figures for Komi-Zyrian and Moksha are preliminary, however it is clear that the total size of the Moksha *vkontakte* segment is tiny compared to the rest of the languages.

	#Groups	#Users	Uralic part	Russian part
Udmurt	335	979	2.66M	9.83M
Komi-Zyrian	87	408	2.14M	16.12M
Erzya	20 (+ forums)	111 (+ forums)	0.83M (*vk*: 0.4M)	5.23M
Moksha	17	17	0.014M	0.17M

Table 3: Corpus sizes.

In Table 4, year-by-year figures for Udmurt, Komi-Zyrian and Erzya are presented. The figures for 2018 are left out because the data for the entire year is not yet available. However, at least for Komi-Zyrian and Erzya they are projected to continue the trends observed in earlier data.

Vkontakte was launched in early 2007, which is why there are no texts in the corpora before this date. The only exception is one of the Erzya forums, `http://erzianj.borda.ru`, which was started in 2006. The dynamics look different for Erzya on the one hand and the Permic languages on the other. After an initial gradual

Year	Udmurt	Komi-Zyrian	Erzya (*vk*)	Erzya (forums)
2006	0	0	0	15.9
2007	1.0	0.7	0.01	70.7
2008	15.1	1.9	0.7	23.1
2009	14.3	6.0	2.6	64.3
2010	42.7	5.9	3.8	**105.6**
2011	101.7	14.3	11.3	79.0
2012	273.1	33.0	29.2	40.8
2013	424.1	55.4	28.3	15.8
2014	473.6	140.6	79.2	20.4
2015	429.8	251.4	**96.5**	11.3
2016	350.6	259.0	70.8	1.4
2017	505.2	**660.6**	44.5	0.01

Table 4: Size of Uralic parts of corpora by year, in thousands of tokens.

increase in the number of texts, which continued until 2014–2015, number of Erzya *vkontakte* texts started going down. Permic segments of *vkontakte*, by contrast, continued growing, although Udmurt had a two-year plunge. The number of groups also seems to grows continuously: Pischlöger (2017) reported 90 groups in 2013 and 162 groups in 2016 for Udmurt. Komi-Zyrian speakers were adopting social media at a lower pace, but at the moment, Komi-Zyrian segment outnumbers the Udmurt one in terms of token counts. The Erzya forums enjoyed peak popularity around 2010. The reason for that was most probably the discussions about development of an artificial unified Mordvin language out of the two existing literary standards, Erzya and Moksha. This idea was advocated by Zaics (1995) and Keresztes (1995) and supported by Mosin (2014). The initiative belonged to people in the position of power rather than e.g. writers or teachers (Rueter, 2010, 7) and was vehemently opposed by Erzya language activists. This possibility was actively discussed in 2009, which energized the activists and led to the spike in the number of forum posts. The controversy seems to have abated since then, and both forums are now defunct (although still accessible).

The gender composition is even more different in Udmurt and Erzya (counting only *vkontakte* texts), as can be seen from the Table 5. Three quarters of texts authored by users (rather than groups) in Erzya were written by males, while in Udmurt it is the females who contribute more. The Udmurt picture is actually close to the average: according to a 2017 study by Brand Analytics[6], 58.4% of all posts in *vkontakte* are written by females. I do not have any explanation for this disparity.

	F	M
Udmurt	59.5%	40.5%
Erzya	24.7%	75.3%

Table 5: Proportion of tokens by sex of the author in *vkontakte*.

---

[6] https://www.slideshare.net/Taylli01/2017-77172443

3.2 Linguistic properties

Literary standards were developed for minority Uralic languages only in the 1930s, although written literature in them existed earlier. During the Soviet times, the standard language was taught at schools, however, this is not obligatory anymore and even unavailable in many places. Dialectal variation is still significant within each language. While older speakers generally try to follow the literary standard when writing, the younger generation may not know it well enough. Their written speech is therefore influenced by their native dialects, as well as by Russian. This contrasts to official texts and press in these languages, where puristic attitudes prevail. In Udmurt, the official register with its neologisms is hardly comprehensible for many speakers (Edygarova, 2013). In Erzya, neologisms in press are often accompanied by their Russian translations in parentheses because otherwise nobody would understand them (Janurik, 2015). Texts in the social media are much closer to the spoken varieties, which makes them better suited for the research of the language as it is spoken today.

Dialectal variation is observable in vocabulary and morphology. Frequently occurring non-standard suffixes include, for example, the infinitive in *-n* and present tense in *-ko* in Udmurt, or dative in *-ńe* and 1pl possessive in *-mok* in Erzya. This makes dialectological research on the social media corpora possible in principle. The main obstacle to such research is corpus size. Only a minority of users indicate their place of origin. Divided by the number of districts these people were born, this leaves a really small number of geographically attributed tokens for all districts except the most populous ones (several thousand to several dozen thousand tokens in the case of Udmurt). In order to see a reliable areal distribution of a phenomenon, that phenomenon has to be really frequent in texts.

As a test case, I used three dialectological maps collected for Udmurt using traditional methods: the distribution of the affirmative particles *ben/bon* (Maksimov, 2007b); the word for 'forest' (Maksimov, 2007a); and the word for 'plantain (Plantago; a small plant common in Udmurtia)' (Maksimov, 2013). The distribution of the affirmative particles was clearly recoverable from the corpus data: having an average frequency of over 1000 ipm, they had enough occurrences in most districts. The distribution obtained from the corpus coincided with the one from the dialectological map, although it had lower resolution. Out of 7 different names for the forest available on the dialectological map (excluding phonetic variants), 5 were present among the geographically attributed tokens of the corpus (*ńules, tel', śik, ćašša, surd*). The overwhelming majority of occurrences in all districts belonged to the literary variant, *ńules*, while each of the other variants had only a handful of examples. Nevertheless, all these occurrences were attested exactly in the districts where they were predicted to appear by the dialectological map. Finally, the map for the plantain had 27 variants. Given the number of available options and the low frequency of this word, it is not surprising that its distribution turned out to be completely unrecoverable from the corpus. To sum up, it is possible to obtain some information on areal distributions of high- or middle-frequency phenomena from the social media corpora. However, in most cases this information can only be used as a preliminary survey and has to be supplemented by fieldwork or other methods to make reliable conclusions.

4 Availability

All social media corpora (as well as the "support corpora", see Subsection 2.4) are or will be available for linguistic research through an online interface[7]. Udmurt and Erzya corpora are already online. Komi-Zyrian and Moksha are being processed and will be available in December 2018. Komi-Permyak and both Mari corpora are scheduled for release in the first half of 2019.

Unfortunately, due to copyright and privacy protection reasons it is hardly possible to simply redistribute the source files freely. Instead, I currently employ a solution whereby the texts are only available through a search interface where the users can make queries and get search hits. The search hits appear in shuffled order, and for each sentence found, only a limited number of context sentences can be seen for copyright protection. This is a solution that is commonly applied in the web-as-corpus approach.[8] All data is anonymized (see Subsection 2.3). *Tsakorpus*[9] is used as the corpus platform. Queries can include any layer of annotation or metadata and support regular expressions and Boolean functions. Additionally, all code used for data processing will be available under the MIT license in a public repository.

5 Conclusion

In this paper, I described the ongoing project with the goal of creating social media corpora for seven medium-sized minority Uralic languages. The processing pipeline for these corpora includes semi-supervised identification of the texts (mostly in the *vkontakte* social networking service), downloading them through the API, language-tagging, filtering and anonymization, and morphological annotation. The corpora and tools used to build them are or will be publicly available. Sizes of the corpora vary, but do not exceed 3 million tokens written in the Uralic languages. Apart from those, each corpus also contains Russian sentences written by native speakers of the Uralic languages or in groups where Uralic texts have been posted; Russian parts of the corpora are several times larger than the Uralic ones. The corpora are better suited for sociolinguistic research than more traditional resources and contain texts written in a less formal register than those of press and fiction. Greater dialectal variation in the texts make them a possible source for dialectological investigations, which, however, have to be supported by independent sources to make reliable conclusions. In any case, given the scarcity of texts available digitally for the languages in question, the social media corpora will be a valuable resource for any kind of corpus-based linguistic research on them.

Acknowledgments

I am grateful to Irina Khomchenkova, who helped me with filtering URL lists for Erzya, Moksha, Meadow and Hill Mari, to Boglárka Janurik, who pointed me to resources in

---

[7] http://volgakama.web-corpora.net/index_en.html

[8] Although it is really widespread in web-based corpora, this solution is often left implicit. For example, non-public-domain parts of the Leeds Corpora have a context limitation of 150 characters in the KWIC view and slightly larger limitation in the "expanded context" view. However, this limitation, which has existed right from the start, is not mentioned by Sharoff (2006). Similarly, the one-sentence limitation and shuffling in the Leipzig Corpora Collection is not reported by Biemann et al. (2007), although it is mentioned elsewhere (Schäfer and Bildhauer, 2013).

[9] https://bitbucket.org/tsakorpus/tsakonian_corpus_platform

Erzya, and to Svetlana Edygarova, who helped me with translating the abstract into Udmurt.

References

Aller Media Oy. 2014. Suomi 24 2001-2014 (näyte) -korpuksen Helsinki-Korp-versio. http://urn.fi/urn:nbn:fi:lb-2016050901.

Timothy Baldwin, Paul Cook, Marco Lui, Andrew MacKinlay, and Li Wang. 2013. How Noisy Social Media Text, How Diffrnt Social Media Sources. In *International Joint Conference on Natural Language Processing*. Nagoya, Japan, pages 356–364.

Caroline Barrière. 2016. Bilingual Corpora. In *Natural Language Understanding in a Semantic Web Context*, Springer, Cham, pages 105–125.

Chris Biemann, Gerhard Heyer, Uwe Quasthoff, and Matthias Richter. 2007. The Leipzig Corpora Collection: monolingual corpora of standard size. In *Proceedings of Corpus Linguistics 2007*.

Rogier Blokland and Cornelius Hasselblatt. 2003. The Endangered Uralic Languages. In Mark Janse and Sijmen Tol, editors, *Language Death and Language Maintenance. Theoretical, practical and descriptive approaches*, John Benjamins, Amsterdam & Philadelphia, Current issues in linguistic theory, pages 107–142.

Andrei Z. Broder. 2000. Identifying and Filtering Near-Duplicate Documents. In Gerhard Goos, Juris Hartmanis, Jan van Leeuwen, Raffaele Giancarlo, and David Sankoff, editors, *Combinatorial Pattern Matching*, Springer Berlin Heidelberg, Berlin, Heidelberg, volume 1848, pages 1–10. https://doi.org/10.1007/3-540-45123-4_1.

W. B. Canvar and J. M. Trenkle. 1994. N-Gram-Based Text Categorization. In *Proceedings of the 3rd Annual Symposium on Document Analysis and Information Retrieval*. pages 161–176.

Michael Daniel, Nina Dobrushina, and Sergey Knyazev. 2010. Highlander's Russian: Case Study in Bilingualism and Language Interference in Central Daghestan. In Arto Mustajoki, Ekaterina Protassova, and Nikolai Vakhtin, editors, *Instrumentarium of Linguistics: Sociolinguistic Approaches to Non-Standard Russian*, Helsinki, number 40 in Slavica Helsingiensia, pages 65–93.

Svetlana Edygarova. 2013. Ob osnovnyx raznovidnostjax sovremennogo udmurtskogo jazyka [On the fundamental varieties of the modern Udmurt language]. *Ezhegodnik finno-ugorskix issledovanij* 3:7–18.

Boglárka Janurik. 2015. The emergence of gender agreement in Erzya-Russian bilingual discourse. In *Language Empires in Comparative Perspective*, Walter de Gruyter, pages 199–218.

Heidi Jauhiainen, Tommi Jauhiainen, and Krister Lindén. 2015. The Finno-Ugric Languages and The Internet Project. *Septentrio Conference Series* (2):87–98. https://doi.org/10.7557/5.3471.

Tommi Jauhiainen, Marco Lui, Marcos Zampieri, Timothy Baldwin, and Krister Lindén. 2018. Automatic Language Identification in Texts: A Survey. *arXiv:1804.08186 [cs]* ArXiv: 1804.08186. http://arxiv.org/abs/1804.08186.

László Keresztes. 1995. On the Question of the Mordvinian Literary Language. In Gábor Zaics, editor, *Zur Frage der uralischen Schriftsprechen [Questions of Uralic literary languages]*, Az MTA Nyelvtudományi Intézete, Budapest, Linguistica, Series A, Studia et Dissertationes, pages 47–55.

András Kornai. 2016. Computational linguistics of borderline vital languages in the Uralic family. Paper presented at International Workshop on Computational Linguistics for Uralic Languages 2. http://kornai.com/Drafts/iwclul.pdf.

Sergey Maksimov. 2007a. 'Les' v udmurtskix govorax: Dialektologicheskaja karta i kommentarij ['Forest' in Udmurt varieties: A commented dialectological map]. *Idnakar: Metody istoricheskoj rekonstrukcii* 2(2):56–69.

Sergey Maksimov. 2007b. Upotreblenie chastic ben-bon 'da' v udmurtskix dialektax [Use of the ben/bon 'yes' particles in Udmurt dialects]. *Nauka Udmurtii* 2(15):75–82.

Sergey Maksimov. 2013. Nazvanija podorozhnika v udmurtskix dialektax i ix proisxozhdenie [The Names of Plantain (Plantago) in the Udmurt Dialects and Their Origin]. *Ezhegodnik finno-ugorskix issledovanij* (4):7–17.

Mikhail Mosin. 2014. Sozdavat' li edinye literaturnye jazyki dlja ural'skix narodov? [Should unified literary languages be created for Uralic peoples?]. *Trudy Karel'skogo nauchnogo centra RAN* (3):76–82.

Boris Orekhov, I. Krylova, I. Popov, L. Stepanova, and L. Zaydelman. 2016. Russian Minority Languages on the Web: Descriptive Statistics. In *Computational Linguistics and Intellectual Technologies: Proceedings of the International Conference "Dialogue 2016"*. RSUH, Moscow, Computational Linguistics and Intellectual Technologies, pages 498–508.

Boris Orekhov and Kirill Reshetnikov. 2014. K ocenke Vikipedii kak lingvisticheskogo istochnika: sravnitel'noe issledovanie [Evaluating Wikipedia as a linguistic source. A comparative study]. In Yana Akhapkina and Ekaterina Rakhilina, editors, *Sovremennyj russkij jazyk v internete [Contemporary Russian language on the Internet]*, Jazyki slavjanskoj kul'tury, Moscow, pages 309–321.

Saša Petrović, Miles Osborne, and Victor Lavrenko. 2010. The Edinburgh Twitter Corpus. In *Proceedings of the NAACL HLT 2010 Workshop on Computational Linguistics in a World of Social Media*. Association for Computational Linguistics, Stroudsburg, PA, USA, WSA '10, pages 25–26. http://dl.acm.org/citation.cfm?id=1860667.1860680.

Christian Pischlöger. 2017. Udmurtskij jazyk v social'noj seti "VKontakte": Kvantitativnye i (vozmozhnye) kvalitativnye issledovanija [Udmurt in the Vkontakte Social Network: Quantitative and (Possible) Qualitative Research. In *Elektronnaja pis'mennost' narodov Rossijskoj Federacii: Opyt, problemy i perspektivy [Digital literacy of the nations in Russia: Experience, challenges and perspectives]*. GOU VO KRASGSiU, Syktyvkar, pages 154–162.

Jack Rueter. 2010. *Adnominal Person in the Morphological System of Erzya*. Number 261 in Mémoires de la Société Finno-Ougrienne. Société Finno-Ougrienne, Helsinki.

Kevin P. Scannell. 2007. The Crúbadán Project: Corpus building for under-resourced languages. In *Building and Exploring Web Corpora: Proceedings of the 3rd Web as Corpus Workshop*. volume 4, pages 5–15.

Roland Schäfer and Felix Bildhauer. 2013. *Web Corpus Construction*. Synthesis Lectures on Human Language Technologies. Morgan & Claypool.

Ilya Segalovich. 2003. A fast morphological algorithm with unknown word guessing induced by a dictionary for a web search engine. In *MLMTA-2003*. Las Vegas.

Serge Sharoff. 2006. Creating general-purpose corpora using automated search engine queries. In *WaCky! Working papers on the Web as Corpus*, pages 63–98.

Natalya Stoynova. 2018. Differential object marking in contact-influenced Russian Speech: the evidence from the Corpus of Contact-influenced Russian Speech of Russian Far East and Northern Siberia. In *Computational Linguistics and Intellectual Technologies: papers from the Annual conference "Dialogue"*. RSUH, Moscow, pages 721–734.

Viljami Venekoski, Samir Puuska, and Jouko Vankka. 2016. Vector Space Representations of Documents in Classifying Finnish Social Media Texts. In Giedre Dregvaite and Robertas Damasevicius, editors, *Information and Software Technologies*, Springer International Publishing, Cham, volume 639, pages 525–535. https://doi.org/10.1007/978-3-319-46254-7₄2.

J. Vinosh Babu and S. Baskaran. 2005. Automatic Language Identification Using Multivariate Analysis. In Alexander Gelbukh, editor, *Computational Linguistics and Intelligent Text Processing: Proceedings of CICLing 2005*, Springer, Berlin, Heidelberg & New York, pages 789–792.

Gábor Zaics. 1995. Skol'ko jazykov nuzhno erze i mokshe? [How many languages do the Erzya and the Moksha need?]. In *Zur Frage der uralischen Schriftsprechen [Questions of Uralic literary languages]*, Az MTA Nyelvtudományi Intézete, Budapest, number 17 in Linguistica, Series A, Studia et Dissertationes, pages 41–46.

Is this the end?
Two-step tokenization of sentence boundaries

Linda Wiechetek
UiT Norgga árktalaš universitehta
Divvun
`linda.wiechetek@uit.no`

Sjur Nørstebø Moshagen
UiT Norgga árktalaš universitehta
Divvun
`sjur.n.moshagen@uit.no`

Thomas Omma
UiT Norgga árktalaš universitehta
Divvun
`thomas.omma@uit.no`

Abstract

A period does not only mark the end of a sentence; it can also be part of an abbreviation and numerical expressions. When analysing corpus text linguistically we need to know where a sentence begins and where it ends. In traditional corpus analysis, typically a sentence is identified before linguistic analysis is performed. In this work we propose an approach where we do basic linguistic analysis before we decide what a sentence is. As the interpretation of a period after abbreviations and numerical expressions is ambiguous, we leave the ambiguity in the initial tokenization. In a second step we remove the ambiguity based on the linguistic context of the period. We compare the previous approach to the new one and show how the new two-step approach to tokenization improves the identification of sentence boundaries.

Abstract

Piste ei ole vain merkki lauseen päättämisestä, se voi myös olla osa lyhennettä tai numeroa. Kun analysoidaan korpustekstejä kielitieteellisesti, täytyy tietää, missä on lauseen alku ja loppu. Perinteisesti lauseen loppu on löydetty ennen kielitieteellistä analyysia. Tässä artikkelissa ehdotamme menettelyä, jonka mukaan kielitieteellinen perusanalyysi on tehty ennen lauseiden löytämistä. Koska lyhyen ja numeerisen ilmaisun jälkeisen pisteen tulkinta on epäselvä, jätämme epäselvyyden selvittämisen tekemättä prosessoimisen alkuvaiheessa. Toisessa vaiheessa poistamme epäselvyyden lauseen kielellisen kontekstin perusteella. Vertailemme aikaisemmat lähestymistavat uuteen ja näytämme, miten uusi kaksivaiheinen lähestymistapa jäsentämiseen parantaa lauserajojen tunnistamisen.

Abstract

Čuokkis ii dušše mearkkat cealkkaloahpa; muhtumin dat lea oanádusa oassi ja lohkosátnedajaldaga oassi. Go mii analyseret korpusteavstta lingvisttalaččat, de dárbbahit diehtit gokko cealkka álgá ja gokko dat loahppá. Árbevirolaš korpusanalysas láve cealkka mearriduvvot ovdal lingvisttalaš vuođđoanalysa. Dán

Proceedings of the fifth Workshop on Computational Linguistics for Uralic Languages, pages 141–153,
Tartu, Estonia, January 7 - January 8, 2019.

barggus mii árvalit lahkonanvuogi mas mii dahkat lingvisttalaš analysa ovdal go mearridit mii cealkka lea. Danin go čuoggá manná dulkot guovtti ládje oanádusa ja lohkosátnedajaldaga maŋis, de mii diktit ambiguitehta orrut álgotokeniseremis. Nuppi lávkkis mii fas dulkot daid nu ahte ambiguitehta jávká - čuoggá lingvisttalaš birrasa vuodul. Mii buohtastahttit ovdalaš lahkonanvuogi dainna odda vugiin ja čájehit got odda guovttelávkkat vuohki tokeniseret dahká álkibun mearridit cealkkarájiid.

1 Introduction

North Sámi is a Uralic language with a complex morphological structure spoken in Norway, Sweden and Finland by approximately 25 700 speakers (Simons and Fennig, 2018). In corpus analysis the first challenge is the correct identification of the basic syntactic frame, the sentence. While a combination of period and whitespace is typically seen as a reliable indicator for the sentence, there are many contexts in which this is not the case. In this paper we challenge this rather rigid and local analysis of potential sentence boundaries and suggest a flexible approach initially assuming ambiguity and later disambiguating this ambiguity by means of morpho-syntactic context conditions.

In the method we present we are using a morphological analyser as a center piece of tokenization of free text using *hfst-pmatch* and *hfst-tokenise*, and we specifically look at sentence boundary detection and disambiguation, using the morphological analysis of various abbreviated expressions to help identify sentence boundaries. Combining a transducer with a tokenization tool lets us delay the resolution of ambiguous tokenization, including sentence boundaries. We then use a Constraint Grammar (CG - see below) module that looks at the context of the ambiguous sentence boundaries to disambiguate and decide whether a period is also an end of sentence mark, or just part of an abbreviated expression or numerical expressions like dates and ordinals.

Due to the typology of North Sámi combined with the scarcity of corpus resources, using a lexicon-based finite state transducer (Beesley and Karttunen, 2003) for morphological analysis it is the only viable option. Both the typology and lack of corpus material are shared with most other Uralic languages, so what is done for North Sámi should be quite relevant for the other languages in the family, as well as for other languages with similar typology. For the same reason we do not consider statistical approaches fruitful, there just is not enough material for most of these languages. A comparison with deep machine learning methods would be an interesting task for a future project.

2 Background

In this section we will present the general framework and infrastructure for our approach and the motivation for replacing our previous approach to tokenization and sentence identification with a newer one.

2.1 Framework

The central tools used in corpus analysis in the *Giella*-framework are *finite state transducers* (FST's) and *Constraint Grammars* (CG). CG is a rule-based formalism for writing disambiguation and syntactic annotation grammars (Karlsson, 1990; Karlsson et al., 1995). The *vislcg3* implementation[1] we use also allows for dependency annotation. CG relies on a bottom-up analysis of running text. Possible but unlikely analyses are discarded step by step with the help of morpho-syntactic context.

Preprocess was built in the early days of the *Giella* infrastructure. It encodes some amounts of linguist knowledge, but isolated from the rest of the linguistic facts of each language. The fact that it is written in Perl makes it hard to include in shipping products such as grammar checkers. The major issue, though, is the fact that it makes linguistic decisions before there has been any linguistic analysis at all, which this article is all about.

All components are compiled and built using the *Giella* infrastructure (Moshagen et al., 2013). This infrastructure is useful when coordinating resource development using common tools and a common architecture. It also ensures a consistent build process across languages, and makes it possible to propagate new tools and technologies to all languages within the infrastructure. That is, the progress described in this paper is immediately available for all languages in the *Giella* infrastructure, barring the necessary linguistic work.

The North Sámi Constraint Grammar analysers take morphological ambiguous input, which is the output from analysers compiled as FST's. The source of these analysers is written in the Xerox *twolc* and *lexc* (Beesley and Karttunen, 2003) formalisms, compiled and run with the free and open source package HFST (Lindén et al., 2011).

We also rely on a recent addition to HFST, *hfst-pmatch* (inspired by Xerox pmatch (Karttunen, 2011)) with the runtime tool *hfst-tokenise* (Hardwick et al., 2015). Below we describe how this lets us analyse and tokenise in one step, using FST's to identify regular words as well as multiword expressions with full morphology.

The choice of purely rule-based technologies is not accidental. The complexity of the languages we work with, and the general sparsity of data, makes purely data-driven methods inadequate. Additionally, rule-based work leads to linguistic insights that feed back into our general understanding of the grammar of the languages.

2.2 Motivation

In the OLD (but still used) corpus analysis pipeline in the *Giella*-framework, sentence boundary identification is performed by the perl script *preprocess* before any other linguistic analysis of the sentence is made, cf. Figure 1.

In sentence boundary identification, the following expressions that are typically followed by a period need to be disambiguated: **abbreviations**, and **numerical expressions** (for example ordinals and dates). The full stop can either be part of the expression itself, with no sentence boundary implied, or it can also entail the end of the preceding sentence.

Preprocess is based on the following assumptions: It distinguishes between 'transitive' and 'intransitive' abbreviations. 'Transitive' and 'intransitive' are used in the following way in this context: Transitive abbreviations are for example *ee.= earret eará* 'amongst others', *vrd.=veardit* 'compare'. Intransitive abbreviations are for example *bearj.= bearjadat* 'Friday', *eaŋg.= eŋgelasgiella* 'English', *jna.= ja nu ain* 'and so on', *milj.= miljovdna* 'million', *ru.= ruvdnu* 'crowns'. In addition, abbreviations typically followed by numbers are listed separately, fore example, *nr.= nummar* 'number', *kap.= kapihttal* 'chapter', *tlf.= telefovdna* 'telephone'.

---

[1]`http://visl.sdu.dk/constraint_grammar.html` (accessed 2018-10-08), also Bick and Didriksen (2015)

While the period after transitive abbreviations like *vrd.=veardit* 'compare' in ex. (1) is never interpreted as a sentence boundary if followed by a word (capitalized or not) or a numerical digit, it is always interpreted as a sentence boundary after intransitive abbreviations like *jna.= ja nu ain* 'and so on' in ex. (2). In the case of abbreviations typically followed by numbers, the period is interpreted as a sentence boundary if followed by a capitalised word, but not if followed by a word with lower case letters or numerical digits like *13* after *kap.* 'chapter' in ex. (3).

(1) **vrd.** máinnašumiin kapihttalis 14
cmp. mention.COM chapter.LOC 14
'compare with the mentioning in chapter 14'

(2) ...mas lea dieđusge
...where is of.course
smávva oasit nugo rap, rocka **jna.**
small parts like rap, rock and.so.on.
Jietnateknihkkáriid mii maid šaddat
Sound.technician.ACC.PL we also become
hui dávjá bivdit boahtit lulde.
very often ask come from.south
'...where are of course small parts like rap, rock and so on. We also often have to ask sound technicians to come from the south'

(3) gč. **kap.** 13.
see chapter 13
'See chapter 13'

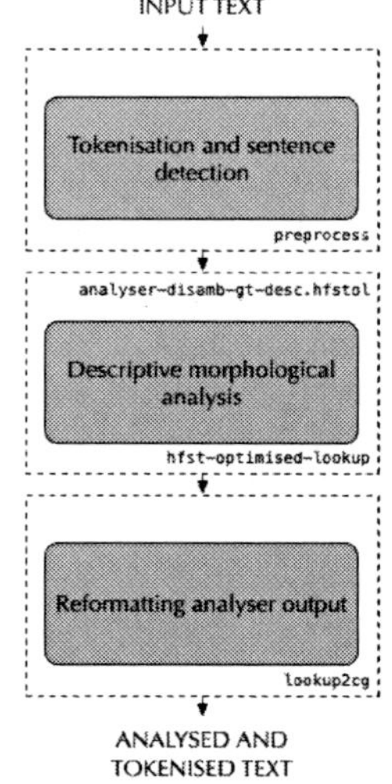

Figure 1: OLD tokenization architecture

While these are reasonable criteria to distinguish between sentence boundaries and periods that are parts of the actual expression, there are a number of cases that cannot be resolved. *Preprocess* has absolutely no access to any linguistic criteria. That means that it cannot distinguish between nouns and proper nouns. If the capitalized word after a period is a proper noun, which is captialized also in the middle of a sentence, *preprocess* cannot take that into consideration. This is the case in the example below, where the intransitive currency abbreviation *ru.* 'crown(s)' is followed by a proper noun. In ex. (4), the period after the intransitive abbreviation *ru.* 'crown(s)' followed by the proper noun *Sámeálbmotfondii* 'Sámi people's fond (Ill.)' is interpreted as a sentence boundary by *preprocess*, cf. Figure 2, while it is interpreted as part of the expression with *ru.* before *fondii* 'fund (Ill.)'.

(4) ...lea várrejuvvon 16 000 000 **ru.** Sámeálbmotfondii 2009:s.
...is reserved 16 000 000 crowns Sámeálbmot.fond.ILL 2009.LOC
'...it is reserved 16 000 000 crowns to the Sámeálbmot-fond 2009.'

(5) ...lea várrejuvvon 16 000 000 **ru.** fondii 2009:s.
...is reserved 16 000 000 crowns fond.ILL 2009.LOC
'...it is reserved 16 000 000 crowns to the fond 2009.'

Also ordinals and date expressions like *02.03* in ex. (6) at the end of sentences can

```
Áššis
25/08
lea
várrejuvvonr
16 000 000
ru.
.
Sámeálbmotfondii
2009:s
.
```

```
Sámi parlamentáralaš ráđđi
čoahkkanii
Kárášjogas
02.03
.
```

Figure 3: Preprocess analysis of ex. (6)

Figure 2: Preprocess analysis of ex. (5)

cause problems when analyzed by *preprocess*.

(6)   Sámi parlamentáralaš ráđđi   čoahkkanii Kárášjogas   02.03.
      Sámi parliament   council met   Kárášjohka.LOC 02.03.
      'The Sámi parliament council met in Kárášjohka on the 02.03.'

In the analysis of *preprocess* in Figure 3, the date expression is not recognized as such
as the period is categorically removed from after **02.03** although it is part of the expression. The same is the case if the last expression in the sentence is an ordinal.

3   Our two-step approach

Below we describe our new approach to tokenization, which includes a two-step identification of sentence boundaries. We will then evaluate our new method and compare
its results to the results of our previous approach. The new approach consists of two
steps:

1. ambiguous tokenization with *hfst-tokenise* and

2. disambiguation of ambiguous tokenization with *mwe-dis.cg3*.

It has originally been introduced as a part of the North Sámi grammar checker to
resolve compound error detection, cf. (Wiechetek, 2012, 2017).

The North Sámi corpus analysis consists of different modules that can be used
separately or in combination, cf. Figure 4. The text is initially tokenised and morphologically analysed by the descriptive morphological analyser and tokeniser *tokeniser-
gramcheck-gt-desc.pmhfst*. Any ambiguous tokenization is left as is, to be resolved
later on. The following module, *analyser-gt-whitespace.hfst*, detects and tags certain
whitespace delimiters, so that it can tag, for example the first word of paragraphs and
other whitespace delimited boundaries. This can then be used by the sentence boundary detection rules later on, which enables detecting, for example, headers based on
their surrounding whitespace. The valency annotation grammar *valency.cg3* adds valency tags to potential governors, i.e. (predominantly) verbs, nouns, adverbs and adjectives.

The subsequent module is the heart of the disambiguation of ambiguous tokenization. The Constraint Grammar file *mwe-dis.cg3* decides, among other things, whether a period is a sentence boundary or not, based on the morphological and other linguistic analysis of the surrounding tokens. Finally, the command line tool *cg-mwesplit* (part of the *vislcg3* package) reformats the disambiguated cohorts into their final form for further consumption by other *vislcg3* grammars.

3.1 Hfst-tokenize

A novel feature of our approach is the support for different kinds of ambiguous tokenizations in the analyser, and how we disambiguate ambiguous tokens using Constraint Grammar rules.

We do tokenization as part of the morphological analysis using the *hfst-tokenise* tool, which does a left-to-right longest match analysis of the input, where matches are those given by a *pmatch* analyser.

```
Define morphology @bin"analyser.hfst" ;
Define punctword  morphology &
                  [ Punct:[?*] ] ;
Define blank      Whitespace |
                  Punct ;
Define morphoword morphology
                  LC([blank | #])
                  RC([blank | #]) ;
regex [ morphoword | punctword ];
```

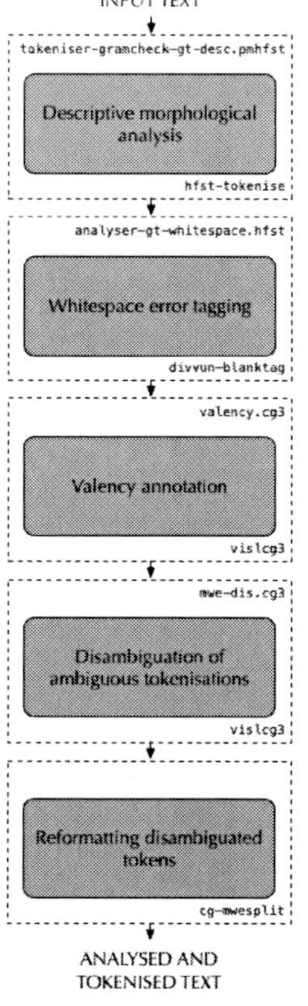

Figure 4: NEW tokenization architecture

The above *pmatch* definitions say that a word from the lexicon (*analyser.hfst*) has to be surrounded by a "blank", where a blank is either whitespace or punctuation. The LC/RC are the left and right context conditions. We also extract (intersect) the subset of the lexicon where the form is punctuation, and allow that to appear without any context conditions.

We insert *re-tokenization* hints in the lexicon at places were we assume there is a possible tokenization border, and our changes to *hfst-tokenise* let the analyser backtrack and look for other tokenizations of the same input string. That is, for a given longest match tokenization, we can force it to *redo* the tokenization so we get other multi-token readings with shorter segments alongside the longest match. This solves the issue of combinatorial explosion.

As a simple example, the ordinal analysis of *17.* has a backtracking mark between the number and the period. If the lexicon contains the symbol-pairs/arcs

```
1:1 7:7 ε:@PMATCH_BACKTRACK@
ε:@PMATCH_INPUT_MARK@ .:A ε:Ord
```

then, since the form-side of this analysis is 17., the input *17.* will match, but since there was a backtrack-symbol, we trigger a retokenization. The input-mark symbol says where the form should be split.[2] Thus we also get analyses of *17* and . as two separate tokens.

```
"<17.>"
        "17" A Ord Attr
        "." CLB "<.>"
                "17" Num "<17>"
```

To represent tokenization ambiguity in the Constraint Grammar format, we use *vislcg3 subreadings*,[3] where deeper (more indented) readings are those that appeared first in the stream, and any reading with a word-form-tag ("<.>" above) should (if chosen by disambiguation) be turned into a cohort of its own. Now we may run a regular Constraint Grammar rule to pick the correct reading based on context, for example SELECT (".") IF (1 some-context-condition) ...; which would give us

```
"<17.>"
        "." CLB "<.>"
                "17" Num "<17>"
```

Then a purely mechanical reformatter named *cg-mwesplit* turns this into separate tokens, keeping the matching parts together:

```
"<17>"
        "17" Num
"<.>"
        "." CLB
```

3.2 Tokenization disambiguation

As mentioned above, disambiguation of ambiguous tokenization is done after the morphological analysis. Consequently, this step has access to undisambiguated morphological (but not full syntactical) information. In addition, lexical semantic tags and valency tags are provided. The rules that resolve sentence boundary ambiguity are based on transitivity tags of abbreviations, lexical semantic tags, and morphological tags. Some of them are specific to one particular abbreviation.

Version r173258 of the tokenization disambiguation grammar *mwe-dis.cg3* has 22 rules that handle sentence boundary disambiguation. The rule below removes a sentence boundary reading ("." CLB) if it is part of a numerical expression and there is noun of the lexical semantic category *currency* (Sem/Curr) to the right of it.

```
REMOVE:num-before-curr ("." CLB) IF (0 Num)(1*> (>>>)
BARRIER (>>>) LINK 1 Sem/Curr OR ("kr"));
```

In the case of *mill.* 'million', the period can be both the end of the sentence (cf. ex. (7)) or not (cf. ex. (8)), depending on the semantic tag of the following token. If a noun of the type currency follows (for example *ruvnno* 'crown (Gen.)' in ex. (8)) the period should be part of the abbreviation expression.

(7)   Eará buvttaduvvon dietnasat: 4,6 **mill.**
        other manufactured profits: 4.6 millions
        'Other manufactured profits: 4.6 millions'

---

[2] This also means we cannot reshuffle the input/output side of the FST. In practice, we use a flag diacritic in the lexicon, which will keep its place during minimisation, and after the regular lexicon is compiled, we turn the flag into the ϵ:@PMATCH_INPUT_MARK@ symbol-pair.

[3] https://visl.sdu.dk/cg3/chunked/subreadings.html (accessed 2018-10-10)

(8)   1,0 **mill.** ruvnno nissondoaimmaide
       1.0 mill. crowns women.activity.ILL.PL
       '1.0 mill. crowns to women's activities'

In ex. (9), the affiliation **Bb.=Bargiidbellodat** 'labor party' is abbreviated and followed by a capitalized proper noun. However it is not a sentence boundary as it is
followed by a female proper noun.

(9)   **Bb.**   Vibeke Larsen ii   jurddaš nie.
       Labor.party Vibeke Larsen not think   so
       'Vibeke Larsen from the labor party doesn't think that way'

The first rule below removes a sentence boundary reading ("." CLB) if it is part
of an abbreviation expression and there is a noun of the lexical semantic category
currency (Sem/Curr) to the right of it.

The second rule removes a sentence boundary reading ("." CLB) if it is part of an
abbreviation expression of the lexical semantic category organization (*Sem/Org*) and
it is followed by a human name (*Sem/Sur OR Sem/Fem OR Sem/Mal*).

```
REMOVE ("." CLB) IF (0 Num)
(1*> (>>>) BARRIER (>>>) LINK 1 Sem/Curr OR ("kr"));

REMOVE ("." CLB) IF (0 Sem/Org + ABBR)
(1*> Sem/Sur OR Sem/Fem OR Sem/Mal);
```

In ex. (10), the date is removed because it is preceded by an item of the class
category (*kap=kapihttal* 'chapter').

(10)   Dás čujuhuvvo Sámedikki   jahkediečáhussii kap   2.11.
       here referred   Sámi.parliament report.ILL   chapter 2.11.
       'Here, they refer to The Sámi parliament's report chapter 2.11.'

```
REMOVE (Sem/Date) IF (-1 KLASS)(0 CLB LINK 0/1 (Num Arab));

LIST KLASS = "art" "ášši" "bálkáceahkki" č"uokkis"
"ddie.nr" "nr" "s" "siidu" "§" "§§" "paragráfa" "S.nr"
"st.ddie. nr" "od.prp.nr" "Ot.prp. nr" "oassi" "kap"
"kapihttal" "kapihtal";
```

4   Evaluation

In this section we are going to evaluate our new approach to tokenization. A common method for splitting sentences in a complete pipeline (used for example by *Lan-
guageTool*) is to tokenise first, then do sentence splitting, followed by other stages of
linguistic analysis.

The quantitative evaluation is split in two: the first part only looks at expressions
ending in a full stop that are truly ambiguous with respect to sentence boundaries —
the full stop can both be and not be a sentence boundary depending on the context.
The evaluation looks at the performance of the pipeline for this specific subset of the
corpus. The second evaluation looks at all instances of expressions ending in full
stops, both the unambiguous and the ambiguous ones, and compare the performance

of two different approaches as measured to a gold standard version of the tokenized text. Again, we only look at sentence boundaries, but in this evaluation we look at the overall performance. The two pipelines evaluated are the old pipeline and the new pipeline described elsewhere in this article.

Within the qualitative evaluation where we analyze the cases of unsuccessful sentence boundary identification and analyze the reasons for the shortcomings.

4.1 Quantitative evaluation of the NEW approach

In this part of the evaluation, we particularly focus on the performance of the tokenizer in contexts that are ambiguous, and we evaluate the identification of sentence boundaries rather than successful tokenization in general. In the quantitative evaluation of ambiguous sentence boundary (SB) detection we calculated both precision (correct fraction of all decisions), recall (correct fraction of all targeted constructions) and accuracy (all correct decisions as fraction of all decisions). As an evaluation corpus we chose a newspaper corpus containing the 2014 texts of the daily North Sámi newspaper *Ávvir*[4].The corpus used contains 556 644 space separated strings, as reported by the Unix tool wc. The exact number of tokens will vary depending on tokenization methods, as described below.

In Table 1, we evaluate the identification of sentence boundaries in ambiguous expressions, i.e. NOT all sentence boundaries. As true positives we count ambiguous sentence boundaries that have been correctly identified. As false positives we count ambiguous expressions that do not involve a sentence boundary that have falsely been identified as sentence boundaries. As true negatives we count the cases of ambiguous expressions that are not sentence boundaries and have not been identified as such. As false negatives count sentence boundaries that have not been identified as such. Precision is 48% and recall is 62% and can still be improved. However, due to the fact that abbreviations and time expressions hardly ever occur at the end of a sentence, the number of true positives is naturally low. The accuracy of the NEW pipeline is 97%, i.e. 97% of all ambiguous periods are correctly analyzed as either parts of the abbreviation or as a sentence boundary.

Measures	
True positives	64
False positives	69
True negatives	3 425
False negatives	39
Precision	48.1%
Recall	62.1%
Accuracy	97.0%

Table 1: Quantitative evaluation of ambiguous sentence boundary tokenization after morphological analysis

4.2 Comparison with the old pipeline

We also evaluated the NEW pipeline against the OLD one with respect to the identification of all sentence boundaries (not only the morphologically ambiguous ones). Using the manually annotated section of the corpus as the base, we constructed a smaller, gold standard (GS) corpus to compare against. The GS corpus contains 221 620 tokens as measured by the Unix tool *wc*, and 14 811 sentence delimiting full stops out of a total of 16 057 tokens ending in or consisting of full stops. This also implies that 1 246 tokens ending in full stops do *not* constitute a sentence boundary.

---

[4] `https://avvir.no/` (accessed 2018-10-08)

The result of comparing both the OLD and the NEW pipelines against the gold standard is summarised in Table 2. These numbers have been checked by manual search for problematic pairs, and by diffing the OLD and NEW directly against each other, to see whether we get similar results for true positives.

As documented by the recall results, both tokenization approaches are almost equally successful regarding the true positives. But when looking at the other numbers, the difference is quite striking. While precision and accuracy hover around 96% for the OLD pipeline, all measures for the NEW pipeline are around 99.9%. Most of the remaining errors can be removed by lexicon fixes and improved Constraint Grammar rules. Some of the problematic issues are discussed below.

Measures	OLD	NEW
True positives	14 727	14 798
False positives	592	17
True negatives	669	1 228
False negatives	69	4
Precision	96.14%	99.89%
Recall	99.53%	99.97%
Accuracy	95.88%	99.81%

Table 2: Quantitative evaluation and comparison of the OLD and the NEW sentence boundary detection pipelines.

4.3 Qualitative evaluation

While some errors in the sentence boundary identification are due to problems in the lexicon, others require more precise rules in the disambiguation grammar *mwe-dis.cg3*.

(11) Lean   veallán   dás ja geahččan **su.**
have.PRS.1SG lie.PRFPRC here and watch.PRFPRC her;him
'I have lain here and watched her;him.'

In ex. (11), the period after the pronoun *su* 'her, his' is not correctly identified as a sentence boundary, it is a false positive. Instead *su=sulli* 'approximately' is identified as an abbreviation with the period being part of the expression. The pronoun reading does not even appear in the analysis.

```
"<su.>"
    "su" Adv ABBR Gram/NumNoAbbr <W:0.0000000000>
;   "." CLB <W:0.0000000000> "<.>"
;   "su" Adv ABBR Gram/NumNoAbbr <W:0.0000000000> "<su>"
```

This is due to an issue in the lexicon that is easily solvable, but had not been detected at the time of doing the analysis used as basis for the evaluation. The core of the issue is that some pronouns, such as *su* above, can also be abbreviated adverbs with obligatory full stops. What was missing in the lexicon is a signal for such abbreviated adverbs that will trigger retokenization. Such triggers are easy to add, and needs to be added only once for the whole category.

In ex. (12), the time expression *20.00* (Sem/Time-clock) is ambiguous with a date expression (Sem/Date). This needs to be corrected in the morphological analyzer as *20.00* is not a valid date. The time expression is erroneously removed and the sentence boundary is not identified.

(12) gaskal   13.00 ja **20.00.**
between 13.00 and 20.00

'between 1 and 8 pm.'

```
"<13.00>"
        "13.00" Num Arab Sg Gen <W:0.0000000000>
        "13.00" Num Sem/Time-clock Sg Gen <W:0.0000000000>
:
"<ja>"
        "ja" CC <W:0.0000000000>
:
"<20.00.>"
        "20.00" Num Sem/Date Sg Gen <W:0.0000000000>
;       "." CLB <W:0> "<.>"
;               "20.00" Num Sem/Time-clock Sg Nom <W:0> "<20.00>"
     REMOVE:2426:longest-match
;       "." CLB <W:0> "<.>"
```

In other cases, the error in the analysis is due to shortcomings in the disambiguation file *mwe-dis.cg3*. In ex. (13), the name is is followed by two initials before the surname. The period after the first initial is erroneously interpreted as a sentence boundary. There is a rule that removes the sentence boundary reading if there is one initial after a first and before the surname.

(13)   Hilde C.J. Mietınen álgá   maŋŋel geasi
        Hilde C.J. Mietinen begins after   summer.GEN
        'Hilde C.J. Mietinen begins after the summer'

5   Conclusion

We have questioned the traditional approach to identifying sentence boundaries as the first step of text processing, before any linguistic analysis is done, and usually completely independent of any linguistic parsing at all. This introduces errors that are almost impossible to recover from in the remaining analysis steps.

We have demonstrated that by means of a basic linguistic analysis prior to tokenization sentence boundary detection can be substantially improved. We proposed a two step tokenization that leaves initial ambiguity in sentence boundary detection until it can be disambiguated by means of linguistic context.

Our experiment showed that our system outperforms a state-of-the-art traditional sentence tokenizer. 97% of all ambiguous periods are correctly analyzed in the new tokenization approach. Disambiguation of all sentence boundaries give good results both in terms of precision, recall and accuracy, i.e. all are above 99.8%, and recall approaching 99.99%. Our method of ambiguous tokenization and ambiguity resolution by means of grammatical context allows us to improve tokenization significantly compared to the previous one-step-approach.

It would be an interesting topic for future work to compare our results with deep machine learning approaches, and whether deep learning can approach our results given the sparsity of data for the languages we work on.

The main new insight gained is that linguistic context is relevant and necessary when identifying sentence boundaries, and ambiguous tokenization should not be handled solely by a tokenizer without linguistic knowledge. Tokenization is not only important in corpus analysis but also in other tasks like grammar checking, machine translation and all other text processing of free text.

Acknowledgments

We especially would like to thank Kevin Unhammer for his work on the gramar
checker framework that is the foundation of our work discussed above, and our col-
leagues in *Divvun* and *Giellatekno* for their daily contributions to our language tools
and the infrastructure.

References

Kenneth R. Beesley and Lauri Karttunen. 2003. *Finite State Morphology*. CSLI Studies
in Computational Linguistics. CSLI Publications, Stanford.

Eckhard Bick and Tino Didriksen. 2015. CG-3 – beyond classical Constraint Grammar.
In Beáta Megyesi, editor, *Proceedings of the 20th Nordic Conference of Computational
Linguistics (NoDaLiDa 2015)*. Linköping University Electronic Press, Linköpings
universitet, pages 31–39.

Sam Hardwick, Miikka Silfverberg, and Krister Lindén. 2015. Extracting
semantic frames using hfst-pmatch. In *Proceedings of the 20th Nordic
Conference of Computational Linguistics, (NoDaLiDa 2015)*. pages 305–308.
http://aclweb.org/anthology/W/W15/W15-1842.pdf.

Fred Karlsson. 1990. Constraint Grammar as a Framework for Parsing Running Text.
In Hans Karlgren, editor, *Proceedings of the 13th Conference on Computational Linguistics (COLING 1990)*. Association for Computational Linguistics, Helsinki, Finland, volume 3, pages 168–173.

Fred Karlsson, Atro Voutilainen, Juha Heikkilä, and Arto Anttila. 1995. *Constraint
Grammar: A Language-Independent System for Parsing Unrestricted Text*. Mouton
de Gruyter, Berlin.

Lauri Karttunen. 2011. Beyond morphology: Pattern matching with FST. In *SFCM*.
Springer, volume 100 of *Communications in Computer and Information Science*,
pages 1–13.

Krister Lindén, Miikka Silfverberg, Erik Axelson, Sam Hardwick, and Tommi Pirinen. 2011. Hfst—framework for compiling and applying morphologies. In Cerstin
Mahlow and Michael Pietrowski, editors, *Systems and Frameworks for Computational Morphology*, Springer-Verlag, Berlin, Heidelberg, volume Vol. 100 of *Communications in Computer and Information Science*, pages 67–85.

Sjur N. Moshagen, Tommi A. Pirinen, and Trond Trosterud. 2013. Building an open-
source development infrastructure for language technology projects. In *NODAL-
IDA*.

Gary F. Simons and Charles D. Fennig, editors. 2018. *Ethnologue: Languages of the World*. SIL International, Dallas, Texas, twenty-first edition.
http://www.ethnologue.com (Accessed 2018-10-09).

Linda Wiechetek. 2012. Constraint Grammar based correction of grammatical errors
for North Sámi. In G. De Pauw, G-M de Schryver, M.L. Forcada, K. Sarasola, F.M. Tyers, and P.W. Wagacha, editors, *Proceedings of the Workshop on Language Technology*

for Normalisation of Less-Resourced Languages (SALTMIL 8/AFLAT 2012). European Language Resources Association (ELRA), Istanbul, Turkey, pages 35–40.

Linda Wiechetek. 2017. *When grammar can't be trusted – Valency and semantic categories in North Sámi syntactic analysis and error detection.* PhD thesis, UiT The arctic university of Norway.

Learning multilingual topics through aspect extraction from monolingual texts

Johannes Huber
Otto-von-Guericke-Universität Magdeburg
& TrustYou GmbH, Munich
`johannes@trustyou.net`

Myra Spiliopoulou
Otto-von-Guericke-Universität Magdeburg
Faculty of Computer Science
Working Group "Knowledge Management & Discovery"
`myra@ovgu.de`

Abstract

Texts rating products and services of all kind are omnipresent on the internet. They come in various languages and often in such a large amount that it is very time-consuming to get an overview of all reviews. The goal of this work is to facilitate the summarization of opinions written in multiple languages, exemplified on a corpus of English and Finnish reviews. To this purpose, we propose a framework that extracts aspect terms from reviews and groups them to multilingual topic clusters.

For aspect extraction we work on texts of each language separately. We evaluate three methods, all based on neural networks. One of them is supervised, one unsupervised, based on an attention mechanism and one a rule-based hybrid method. We then group the extracted aspect terms into multilingual clusters, whereby we evaluate three different clustering methods and juxtapose a method that creates clusters from multilingual word embeddings with a method that first creates monolingual clusters for each language separately and then merges them.

We report on our results from a variety of experiments, observing the best results when clustering aspect terms extracted by the supervised method, using the k-means algorithm on multilingual embeddings.

Tiivistelmä

Tekstejä, jotka arvostelevat erilaisia tuotteita ja palveluja löytyy kaikkialta netistä. Niitä on usealla kielellä ja niin monia, että on hyvin aikaa vievää luoda yleiskuva kaikista arvosteluista. Tämän työn päämäärä on helpottaa objektiivisen yhteenvedon luomista mielipiteistä, jotka ovat kirjoitettu useammalla kielellä, mikä työssä on havainnollistettu niin englannin- kuin suomenkielisellä aineistolla. Tähän tarkoitukseen työ ehdottaa viitekehystä joka poimii aspektisanat arvosteluista ja ryhmittää ne monikielisiin aiheklustereihin.

Proceedings of the fifth Workshop on Computational Linguistics for Uralic Languages, pages 154–183,
Tartu, Estonia, January 7 - January 8, 2019.

Poimimivaihe tehtiin erikseen molempien kielien kohdalla. Vertailemme kolmea metodia, jotka kaikki käyttävät neuroverkkoja. Ensimmäinen metodi on valvottu ja toinen on hybridi, sääntöihin perustuvan poimimisen sekä valvotun opettamisen välimuoto. Viimeinen metodi on valvomaton ja perustuu huomiointimekanismiin. Sen jälkeen poimitut aspektitermit ryhmitetään monikielisiin aiheklustereihin. Testaamme kolme eri klusterointialgoritmia ja vertailemme kahta eri metodia monikielisten klustereiden tekemiseen: yksikielisten sanaedustumisen kohdistamista yhteen vektoritilaan sekä erikseen yksikielisille klustereille ryhmittämistä ja jälkeenpäin klustereiden kohdistamista.

Raporttina voimme muun muassa kertoa saaneemme parhaimmat tulokset poimimalla aspektisanat valvotulla metodilla ja ryhmittämällä k-means algoritmin monikielisten sanaedustumisen kanssa.

1   Introduction

Texts expressing opinions about products are becoming important for a constantly increasing number of people. From 2011 to 2017, the percentage of customers in the United States that reads online reviews to determine if a business is good or bad at least occasionally has grown from 71% to 93% (Anderson, 2017). Summarizing these reviews objectively can help customers in their choice of a product. As only about 40% of internet content is in English (Pimienta et al., 2009), analyzing reviews also in other languages appears vital to give a full picture of opinions about an entity. In this work, we propose a framework that derives aspect terms from reviews written in different languages and then summarizes them into multilingual topics.

Aspect term extraction is a part of aspect-level sentiment analysis (ALSA). ALSA is able to provide a detailed analysis of opinions conveyed in a text by extracting the sentiment expressed towards each mentioned aspect. For example, given the sentence "the waitress was friendly", it should extract a positive sentiment towards the aspect "waitress". As creating summaries or statistics on these aspects alone would result in a lot of clutter, it is beneficial to group semantically similar words into "topics"; for example, aspect terms "waitress", "waiter" and "bartender" could form a topic "staff".

A survey by Schouten and Frasincar (2016) provides an overview about ALSA, but reports nearly exclusively on research on English corpora. Indeed, the vast majority of research on Sentiment Analysis and also natural language processing (NLP) in general has been done with English. Crosslingual NLP tries to utilize resources from a source language (generally English) for application on another target language. This is of advantage for languages where resources (in our work: opinions) are very rare. Multilingual NLP rather combines resources from different languages to analyze content written in them (Utt and Padó, 2014). In our work, we adhere to the second approach, in order to make full use of documents available in each of the languages under consideration.

We address the question "How can we extract mono-lingual aspect terms from reviews in different languages and then combine them into multilingual topics that describe the multilingual corpus?". We evaluate different methods for both the aspect extraction and the clustering step, focusing on ways of reducing human involvement and automating the learning process with minimal human input.

As proof of concept of our approach, we study a corpus containing English and Finnish reviews of restaurants. These two languages belong to unrelated families (Indoeuropean vs Uralic), differ in the amount of available resources (Finnish resources are sparse), and are linguistically very different: English is a language with comparatively little morphology, while Finnish is an agglutinative language with very rich morphology (Pirkola, 2001). Our results show that multilingual topics can be extracted for even so different languages, making full use of the resources available in each language.

This study is organized as follows. In the next section we discuss relevant research advances. In section 3 we describe our framework, its components and the mechanisms used to evaluate each component. Our experiments and results are presented in section 4. In section 5 we discuss our findings. The last section concludes the paper with and outlook on future work and extensions.

2   Current Research State

2.1   Aspect extraction

Schouten and Frasincar in their 2016 survey classify the approaches to aspect detection into five different general methods: frequency-based, syntax-based, based on supervised learning, based on unsupervised learning and hybrids between the aforementioned.

2.1.1   Unsupervised approaches

The unsupervised methods presented in the survey are mostly based on Latent Dirichlet Allocation (LDA), in variants to make it work on the aspect level, which is far finer grained than the document level LDA was designed for. For example, the relatively recent Amplayo and Song (2017) combine LDA with Biterm Topic Models. Asnani and Pawar (2017) use more or less default LDA but combines it with semantic information from a multilingual dictionary, which allows them to extract aspects from code-mixed text, in this case social media content written in a combination of Hindi and English.

There are also some unsupervised approaches not based on LDA. Schouten et al. (2018) presents an unsupervised method based on association rule mining on co-occurrence frequency data. Also very recently, Dragoni et al. (2018) use NLP methods to get grammar dependencies and POS of a sentence and use rules based on that information to extract aspects from real-time stream data. A different approach is taken in the paper by He et al. (2017), which is based on an attention model, and which is the unsupervised method we decided to evaluate in this work.

2.1.2   Supervised approaches

For supervised approaches, we only examined methods that do not require the definition of a static set of aspects, but see the problem as a sequence labeling task.

State-of-the-art approaches train Deep Neural Networks on word embeddings for aspect term extraction. Usually general purpose word embeddings are used, however Pham et al. (2017) focuses on training word embeddings specifically for aspect extraction. The first deep learning based method was Poria et al. (2016), which uses word embeddings enriched by POS tags to surpass all previous approaches to aspect extraction significantly. The Xu et al. (2018) builds up on that, using double embeddings, which in this case means a combination of general-purpose embeddings with domain specific ones. Other recent supervised approaches using deep learning include Luo et al. (2018), which uses embeddings acquired from a bidirectional dependency tree network to train a classifier, and Li et al. (2018), which uses an attention-based model in combination with selective transformation to not only extract aspect terms but also the corresponding opinion words. The last three papers mentioned report very similar performance values. We used (Xu et al., 2018) as the supervised method for our experiments.

2.1.3 Hybrid approach

A hybrid system, combining unsupervised extraction with training a Neural Network is described in Wu et al. (2018). We also tested this approach in our experiments.

2.2   Multi- and Crosslingual NLP

Multi- and crosslingual NLP has been dominated by methods utilizing word embeddings in the last years. A relatively recent *not* embedding-based approach is described by Täckström et al. (2012), where crosslingual word clusters are used to transfer models to predict linguistic structure between languages. These semantic clusters are built first for one language in the way described in by Brown et al. (1992) and then combined by projection.

A survey on crosslingual word embeddings was compiled by Ruder et al. (2017). It suggests a taxonomy of training crosslingual word-embedding models, which is classifying them based on the training data required: parallel or just comparable, aligned on word, sentence or document level.

Dufter et al. (2018) claim the current state-of-the-art model for sentence-aligned methods, called "concept induction". A parallel corpus is taken as input and used to induce dictionary graphs. From the dictionary graphs, concepts and words-concept pairs are then induced from the dictionary graph. Finally, embeddings are learned from the word-concept pairs using the standard Word2Vec method (Mikolov et al., 2013).

Word-aligned models usually use both bi- or multilingual dictionaries and big monolingual corpora in the target languages. The method we used for our experiments was presented by Joulin et al. in 2018. It is based on creating a restrained mapping between the two target vector spaces using the entries from the bilingual dictionary as anchor points. Artetxe et al. (2017) use a similar approach, but focus on reducing the amount of training data required by a self-learning method.

Some recent papers present ways to align word embeddings without any training data at all. Lample et al. (2018) and Zhang et al. (2017) use adversial training for this. In adversial training, two networks are used to provide training signals for each other. Lample et al. (2018) is also remarkable for presenting *MUSE*, an evaluation framework for multilingual embeddings that we also used as the basis for some of our experiments. Hoshen and Wolf (2018) instead of adversial training use iterative matching methods and Alvarez-Melis and Jaakkola (2018) see the task as an optimal transport problem and use the Gromov-Wasserstein distance to align embedding spaces.

3   Framework for extracting aspect terms and learning multilingual topics

Figure 1 shows the components of the system and the data passed between them, together with task descriptions for the more complex components. The tasks and

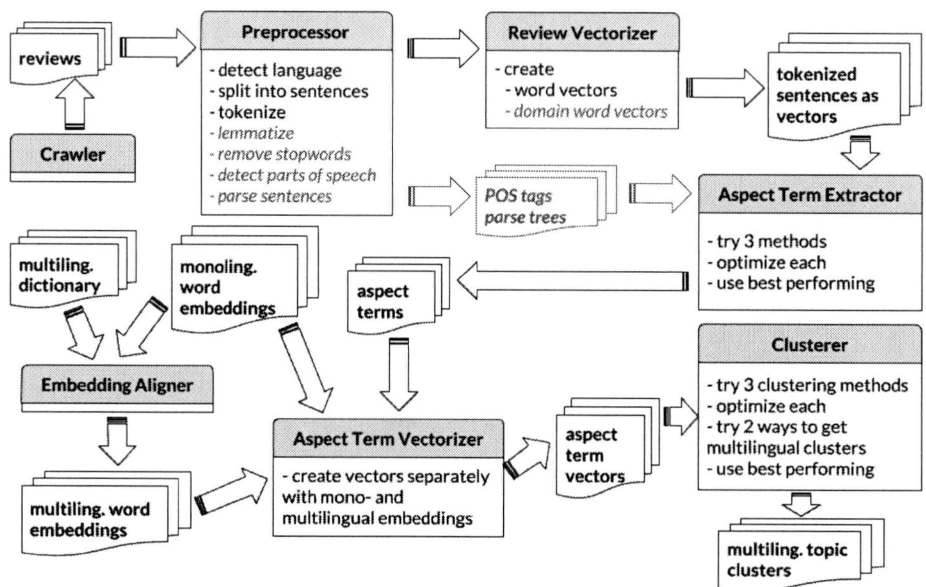

Figure 1: Architecture of system components and passed data

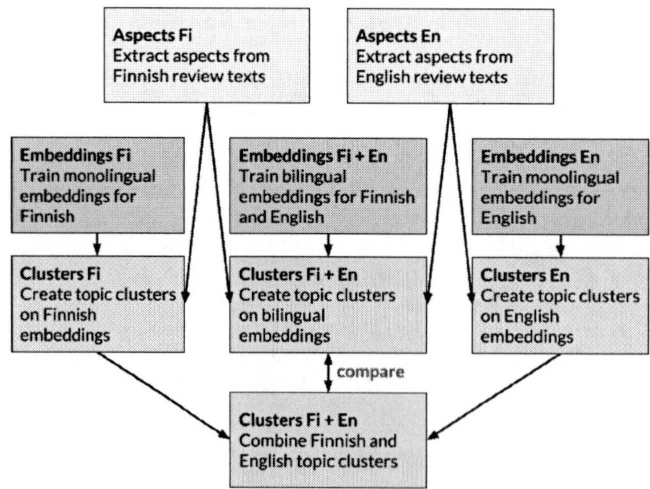

Figure 2: Multilingual workflow of the system

data printed in greyed out, italic letters are only relevant for some of the methods evaluated for the Aspect Term Extractor. Figure 2 shows the workflow of the system, with the focus put on exhibiting which parts are monolingual and which multilingual.

First, reviews are crawled from internet sources, then preprocessed and vectorized as required by the method to be tested in the Aspect Term Extractor. Each method is optimized, the best performing one is used to extract the set of aspect terms required for the next steps. This happens independently for each language.

In parallel, a set of multilingual word embeddings is created by aligning monolingual word embeddings of the target languages, using a dictionary that maps words between the languages to train the alignment.

The Aspect Term Vectorizer uses the aspect terms as well as both the monolingual and the previously obtained multilingual embeddings to create aspect term vectors - for each aspect terms once with the monolingual and once with the multilingual embeddings.

These vectors are then clustered to topics. From the monolingual embeddings, monolingual clusters are formed and then combined; from the multilingual ones, the multilingual clusters are formed directly. The performance of both the two ways of getting multilingual clusters and of the three different clustering methods that are evaluated is compared. The best performing method is used to create the final set of multilingual topic clusters.

In the following subsections, the different components are outlined in detail.

3.1 Preparing review texts for classification

This section describes the "Preprocessor" and "Review Vectorizer" components.

The language of each review is identified using *langid.py* (Lui and Baldwin, 2012), reviews not belonging to one of the target languages are filtered. Reviews are split into sentences with the PUNKT sentence segmenter (Kiss and Strunk, 2006), using the default NLTK (Bird et al., 2009) model for the respective language. The Penn Treebank tokenizer (Marcus et al., 1993) was then used to split the sentence into tokens.

To improve the performance of both sentence segmentation and tokenization, if a fullstop, colon, exclamation mark or quotation mark was directly followed by an upper-case character, a space was inserted in between. Without this step, the sentence segmenter would usually not split the sentence in case of this relatively common error.

The reason to choose these relatively simple methods over more sophisticated ones is their applicability to many languages: PUNKT was specifically designed as a multilingual method and the tokenizer is using relatively simple regular expressions that work for most languages.

The tokens in each sentence are then vectorized by assigning them a word embedding from a general-purpose dataset of pretrained word embeddings.

Some of the methods tested in the Aspect Term Extractor require additional preprocessing steps or use additional data in their vectors. These method-dependent preprocessing steps are outlined in the method descriptions.

3.2 Aspect term extraction

This section describes the "Aspect Term Extractor" component. The task of this component is to extract aspect terms from review sentences. We see aspects in the sense of the SemEval Task 2016/5 (Pontiki et al., 2016), called there "opinion target expression":

> [...] an explicit reference (mention) to the reviewed entity of the [entity-aspect] pair. This reference can be a named entity, a common noun or a multi-word term [...]

In other words, in a phrase expressing an opinion towards an aspect of the reviewed entity, it is the term explicitly referring to the aspect. It can be

- a named entity, like *"My **Sprite** was lukewarm when I got it."*

- a common noun, like *"The **bartender** excelled in his job."*

- a multi-word term, like *"I loved the **meat balls with mashed potatoes!**"*

To represent the positions of aspects in a sentence, sequence labelling with labelling space $\{B, I, O\}$ is performed. That means that each word in a sentence gets assigned a tag: either O when it is not part of an aspect, B when it is a single-word term or the first word of a multi-word term or I when it is a later word of a multi-word aspect term. An example:

The/O chicken/B wings/I were/O tasty/O and/O their/O price/B moderate./O

We evaluated the supervised method by Xu et al. (2018), the hybrid method by Wu et al. (2018) and the unsupervised method by He et al. (2017) which we outlined in the previous chapter. All methods evaluated operate on a sentence level, so each sentence is seen as independent.

3.2.1 Supervised method: Xu et al. (2018)

The supervised method was presented by Xu et al. in the paper "Double Embeddings and CNN-based Sequence Labeling for Aspect Extraction".

Their main contribution is to use what the authors call "double embeddings" as features. Double embeddings are concatenated general and domain-specific word embeddings. The general embeddings are trained on a huge, general dataset, the domain-specific embeddings on a dataset matching the target domain as exactly as possible. Labeled review sentences represented by these embeddings are used to train a relatively simple convolutional neural network.

This method requires the creation of domain-specific word vectors in the Review Vectorizer. We used this method without any changes. Besides in preprocessing, no changes were required to use this method for Finnish.

3.2.2 Hybrid method: Wu et al. (2018)

Wu et al. presented the hybrid method we are evaluating in the paper "A hybrid unsupervised method for aspect term and opinion target extraction".

The basic idea is to create training data for a deep-learning classifier by using some linguistic rules to create possible candidates, which are then filtered according to their domain correlation. The trained neural network is used to improve the domain correlation filter, which results in better training data for the next iteration, and so on. We evaluate the system performance either using the filtered candidates as the prediction or using the neural network to predict the tags.

While we tried to implement the model following the description in the paper as closely as possible, we had to make some adjustments in the selection of initial aspect candidates and the domain correlation filtering. The general architecture and the classifier remain unchanged.

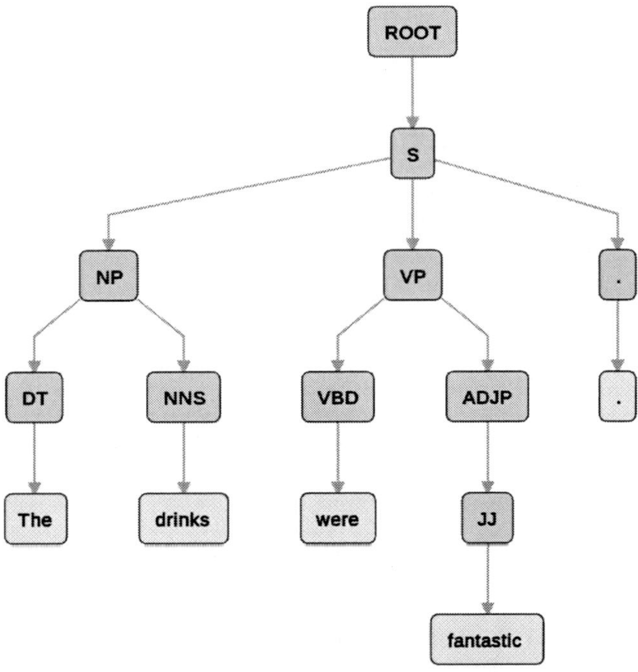

Figure 3: Constituency parse tree

English   Since the original paper doesn't describe the initial creation of candidates to the last detail and we slightly diverged from it, we are presenting the full process we implemented in the following paragraphs.

First, for each sentence a parse tree like the one displayed in figure 3 is created using the NTLK (Bird et al., 2009) interface to the Stanford CoreNLP phrase constituency parser (Manning et al., 2014). All subtrees with "NP" (noun phrase) as the root node that have a height of 3 or 4 are extracted from the tree. A height of 3 means the level directly over part-of-speech (POS) tags and manages to capture mainly simple phrases like those consisting of just a noun; a NP with a height of 4 could for example be two nouns connected by a conjunction.

The noun phrases are filtered to only keep those which either include an adjective, adverb or a modal verb themselves or have a verbal phrase which includes one of these parts of speech as their right neighbor. Additionally, noun phrases that have a verb in base form as their left neighbour are kept, this is meant to capture phrases like "try the sushi".

Next, we remove overlapping phrases, which can exist because we initially picked phrases of both height 3 and 4. This is done as follows: The tree of height 4 is discarded if all of its NP-subtrees are also included in the set of trees eligible at this point. If that is not the case, the subtrees of height 3 are discarded.

From the remaining phrases, we remove all words that are not nouns of some kind or connectors. If connectors are at the beginning or the end of a phrase, they are, as the next step, also removed. The remaining words are seen as the final aspect term candidates and passed to the domain correlation filter.

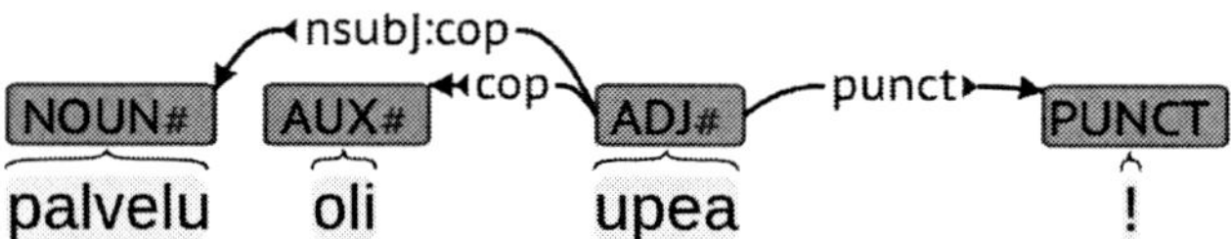

Figure 4: Dependency parse with TurkuNLP

Finnish For Finnish, we had to take a different approach to extracting initial candidates, since no phrase constituency parser is available for that language. However, a good dependency parser, created by TurkuNLP group (Kanerva et al., 2018) exists, which yields POS-tags and depencies between words as shown in figure 4. That allowed us to extract candidates in the following way:

We first extract all nouns that either are modified by an adjective directly or had a copula verb relation to any word. An example for a sentence with a copula verb relation is "palvelu oli upea" ("the service was great"), where "oli" ("was") is the copula verb. In a second step, if another noun is either part of a compound with a noun chosen in the first step or a nominal modifier of such, this other noun is added to the term. The resulting noun phrases are the final aspect candidates.

Different than English, Finnish is a language with extremely many variations of each word. Because of that, we experimented with doing domain correlation filtering on lemmas instead of the word forms: all forms of a lemma should have the same domain correlation. The lemmas are created as part of the TurkuNLP parsing pipeline. As it is not guaranteed that a meaningful word embedding exists for a lemma, we represent a lemma by the embedding of its most frequent form. We always used lemmas to create the set of "domain words" against which every other word is compared in order to decide on its domain correlation. For the sentences used to train the classifier, we did experiments both with and without lemmatizing each word in them.

Besides that, the architecture is the same as for English and as described in the paper.

3.2.3   Unsupervised method: He et al. (2017)

The unsupervised method was presented in the paper "An Unsupervised Neural Attention Model for Aspect Extraction" by He et al.. This method does not train any classifier, but instead tries to compute representations for a set of topics[1], in the same vector space as the word embeddings. These topics are not predefined, but the number of topics is a fixed hyperparameter. The topic embeddings can be interpreted by looking at the closest words around them, which should be a set of semantically related words. They are learned by first determining a sentence representation using an attention model to determine the weight of each word in it and then reducing the error of recreating this sentence from the topic embeddings. As the model extracts the words that are most important both for a topic and in a sentence, this can be used to extract aspect words as well.

---

[1]In the paper, the authors are using the term "aspects" for what we call "topics". We adopted this to our terminology for consistence.

We used the method basically as suggested in the original paper. It requires lemmatization, stopword removal and part-of-speech tagging as additional preprocessing steps.

The focus of the paper is on forming coherent topic clusters from words and not on extracting aspect terms in our sense. The clusters presented in their paper therefore contain also many words that are not aspect terms in the sense desired for this work. However, since the goal of the attention model is to put focus on words that have a high importance both towards the sentence and towards the aspect, the vectors representing the weight of each word in a sentence create a good basis to extract aspect terms from them. We did so by simply using all nouns whose weight is over a specified threshold as aspect terms.

3.2.4 Baseline values

To put the performance of the three models in relation, the following simple baseline values are given:

- Taking all nouns as aspect terms; if multiple nouns follow in a row, the later nouns get an I tag.

- Using the aspect term candidates extracted for the hybrid method as described in section 3.2.2 directly.

3.2.5 Evaluation

As evaluation metrics for the aspect term extractor, precision, recall and F1-value are computed by comparing the output of a classifier with labeled data. A correctly identified aspect term is seen as a correct match, if it is not correctly identified it's a false one. This means that correctly set O tags do not increase the precision or recall. This method is described for example in Tjong Kim Sang and Buchholz (2000).

For example, if one of the methods would return the following tag sequence:

B   O   B   I   O   O   O   B

and the ground truth is the following sequence:

B   O   B   O   O   B   B   O

the precision would be 0.333, since only one of three detected matches is correct; the recall would be 0.250, since only one of four actual matches is found. The F1 score would be 0.286, as it is the harmonic mean between precision and recall.

As seen in the example, only full matches are seen as correct, partial matches are treated the same as wrong matches.

3.3   Training Multilingual Embeddings

This section describes the "Embedding Aligner" component. The goal of training multilingual word embeddings is to create embeddings for words from multiple languages in the same vector space. These embeddings should have the same properties across languages as embeddings for one language, i.e. similar words should appear closely together in the vector space.

To obtain multilingual embeddings, we use pretrained monolingual embeddings and use the method described by Joulin et al. (2018). It works as follows: First, a linear mapping between the vectors of the words that are in the training dictionary is learned. The mapping is optimized by minimizing the average of the loss between the mapped vectors of the source language and the vectors of the target language. The used loss function is based on the cosine similarity between the two vectors and symmetrically the average cosine similarity between one vector and the k nearest neighbours of the other vector (with k being a hyperparameter). The mapping is restrained to be orthogonal, which leads to the distances between the vectors being preserved from the original monolingual embeddings.

We used the reference implementation provided by the authors completely unchanged, also using their recommended hyperparameters.

3.4 Term Clustering

In this section, we describe the components "Aspect Term Vectorizer" and "Clusterer".

The goal of the clustering task is to create groups of words that are semantically coherent, i.e. describe the same topic. We are evaluating three different clustering methods: k-means (in the k-means++ variant (Kanungo et al., 2004)), Affinity Propagation (Frey and Dueck, 2007) and the attention-based method by He et al. described in section 3.2.3. K-means and Affinity Propagation are widely used general clustering algorithms that have been successfully used for the clustering of word embeddings (e.g. Kutuzov (2018); Cha et al. (2017); Suárez-Paniagua et al. (2015)), while the attention-based method was specifically developed for our target task.

We first vectorize the aspect terms, using either the multilingual embeddings obtained from the aligner or the monolingual embeddings directly. Then we try the different clustering methods and ways of obtaining multilingual clusters and use the best performing one to create the desired multilingual clusters.

3.4.1 K-means

The k-means algorithm is based on determining k centroid points, each of which defines a cluster as the points that are closer to it than to any other centroid. The distance used is the euclidean distance. The centroids are initialized randomly and then in each iteration chosen as the mean of the points in the centroid's cluster. After updating the centroids, the assignments of points to clusters are recomputed. This procedure is repeated until updating the centroids no longer leads to changes in the clustering, i.e. until the algorithm converged. The k-means++ variant we used differs from original k-means in the initialization of centroids, which is optimized for faster convergence.

3.4.2 Affinity propagation

Affinity propagation is an algorithm that does not require specifying the number of clusters. It uses the concept of passing messages between points in order to determine which points are chosen as *exemplar points*. Each non-exemplar point is assigned to exactly one exemplar point and all points that belong to the same exemplar form a cluster.

The algorithm starts with considering all points as possible exemplars. In each iteration, messages are passed between points in two steps, *responsibility* and *availability*. Responsibility values are sent towards candidate exemplar points, indicating how likely a point considers the candidate to be its exemplar. Availability values are the reverse, being sent from the candidate exemplars towards other datapoints and reflecting how suitable the exemplar would be as an exemplar for a point. Responsibility is calculated using the distance between the two points and takes both availability of the previous iteration and distance towards other possible exemplars for the point into account. This results in the responsibility value being lowered if there are many other good exemplar candidates. Availability values are calculated from the responsibility of an exemplar candidate with itself and with other points. This results in a higher value if many other points see the candidate as suitable to be an exemplar.

The algorithm terminates either after a set number of iterations or when the number of clusters hasn't changed for some iterations. After termination, for each point the exemplar candidate with the highest value for summed availability and responsibility is chosen as its exemplar. If this candidate is the point itself, that point is an exemplar.

There are two main hyper-parameters for this algorithm to tune: The damping factor is used to determine the extent to which responsibility and availability values are updated over iterations, i.e. how big the impact of the value in the previous iteration is. A higher damping value indicates a higher weight to the previous value. The second hyper-parameter is the preference, which indicates how likely each point is chosen to be a exemplar. A higher preference value correlates with more clusters being created.

3.4.3 Attention based clustering

The method for attention-based clustering has already been described in section 3.2.3. Each topic embedding defines a cluster, with each point being assigned to the topic embedding closest to it.

3.4.4 Assigning multi-word terms to a cluster

All of the clustering methods are done on word embeddings, assigning each embedding of an aspect term to a cluster. This works well for single-word aspect terms, since their embeddings are either directly in the embedding set or can be inferred from sub-word information (Bojanowski et al., 2017). For aspects terms consisting of more than one word, this is not possible. While in theory it is possible to train embeddings for n-grams (Zhou et al., 2017), this would require training word embeddings specifically for our dataset and wouldn't allow us to use pretrained embeddings.

Therefore, we use the following approach: We train the clusterings on only single-word terms. Then, we check for each word in the multi-word term which cluster it would be assigned to. The full multi-word term is assigned to the cluster most of the words in it are assigned to. In case there isn't one cluster assigned more often than all others, we assign one of the most frequent clusters randomly for affinity propagation. For k-means and the attention-based method, we use the distances between the words in the term and the centroid (resp. topic embedding) of the cluster as a tie-breaker; the cluster with the lowest distance gets assigned.

3.4.5 Merging monolingual to multilingual clusters

To merge mono-lingual clusters of the different languages to multilingual ones, we used the bilingual dictionary also used for creating the multilingual clusters. For each cluster in the source language we checked in which clusters the translations of the words in it are in the clustering of the target language. The cluster gets merged with the cluster containing most translations.

3.4.6 Evaluation

Clusterings are evaluated against a pre-defined clustering. While this is in some ways slightly against the original purpose of dynamically creating topic clusters without pre-defining the set of topics, it appears to be the only way of providing an objective evaluation. In order to maintain the sense of dynamic clustering, we are mainly interested in seeing if clusters contain only terms belonging to one topic and not so much if there are clusters that could maybe be merged. To give an example, we would like to penalize if *bartender* and *salmon steak* are in the same cluster, since they very clearly do not belong to the same topic. We do not care much though if *salmon steak* and *beef tenderloin* are in the same cluster or not, since this is just a matter of how fine-grained the topic clustering is.

In order to meet this evaluation goal, we only define very few, broad clusters to evaluate against and see the *homogeneity* score (Rosenberg and Hirschberg, 2007) as our primary evaluation metric. Homogeneity is maximized when all clusters contain only elements from one ground-truth class, with 1 being the maximum and 0 the minimum value. Homogeneity strongly prefers fine-grained clustering over coarse grained ones; in the most extreme case, if a clustering would contain one cluster for each datapoint, homogeneity would be maximised. We therefore don't accept too fine-grained clusterings and also report the complementing score, *completeness*, which is maximized when all ground-truth classes contain only elements of one cluster.

This evaluation method is based on the way He et al. (2017) are evaluating their results. The main difference is that they manually assign clusters to ground-truth classes, which we avoid.

4 Experiments and Results

4.1 Implementation

All code is written in Python 3. We use PyTorch (Paszke et al., 2017) as the framework for all deep learning methods except for the unsupervised aspect extraction method, which uses TensorFlow (Abadi et al., 2016). The clustering methods use the implementations from the Scikit-learn framework (Pedregosa et al., 2011).

We implemented the crawling, preprocessing and vectorization components ourselves. For the other components, we used existing implementations of the tested methods as the base when they were available and extended and adjusted them to fit into our architecture. The only method completely implemented from scratch is the hybrid aspect extraction method, as no reference implementation has been published for it.

4.2 Aspect Term Extraction

In this section we present the experiments done in the Aspect Term Extractor, which are aimed at finding the best method of extracting aspect terms from review sentences.

4.2.1 Dataset

This subsection describes the datasets used for the experiments. Which data was used for which experiment is explained in detail in the subsections for each method.

English   For English, we used SemEval 2016 Task 5 (Pontiki et al., 2016) as the annotated dataset. This dataset consists of 2674 sentences, of which 2000 are considered training and 674 testing data. Some of these sentences are marked as "out of scope" in the dataset and not annotated, so these were removed here. 2579 sentences remain. For the hybrid and unsupervised methods, an additional corpus of 75000 restaurant reviews, which consist of 368551 sentences, was used. These reviews are a random selection of reviews provided by *TrustYou GmbH*[2], which is a company focusing on review management for hotels and restaurants . The reviews were collected from different public sources, including *TripAdvisor, Google, OpenTable, Facebook* and *Zomato.*

We use the pretrained word embeddings provided by the GloVe project (Pennington et al., 2014), as this embedding set was used also in the original experiments for the supervised method (Xu et al., 2018). It was trained on the CommonCrawl corpus, a general-purpose text corpus that includes text from several billion web pages; the GloVe embeddings were trained on 840 billion tokens. The GloVe set includes embeddings for 2.2 million words, the embeddings have 300 dimensions. As domain-specific embeddings for the supervised method, we use the embedding set provided by the authors, which is 100-dimensional and was trained with *FastText* (Bojanowski et al., 2017) on a dataset provided by *Yelp.*

Finnish   For Finnish, it was more difficult to obtain a sizable corpus of restaurant reviews. We ended up crawling the page *eat.fi*, a website for reviews of restaurants in Finland. After filtering out all reviews written in a language different than Finnish with *langid.py* (Lui and Baldwin, 2012), the obtained dataset consists of 71730 reviews, or 346144 sentences. 250 of these reviews, consisting of 1076 sentences, were labelled manually by the author. A subset of 70 reviews was additionally labelled by a native speaker; no major discrepancies in annotation were discovered. As general word embeddings, we use the Finnish word embeddings provided by *FastText* (Grave et al., 2018), which are also 300 dimensional and were trained on both CommonCrawl and Wikipedia data, together about 6 billion tokens. The provided dataset contains embeddings for exactly 2 million words, but also includes sub-word information that allows inferring embeddings for unknown words (Bojanowski et al., 2017). We trained domain-specific embeddings ourselves with *FastText* on the full dataset of restaurant reviews. We used the default parameters of *FastText* to train 100-dimensional vectors.

4.2.2   Baseline

Table 1 shows the baseline values for the aspect extraction task. For both languages, these values were computed on the complete annotated datasets, consisting of 2579 sentences for English and 1076 sentences for Finnish.

	English		Finnish	
	Nouns	Rules	Nouns	Rules
Precision	0.204	0.375	0.355	0.520
Recall	0.802	0.563	0.822	0.554
F1	0.430	0.450	0.496	0.537

Table 1: Baseline values for English and Finnish

---

[2]www.trustyou.net

4.2.3 Supervised

Datasets For the supervised method, the annotated data for Finnish was split to use 80% of the data for training and 20% for testing. This amounts to 216 testing and 860 training sentences. 128 of the training sentences were held out for choosing the best model and optimizing hyperparameters. For English, we used the SemEval 2016 Task 4 (Pontiki et al., 2016) dataset as suggested. After filtering "out-of-scope" sentences, that's 642 sentences for testing and 1937 for training. 150 training sentences were used for optimization.

English We attempted to recreate the English results from the paper (which uses the same dataset), but ended up with slightly worse values: With exactly the same hyperparameters, the model got an F1-Value of 0.724 (average over 5 runs), compared to the 0.747 reported in the paper. It is however to note that the performance deviation between runs is relatively high, with values ranging from 0.713 to 0.731 in the 5 runs. The best of the 5 runs had a precision of 0.674 and recall of 0.802. These values are all created with the evaluation tool provided by SemEval, which calculates slightly different values than our evaluation tool. With our evaluation script, the F1 value of the best run is 0.730, the averaged one 0.722. Since the difference between the values is very small and a detailed analysis of the differences is made difficult by the SemEval tool not being Open Source, we omit a further investigation. All other values reported in this paper are created with our evaluation script.

Finnish For Finnish, we tested different learning rates and dropout values. The results are displayed in table 2. All values are the average of three independent runs. The other hyperparameters were kept the same as in the paper.

| Dropout | 40 | | | 55 | | | 70 | | |
Learning Rate	10^{-5}	10^{-4}	10^{-3}	10^{-5}	10^{-4}	10^{-3}	10^{-5}	10^{-4}	10^{-3}
Precision	0.597	0.628	**0.698**	0.591	0.614	0.669	0.000	0.607	0.685
Recall	0.672	0.724	0.719	0.626	0.749	0.732	0.000	**0.781**	0.729
F1	0.632	0.672	**0.707**	0.608	0.675	0.699	0.000	0.683	0.706

Table 2: Results for different dropout and learning rate values in Finnish

The experiments show that the dropout rate has very little influence on the result. The learning rate however has a significant influence, with performance generally increasing with bigger learning rates, despite the high number of training iterations (200). In all experiments, recall was at least slightly higher than precision. The result for a dropout of 70 and a learning rate of 10^{-5} sticks out as the system in this case learned to always predict the label *O*. An explanation for this result could be the choice of the loss function: The negative log-likelihood is calculated for every possible target label, including *O*. With *O* being, naturally for this task, the by far most frequent label, a slight bias towards choosing it can be expected. This is however contrary to our evaluation method, for which always predicting *O* is the worst possible result. It is unclear why this happens only for this specific combination of parameters.

4.2.4 Hybrid

For the hybrid method, we trained the model with the full dataset (annotated and unannotated) for both English and Finnish and evaluated it on the annotated dataset. For English, we additionally did experiments where we used only the annotated dataset for both training and evaluation.

We used a mini-batch size of 64 for all experiments. This value is not given in the original paper, as well as the learning rate. The latter we optimized as explained in the following subsection.

English For English, we first did some experiments to determine good hyper- parameters using only the annotated data for training. Training for six iterations (updating the domain correlation filter and thereby the training data after each iteration) and ten epochs per iteration, we optimized separately the learning rate and the minimum correlation required to pass the correlation filter. All other hyper-parameters were kept as reported in the paper. Results for different learning rates can be found in table 3; we used 0.50 as the minimum correlation here. Table 4 shows results for different minimum correlation values, with the learning rate set to the best value found, 0.001. The columns in the section "Classifier" mean the performance of the trained classifier, the columns in the "Filter" section mean the performance when using the filtered aspect candidates as the prediction.

	Classifier			Filter		
Learning rate	0.0001	0.001	0.01	0.0001	0.001	0.01
Precision	0.263	0.299	0.266	0.390	0.390	**0.704**
Recall	0.668	**0.685**	0.582	0.333	0.331	0.086
F1	0.377	**0.416**	0.365	0.360	0.358	0.153

Table 3: Results for using different learning rates for English

	Classifier				Filter			
Min correlation	0.40	0.45	0.50	0.55	0.40	0.45	0.50	0.55
Precision	0.300	0.301	0.299	0.286	0.373	0.373	0.390	**0.508**
Recall	**0.725**	0.712	0.685	0.685	0.473	0.414	0.331	0.241
F1	**0.424**	0.423	0.416	0.404	0.417	0.393	0.358	0.327

Table 4: Results for using different correlation value cut-offs for English

The experiments show that the influence of the learning rate is again relatively big, similarly to the supervised method. On the other hand, changing the minimum correlation value to pass the filter has a quite low influence. Using a lower minimum correlation value slightly increases the recall and the F1 value, as the precision stays about constant.

Using the best values of these two experiments, we also used the full dataset, including both annotated and unannotated data, for training. We set the minimum frequency to be included into the set of domain words to 75. The result barely changed compared to training on only the annotated data: The classifier's precision slightly increased to 0.321, however recall fell to 0.626, resulting in an unchanged F1 value of

0.424. For using the output after the filtering step, the precision rose to 0.580, but with a significantly lower recall of 0.183, the F1 value dropped to 0.278.

Finnish Since the amount of annotated data available is significantly lower for Finnish than for English, we for Finnish only ran experiments using the full dataset, both annotated and unannotated, for training. Using the same hyperparameters as for training on the full English dataset, we got the results for Finnish shown in table 5.

	Classifier		Filter	
	Not lemmatized	Lemmatized	Not lemmatized	Lemmatized
Precision	0.391	0.367	**0.851**	0.678
Recall	**0.703**	0.657	0.196	0.471
F1	0.503	0.471	0.318	**0.556**

Table 5: Results for Finnish with and without lemmatization

4.2.5 Unsupervised

For the unsupervised, attention-based method we did most tests using the full dataset, containing both annotated and unannotated data, for training and evaluated the performance on the complete annotated dataset.

We kept all hyper-parameters as in the paper. We tested the influence of the numbers of created clusters on the performance, which turned out to be negligible, so we kept it at 14 (which is the number used in the paper).

For our modification of the method to obtain aspect terms, we had to introduce an additional hyper-parameter, which is the minimum weight of a word to be used as an aspect term. The performance for different values, both for English and Finnish, can be seen in table 6.

	English				Finnish			
Min weight	0.05	0.10	0.15	0.20	0.05	0.10	0.15	0.20
Precision	0.346	0.415	0.433	**0.453**	0.409	0.471	0.489	**0.507**
Recall	**0.696**	0.555	0.510	0.462	**0.744**	0.588	0.546	0.507
F1	0.462	**0.473**	0.468	0.458	**0.528**	0.523	0.516	0.507

Table 6: Results for experiments with different minimum aspect weights

This shows a precision/recall trade-off: The lower the minimum weight, the higher the recall but the lower the precision. This result proves that the attention of a word generally is correlated to the likelihood of it being a aspect term. However, since recall decreases stronger than precision increases, a lower minimum weight leads generally to a higher F1 score.

For English, we additionally tested the performance when training and testing on only the annotated dataset. The F1 value was for all weight-cutoffs two to three percentage points lower than when using the full dataset.

4.2.6 Comparison

Table 7 shows a performance comparison between the three different methods and the baseline.

Method	English				Finnish			
	Baseline	Superv.	Hybrid	Unsup.	Baseline	Superv.	Hybrid	Unsup.
Precision	0.375	0.669	0.300	0.415	0.520	0.698	0.678	0.409
Recall	0.563	0.784	0.725	0.555	0.554	0.719	0.471	0.744
F1	0.450	0.722	0.424	0.473	0.537	0.707	0.556	0.528

Table 7: Summary of the best results for all methods

We see that the supervised method works best with a significant margin. The hybrid and unsupervised methods are at about the level of the rule-based baseline. Results for Finnish and English are comparable, with slightly better results for English with the supervised method and for Finnish with the other methods.

4.3 Multilingual embeddings and clusterings

In this section, we present the experiments evaluating the different ways of clustering and of creating multilingual clusters. This concerns primarily the "Clusterer" component, with additionally the "Embedding Aligner" playing a role in the experiments with multilingual embeddings.

4.3.1 Datasets

We use mainly the same datasets as for the aspect extraction task. The English labeled data from SemEval already contains category information, assigning each aspect term one of the classes *ambiance, drinks, food, location, restaurant* and *service*. The *restaurant* category is used for terms describing the restaurant in general and such that don't match one of the other categories. For the Finnish labeled data, we manually assigned each unique aspect term to one of these six classes. The English dataset contains 874 unique aspect terms, the Finnish dataset 623.

Evaluation was done for all experiments with the full labeled datasets. We did experiments both with training the clusters on only the labeled datasets and with training them on the 5000 most frequent single-word aspect terms extracted by the best performing aspect extraction method from the full datasets.

For both English and Finnish, we use as word embeddings the pretrained *FastText* embeddings, which were trained on CommonCrawl and Wikipedia data and include subword information. For Finnish, this is the same embedding set used as for the aspect extraction task, for English, it is different. The reason for this is that we wanted to have embeddings trained in the same way for both languages, since we assumed that this would improve performance for the creation of multilingual embeddings from them.

Both for creating multilingual word embeddings and for clustering we only worked with the embeddings of words actually required. This includes

- all unique aspect terms,

- the full vocabulary of our datasets, preprocessed as for the attention-based aspect extraction and clustering method (which is lemmatized and reduced to only include words that appear at least two times in the corpus),

- words from the evaluation datasets.

In total, this results in 25808 words for English and 28327 words for Finnish. We did this mainly because the script to create multilingual embeddings is very memory-intensive and was not possible to run with the full embedding sets on our machines. Also, this procedure allowed us to utilize the sub-word information of the FastText embeddings and create embeddings for all words in our vocabulary, also such that are not part of the pretrained set.

4.3.2 Multilingual embeddings

We used the default parameters for training multilingual embeddings and ran the training for 25 iterations. We tested if there is a performance difference between aligning English embeddings to the Finnish embedding space or the other way round. The performance was slightly better when treating English as the target embedding space and aligning the Finnish embeddings into it, so we went with this direction.

4.3.3 Clustering

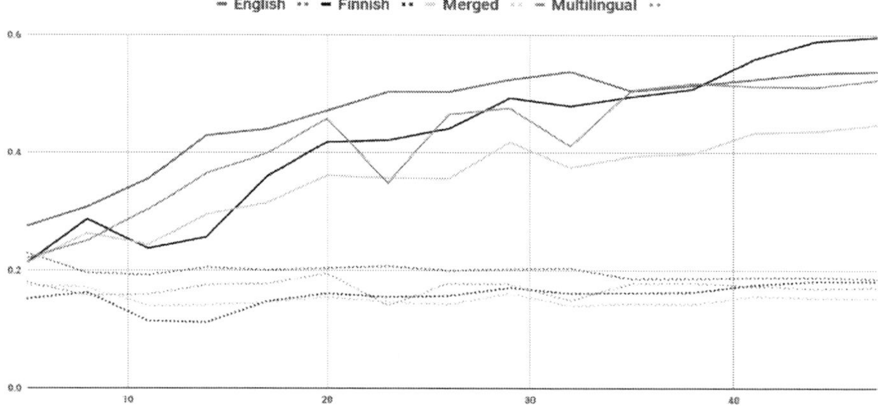

Figure 5: Performance of k-means for different k values. Straight lines: Homogeneity, dotted lines: Completeness

k-means We tested clusterings from 8 to 50 clusters in steps of 3. Figure 5 shows homogeneity and completeness scores for English and Finnish monolingual clusterings, as well as for multilingual clusterings, either based on multilingual embeddings or on merged clusters. As expected, for all of these measurements homogeneity values increased with an increasing number of clusters, up to around 0.60 for Finnish and 0.55 for English. Completeness values stayed more or less constant at a low value of around 0.2.

Using multi-lingual embeddings results in homogeneity scores up to 0.53, the best
score when merging monolingual clusters is about 0.46.

	Finnish	English	Multilingual	Merged
Annotated only	0.493	0.524	0.475	0.418
Full dataset	0.366	0.493	0.381	0.380

Table 8: Homogeneity values for clusters trained on either the full or only the the
annotated dataset

Table 8 shows homogeneity values for cluster size 29, which seemed like a good
trade-off between a not too large number of clusters and a good homogeneity score.
It shows in comparison the results for training clusters on only aspect terms from the
annotated dataset and on also using the terms extracted by the supervised algorithm
from the full dataset. The difference is between 2 and 13 percentage points, with the
smallest difference for the monolingual English clusters and the biggest difference for
monolingual Finnish clusters. This performance trend is also valid for other cluster
sizes. For English, clusters trained on the full dataset work sometimes even slightly,
up to 3 percentage points, better than those trained on only the annotated dataset.
For Finnish, the performance is always at least 5 percentage points lower.

Affinity Propagation Initial experiments showed that the damping factor had nearly
no influence on the resulting performance, so we set it to 0.9, the value suggested by
the authors of the original paper (Rosenberg and Hirschberg, 2007).

The preference value however does have a very significant influence on the number of clusters created and therefore on our performance measurements.

We tested preference values from -42 to -6 in steps of 3, after that in steps of 1
until 0. We discarded any clustering with more than 30 clusters. Table 9 shows the
best homogeneity performance for each experiment setup, together with the number
of clusters created and the chosen preference value.

	Annotated data only				Full dataset			
	En	Fi	ML	Mgd	En	Fi	ML	Mgd
Homogeneity	0.364	0.461	0.344	0.295	0.433	0.393	0.323	0.347
Completeness	0.150	0.158	0.142	0.123	0.171	0.138	0.119	0.145
Clusters	22	30	25	22	30	29	32	30
Preference	-3	-3	-6	-3	-21	-24	-42	-21

Table 9: Best results for clustering with affinity propagation

The experiments show that the number of clusters created with the same preference value is strongly dependent on the amount of data. Comparing the optimal
preference values for the experiments with multilingual embeddings, which contain
about twice the amount of data, to the other experiments, we see that the required
preference value to get a similar number of clusters is also about twice as small.

Another thing to notice is that using the full dataset for training increases the performance of the clustering for English and the merged clusters; it is to notice however
that the number of clusters with the full data is slightly larger for these experiments.

Also it can be seen that merging monolingual clusters works worse than using multilingual embeddings when training on only the annotated dataset, but slightly better when using the full dataset. Completeness scores are about constant for all experiments at values around 0.15.

Attention   Table 10 shows results for clustering with the attention model from He et al. for different numbers of clusters. We ran tests for 14, 28 and 42 different clusters, 14 being the number chosen in the original paper. All other hyper-parameters we set to the best results from the aspect extraction experiments, see section 4.2.5 for details. We created the topic clusters from the complete review dataset.

	14	28	42
English	0.218	0.258	0.125
Finnish	0.171	0.169	0.165
Multilingual	0.107	0.053	0.023
Merged	0.134	0.174	0.076

Table 10: Homogeneity values for clustering with the attention-based model, using different numbers of clusters

Different to the other methods, homogeneity scores don't generally increase with more clusters here; the results for 42 clusters are significantly worse than for 14 or 28 clusters across all setups. 28 clusters work best for English and merged clusters, for Finnish and when using multilingual embeddings 14 clusters work better. Using multilingual embeddings results in significantly worse values than merging clusters, English performs better than Finnish.

Comparison   For all experiments we see that clustering with k-means works, for a similar amount of clusters, better than the other methods. The difference to using affinity propagation is relatively small, the attention based method works a lot worse. This means that the simplest and fastest method works best in our experiments.

For creating multilingual clusters, we see better results when using multilingual embeddings compared to creating monolingual clusters and merging them. Clustering with multilingual embeddings achieves nearly the same performance values as monolingual clusterings. We see that the two languages have generally similar performance in the monolingual experiments, with, depending on the setup, one or the other language performing slightly better. For English and when merging clusters, clustering on the full, automatically extracted set of aspect terms results in about the same performance as clustering on only the manually annotated terms. For Finnish and when using multilingual embeddings, using the full dataset yields worse results.

5   Discussion

5.1   Aspect Term Extraction

In the section about aspect term extraction, we showed that the supervised deep learning method is beating the performance of methods that don't require annotated data by a relatively big margin. This can partly be explained by the nature of the other methods we used. The hybrid method is mainly based on filtering candidates from

the rule-based system. However, as we achieve recall values of only about 0.55 with
the rule-based extraction, it doesn't appear like focusing on removing candidates from
this set is the right approach to increase results. On the other hand, for using the filtered rule-based output to train a classifier, the precision isn't good enough, as can be
seen with the best performance value for the English hybrid model, which achieves
relatively high recall of 0.73 but a precision of only 0.3.

For the unsupervised model, reasons are similar: Since the model gives a weight
to every word in the sentence, not just those that would possibly be aspect terms in
our sense, we had to add some simple rules to get aspect terms comparable to the
other methods. While these rules on their own achieve a recall of about 80% (and a
very low precision), the method can under no circumstances find aspect terms that
don't match these rules. While the attention model does appear to be meaningful in
some way, the precision gains from filtering candidates is lower than the loss of recall,
which results in a relatively poor overall performance.

The supervised model however achieves a good F1 score of about 0.7 both for
English and Finnish. This is especially remarkable with the strict criterion of only
treating exact matches as correct. There have been shared tasks (e.g. Wojatzki et al.
(2017)) that also counted aspect terms as correct when they were only overlapping
with a ground truth term. A subjective look at the terms extracted by the model appears to confirm that the percentage of matches that a human would consider "okay"
is significantly above 70%. Worth noting is also that the performance is about equal
for English and Finnish, despite the very different language structure of English and
Finnish and the significantly lower amount of training data for Finnish.

5.2   Clustering and multilingual embeddings

We showed that clustering with k-means yields better results than the other methods.
The reason for the attention based method to work badly is most likely that the topic
centers it creates are not generally meaningful for the task we evaluate. This is due
to this method creating clusters on the full reviews, not only on the extracted aspect
terms. While in theory the attention mechanism should put weight only on the words
representing aspects, this doesn't appear to always work well in practice. Looking
at the topic clusters the method created on the full dataset in the best performing
experiment (English, 28 clusters), we find for example one cluster containing mainly
first names and one cluster containing predominantly positive adverbs. While there
also are some clusters that look very good, like one containing mostly pasta dishes,
these cannot save the overall bad performance of the method when clustering aspect
terms.

It is not clear why affinity propagation gives worse results than k-means. Previous
works generally report better results for the former, also when working with textual
data, for example Guan et al. (2011). However, Kutuzov (2018), who also clustered
word embeddings, reports that the performance for his experiments was sometimes
better with k-means and sometimes with affinity propagation, so it seems to be highly
dependent on the data used.

The good performance when creating clusters on the set of terms extracted with
the supervised method from the first task further proves its quality.

We showed that by using multilingual embeddings, we can achieve results similar
to monolingual clusterings. Investigating the created clusters in detail, we can find
that while many clusters are nicely merged including related terms from both languages, there are also some clusters that only include words from one language. This

shows that there is still further room for improvement in the task of creating multi-lingual embeddings, either by tuning hyper-parameters or by testing or developing new methods.

5.3 Extensibility to other languages

We showed that supervised aspect extraction methods work significantly better than unsupervised ones, which means training data has to be created for each new language to be added. However, we also show that about 1000 annotated sentences are enough to train a well-performing model. It may well be possible to further reduce this number by using active learning or transfer learning.

The method used for training multilingual embeddings was designed to work for more than two languages; its authors show that aligning 28 languages into the same vector space still works well on their evaluation tasks (Joulin et al., 2018). However, since we noticed several clusters that only contained embeddings from one language, the performance on our clustering task is likely to reduce by some extent. Besides that, clustering would work the same as for two languages though. If clustering with k-means, the number of clusters could just be kept constant, for affinity propagation, the *preference* value would have to be adjusted for the additional data.

To summarize, our method is extensible, but some manual work to integrate another language would be required.

6 Conclusion

6.1 Summary

In our work, we presented a framework to extract aspect terms from monolingual reviews and cluster them to multilingual topics. We showed that for aspect term extraction, the supervised method we tested worked significantly better than the hybrid and unsupervised methods, which did not manage to exceed the performance of our baselines. We showed that for the supervised method, performance for English and Finnish is about equal, without any language-specific adjustments made.

For the clustering subtask, the best performing method was the simplest one we tested, k-means. We showed that when using multilingual embeddings, the performance of the clustering is just slightly worse compared to clustering only Finnish or only English terms monolingually. We also showed that the results when clustering on only annotated aspect terms are only slightly better than when clustering on the set of aspect terms obtained from the supervised aspect extraction method.

6.2 Future work

6.2.1 Technical extensions

There are some smaller, technical improvements that could be done to potentially improve the results in our experiments, mainly in the clustering part. While the homogeneity values for clusters created with multilingual embeddings already are close to the performance of monolingual clusters, we still got some clusters that only included words from one language, indicating further potential for improvements of the alignment process. Potential areas for improvements could be extended training dictionaries (for example by using *PanLex* (Kamholz et al., 2014)) or a more extensive search for the best hyper-parameters.

Another point for improvement of the clustering method is the evaluation method we chose. While using the classification categories from the SemEval data provided an objective truth to measure against and focusing on the homogeneity score allowed for finer-grained clusterings, we still can't really say which number of clusters yields the actually best clustering for the task. Determining which is the best clustering is a very subjective task, which points to a more detailed manual annotation of the resulting clusters being required.

6.2.2 Conceptual extensions

Other directions of improvement are of larger scale. In the last months and years, progress in the field of deep learning has been very rapid. Many of the new developments could also be applied to the tasks of this paper, especially to the part about aspect term extraction. The supervised model which yielded the best performance is based on a relatively simple and straightforward neural network. It is likely that network architectures better suited for the task exist, but manually trying them is extremely time intensive. Methods like *ENAS* (Pham et al., 2018) optimize the architecture search, for example by sharing trained parameters between related architectures. The authors claim that using their method is 1000 times less computationally expensive than trying different architectures without optimization. Also other aspects in the suggested model could potentially be further improved, for example variational, learned dropout rates have shown better results than static ones (Molchanov et al., 2017).

For clustering, we found that one of the most simple clustering methods, k-means, performs better than the more sophisticated methods we tried. Clustering with k-means has several weaknesses, like not being able to handle noise points and expecting non-overlapping clusters of similar sizes. However, especially when clustering the aspect terms extracted automatically, noise points have to be expected in our dataset; also the assumption of similar-sized clusters can not be made, since especially the "food" category is far bigger than the others. This indicates that there should be clustering methods that would be better suited for our problem than k-means. There are many additional methods to cluster high-dimensional data that could be tried. An overview is provided in Kriegel et al. (2009).

For real-world applications to make use of our work, mainly two changes appear to be necessary: For one, the analysis and summarization of reviews is usually desired on the level of the entity they refer to, in our case the restaurant. This is necessary to provide a basis of comparison between the reviews for the different restaurants. Also, it would probably be required to choose an representative name for each topic cluster, so that for example a sentiment score could be displayed for each topic instead of having to list all the aspect terms in this topic. With these extensions, a system to dynamically detect and summarize the most relevant topics for a restaurant could be built. Our work has hopefully provided the basis for that.

Acknowledgments

This work is inspired by the project OSCAR "Opinion Stream Classification with Ensembles and Active Learners" (funded by the German Research Foundation); Myra

Spiliopoulou is principal investigator for OSCAR.

References

Martin Abadi, Paul Barham, Jianmin Chen, Zhifeng Chen, Andy Davis, Jeffrey Dean, Matthieu Devin, Sanjay Ghemawat, Geoffrey Irving, Michael Isard, Manjunath Kudlur, Josh Levenberg, Rajat Monga, Sherry Moore, Derek G. Murray, Benoit Steiner, Paul Tucker, Vijay Vasudevan, Pete Warden, Martin Wicke, Yuan Yu, and Xiaoqiang Zheng. 2016. Tensorflow: A system for large-scale machine learning. In *12th USENIX Symposium on Operating Systems Design and Implementation (OSDI 16)*. pages 265–283. https://www.usenix.org/system/files/conference/osdi16/osdi16-abadi.pdf.

David Alvarez-Melis and Tommi Jaakkola. 2018. Gromov-wasserstein alignment of word embedding spaces. In *Proceedings of the 2018 Conference on Empirical Methods in Natural Language Processing*. Association for Computational Linguistics, Brussels, Belgium.

Reinald Kim Amplayo and Min Song. 2017. An adaptable fine-grained sentiment analysis for summarization of multiple short online reviews. *Data & Knowledge Engineering* 110:54–67. https://doi.org/10.1016/j.datak.2017.03.009.

Myles Anderson. 2017. Local consumer review survey 2017. *BrightLocal* https://www.brightlocal.com/learn/local-consumer-review-survey/.

Mikel Artetxe, Gorka Labaka, and Eneko Agirre. 2017. Learning bilingual word embeddings with (almost) no bilingual data. In *Proceedings of the 55th Annual Meeting of the Association for Computational Linguistics (Volume 1: Long Papers)*. Association for Computational Linguistics, Vancouver, Canada, pages 451–462. https://doi.org/10.18653/v1/P17-1042.

Kavita Asnani and Jyoti D. Pawar. 2017. Automatic aspect extraction using lexical semantic knowledge in code-mixed context. *Procedia Computer Science* 112:693–702. Knowledge-Based and Intelligent Information & Engineering Systems: Proceedings of the 21st International Conference, KES-20176-8 September 2017, Marseille, France. https://doi.org/10.1016/j.procs.2017.08.146.

Steven Bird, Ewan Klein, and Edward Loper. 2009. *Natural Language Processing with Python*. O'Reilly Media, Inc., 1 edition.

Piotr Bojanowski, Edouard Grave, Armand Joulin, and Tomas Mikolov. 2017. Enriching word vectors with subword information. *Transactions of the Association for Computational Linguistics* 5:135–146. http://aclweb.org/anthology/Q17-1010.

Peter F. Brown, Peter V. deSouza, Robert L. Mercer, Vincent J. Della Pietra, and Jenifer C. Lai. 1992. Class-based n-gram models of natural language. *Comput. Linguist.* 18(4):467–479. http://dl.acm.org/citation.cfm?id=176313.176316.

Miriam Cha, Youngjune Gwon, and H. T. Kung. 2017. Language modeling by clustering with word embeddings for text readability assessment. In *Proceedings of the 2017 ACM on Conference on Information and Knowledge Management*. ACM, New York, NY, USA, CIKM '17, pages 2003–2006. https://doi.org/10.1145/3132847.3133104.

Mauro Dragoni, Marco Federici, and Andi Rexha. 2018. An unsupervised aspect extraction strategy for monitoring real-time reviews stream. *Information Processing & Management* https://doi.org/10.1016/j.ipm.2018.04.010.

Philipp Dufter, Mengjie Zhao, Martin Schmitt, Alexander Fraser, and Hinrich Schütze. 2018. Embedding learning through multilingual concept induction. In *Proceedings of the 56th Annual Meeting of the Association for Computational Linguistics (Volume 1: Long Papers)*. Association for Computational Linguistics, Melbourne, Australia, pages 1520–1530. http://aclweb.org/anthology/P18-1141.

Brendan J. Frey and Delbert Dueck. 2007. Clustering by passing messages between data points. *Science* 315(5814):972–976. https://doi.org/10.1126/science.1136800.

Edouard Grave, Piotr Bojanowski, Prakhar Gupta, Armand Joulin, and Tomas Mikolov. 2018. Learning Word Vectors for 157 Languages. In Nicoletta Calzolari (Conference chair), Khalid Choukri, Christopher Cieri, Thierry Declerck, Sara Goggi, Koiti Hasida, Hitoshi Isahara, Bente Maegaard, Joseph Mariani, Hélène Mazo, Asuncion Moreno, Jan Odijk, Stelios Piperidis, and Takenobu Tokunaga, editors, *Proceedings of the Eleventh International Conference on Language Resources and Evaluation (LREC 2018)*. European Language Resources Association (ELRA), Miyazaki, Japan.

Renchu Guan, Xiaohu Shi, Maurizio Marchese, Chen Yang, and Yanchun Liang. 2011. Text clustering with seeds affinity propagation. *IEEE Trans. on Knowl. and Data Eng.* 23(4):627–637. https://doi.org/10.1109/TKDE.2010.144.

Ruidan He, Wee Sun Lee, Hwee Tou Ng, and Daniel Dahlmeier. 2017. An unsupervised neural attention model for aspect extraction. In *Proceedings of the 55th Annual Meeting of the Association for Computational Linguistics (Volume 1: Long Papers)*. Association for Computational Linguistics, Vancouver, Canada, pages 388–397. https://doi.org/10.18653/v1/P17-1036.

Yedid Hoshen and Lior Wolf. 2018. Non-adversarial unsupervised word translation. In *Proceedings of the 2018 Conference on Empirical Methods in Natural Language Processing*. Association for Computational Linguistics, Brussels, Belgium.

Armand Joulin, Piotr Bojanowski, Tomas Mikolov, Hervé Jégou, and Edouard Grave. 2018. Loss in translation: Learning bilingual word mapping with a retrieval criterion. In *Proceedings of the 2018 Conference on Empirical Methods in Natural Language Processing*. Association for Computational Linguistics, Brussels, Belgium.

David Kamholz, Jonathan Pool, and Susan Colowick. 2014. Panlex: Building a resource for panlingual lexical translation. In *Proceedings of the Ninth International Conference on Language Resources and Evaluation (LREC-2014)*. European Language Resources Association (ELRA), Reykjavik, Iceland. http://www.aclweb.org/anthology/L14-1023.

Jenna Kanerva, Filip Ginter, Niko Miekka, Akseli Leino, and Tapio Salakoski. 2018. Turku neural parser pipeline: An end-to-end system for the CoNLL 2018 shared task. In *Proceedings of the CoNLL 2018 Shared Task: Multilingual Parsing from Raw Text to Universal Dependencies*. Association for Computational Linguistics, Brussels, Belgium, pages 133–142. http://www.aclweb.org/anthology/K18-2013.

Tapas Kanungo, David M. Mount, Nathan S. Netanyahu, Christine D. Piatko, Ruth Silverman, and Angela Y. Wu. 2004. A local search approximation algorithm for k-means clustering. *Computational Geometry* 28(2):89–112. Special Issue on the 18th Annual Symposium on Computational Geometry - SoCG2002. https://doi.org/10.1016/j.comgeo.2004.03.003.

Tibor Kiss and Jan Strunk. 2006. Unsupervised multilingual sentence boundary detection. *Computational Linguistics* 32(4):485–525. https://doi.org/10.1162/coli.2006.32.4.485.

Hans-Peter Kriegel, Peer Kröger, and Arthur Zimek. 2009. Clustering high-dimensional data: A survey on subspace clustering, pattern-based clustering, and correlation clustering. *ACM Trans. Knowl. Discov. Data* 3(1):1–58. https://doi.org/10.1145/1497577.1497578.

Andrey Kutuzov. 2018. Russian word sense induction by clustering averaged word embeddings. *CoRR* abs/1805.02258. http://arxiv.org/abs/1805.02258.

Guillaume Lample, Alexis Conneau, Marc'Aurelio Ranzato, Ludovic Denoyer, and Hervé Jégou. 2018. Word translation without parallel data. In *International Conference on Learning Representations*. https://openreview.net/forum?id=H196sainb.

Xin Li, Lidong Bing, Piji Li, Wai Lam, and Zhimou Yang. 2018. Aspect term extraction with history attention and selective transformation. In *Proceedings of the Twenty-Seventh International Joint Conference on Artificial Intelligence, IJCAI-18*. International Joint Conferences on Artificial Intelligence Organization, pages 4194–4200. https://doi.org/10.24963/ijcai.2018/583.

Marco Lui and Timothy Baldwin. 2012. langid.py: An off-the-shelf language identification tool. In *Proceedings of the ACL 2012 System Demonstrations*. Association for Computational Linguistics, Jeju Island, Korea, pages 25–30. http://www.aclweb.org/anthology/P12-3005.

Huaishao Luo, Tianrui Li, Bing Liu, Bin Wang, and Herwig Unger. 2018. Improving aspect term extraction with bidirectional dependency tree representation. *CoRR* abs/1805.07889. http://arxiv.org/abs/1805.07889.

Christopher D. Manning, Mihai Surdeanu, John Bauer, Jenny Finkel, Steven J. Bethard, and David McClosky. 2014. The stanford corenlp natural language processing toolkit. In *Association for Computational Linguistics (ACL) System Demonstrations*. pages 55–60. http://www.aclweb.org/anthology/P/P14/P14-5010.

Mitchell P. Marcus, Mary Ann Marcinkiewicz, and Beatrice Santorini. 1993. Building a large annotated corpus of english: The penn treebank. *Comput. Linguist.* 19(2):313–330. http://dl.acm.org/citation.cfm?id=972470.972475.

Tomas Mikolov, Kai Chen, Greg Corrado, and Jeffrey Dean. 2013. Efficient estimation of word representations in vector space. *CoRR* abs/1301.3781. http://arxiv.org/abs/1301.3781.

Dmitry Molchanov, Arsenii Ashukha, and Dmitry Vetrov. 2017. Variational dropout sparsifies deep neural networks. In Doina Precup and Yee Whye Teh, editors, *Proceedings of the 34th International Conference on Machine Learning*. PMLR, International Convention Centre, Sydney, Australia, volume 70 of *Proceedings of Machine Learning Research*, pages 2498–2507. http://proceedings.mlr.press/v70/molchanov17a.html.

Adam Paszke, Sam Gross, Soumith Chintala, Gregory Chanan, Edward Yang, Zachary DeVito, Zeming Lin, Alban Desmaison, Luca Antiga, and Adam Lerer. 2017. Automatic differentiation in pytorch. In *Proceedings of the NIPS 2017 Autodiff Workshop*.

Fabian Pedregosa, Gaël Varoquaux, Alexandre Gramfort, Vincent Michel, Bertrand Thirion, Olivier Grisel, Mathieu Blondel, Peter Prettenhofer, Ron Weiss, Vincent Dubourg, Jake Vanderplas, Alexandre Passos, David Cournapeau, Matthieu Brucher, Matthieu Perrot, and Édouard Duchesnay. 2011. Scikit-learn: Machine learning in python. *The Journal of Machine Learning Research* 12:2825–2830. http://dl.acm.org/citation.cfm?id=1953048.2078195.

Jeffrey Pennington, Richard Socher, and Christopher D. Manning. 2014. Glove: Global vectors for word representation. In *Empirical Methods in Natural Language Processing (EMNLP)*. pages 1532–1543. http://www.aclweb.org/anthology/D14-1162.

Duc-Hong Pham, Anh-Cuong Le, et al. 2017. Fine-tuning word embeddings for aspect-based sentiment analysis. In *International Conference on Text, Speech, and Dialogue*. Springer, pages 500–508

Hieu Pham, Melody Guan, Barret Zoph, Quoc Le, and Jeff Dean. 2018. Efficient neural architecture search via parameters sharing. In Jennifer Dy and Andreas Krause, editors, *Proceedings of the 35th International Conference on Machine Learning*. PMLR, Stockholmsmässan, Stockholm Sweden, volume 80 of *Proceedings of Machine Learning Research*, pages 4095–4104. http://proceedings.mlr.press/v80/pham18a.html.

Daniel Pimienta, Daniel Prado, and Álvaro Blanco. 2009. *Twelve years of measuring linguistic diversity in the Internet: balance and perspectives*. United Nations Educational, Scientific and Cultural Organization Paris.

Ari Pirkola. 2001. Morphological typology of languages for ir. *Journal of Documentation* 57(3):330–348. https://doi.org/10.1108/EUM0000000007085.

Maria Pontiki, Dimitris Galanis, Haris Papageorgiou, Ion Androutsopoulos, Suresh Manandhar, Mohammed AL-Smadi, Mahmoud Al-Ayyoub, Yanyan Zhao, Bing Qin, Orphée De Clercq, Veronique Hoste, Marianna Apidianaki, Xavier Tannier, Natalia Loukachevitch, Evgeniy Kotelnikov, Núria Bel, Salud Maria Jiménez-Zafra, and Gülşen Eryiğit. 2016. Semeval-2016 task 5: Aspect based sentiment analysis. In *Proceedings of the 10th International Workshop on Semantic Evaluation (SemEval-2016)*. Association for Computational Linguistics, San Diego, California, pages 19–30. http://www.aclweb.org/anthology/S16-1002.

Soujanya Poria, Erik Cambria, and Alexander Gelbukh. 2016. Aspect extraction for opinion mining with a deep convolutional neural network. *Knowledge-Based Systems* 108:42–49. New Avenues in Knowledge Bases for Natural Language Processing. https://doi.org/10.1016/j.knosys.2016.06.009.

Andrew Rosenberg and Julia Hirschberg. 2007. V-measure: A conditional entropy-based external cluster evaluation measure. In *Proceedings of the 2007 Joint Conference on Empirical Methods in Natural Language Processing and Computational Natural Language Learning (EMNLP-CoNLL)*. http://www.aclweb.org/anthology/D07-1043.

Sebastian Ruder, Ivan Vulić, and Anders Søgaard. 2017. A survey of cross-lingual embedding models. *CoRR* abs/1706.04902. http://arxiv.org/abs/1706.04902.

Kim Schouten and Flavius Frasincar. 2016. Survey on aspect-level sentiment analysis. *IEEE Trans. on Knowl. and Data Eng.* 28(3):813–830. https://doi.org/10.1109/TKDE.2015.2485209.

Kim Schouten, Onne van der Weijde, Flavius Frasincar, and Rommert Dekker. 2018. Supervised and unsupervised aspect category detection for sentiment analysis with co-occurrence data. *IEEE Transactions on Cybernetics* 48(4):1263–1275. https://doi.org/10.1109/TCYB.2017.2688801.

Víctor Suárez-Paniagua, Isabel Segura-Bedmar, and Paloma Martı́nez. 2015. Word embedding clustering for disease named entity recognition. In *Proceedings of the Fifth BioCreative Challenge Evaluation Workshop.* pages 299–304.

Oscar Täckström, Ryan McDonald, and Jakob Uszkoreit. 2012. Cross-lingual word clusters for direct transfer of linguistic structure. In *Proceedings of the 2012 Conference of the North American Chapter of the Association for Computational Linguistics: Human Language Technologies.* Association for Computational Linguistics, Stroudsburg, PA, USA, NAACL HLT '12, pages 477–487. http://dl.acm.org/citation.cfm?id=2382029.2382096.

Erik F. Tjong Kim Sang and Sabine Buchholz. 2000. Introduction to the conll-2000 shared task: Chunking. In *Proceedings of the 2Nd Workshop on Learning Language in Logic and the 4th Conference on Computational Natural Language Learning - Volume 7.* Association for Computational Linguistics, Stroudsburg, PA, USA, ConLL '00, pages 127–132. https://doi.org/10.3115/1117601.1117631.

Jason Utt and Sebastian Padó. 2014. Crosslingual and multilingual construction of syntax-based vector space models. *Transactions of the Association for Computational Linguistics* 2:245–258. https://transacl.org/ojs/index.php/tacl/article/view/240.

Michael Wojatzki, Eugen Ruppert, Sarah Holschneider, Torsten Zesch, and Chris Biemann. 2017. Germeval 2017: Shared task on aspect-based sentiment in social media customer feedback. In *Proceedings of the GermEval 2017 – Shared Task on Aspect-based Sentiment in Social Media Customer Feedback.* Berlin, Germany, pages 1–12.

Chuhan Wu, Fangzhao Wu, Sixing Wu, Zhigang Yuan, and Yongfeng Huang. 2018. A hybrid unsupervised method for aspect term and opinion target extraction. *Knowledge-Based Systems* 148:66–73. https://doi.org/10.1016/j.knosys.2018.01.019.

Hu Xu, Bing Liu, Lei Shu, and Philip S. Yu. 2018. Double embeddings and cnn-based sequence labeling for aspect extraction. In *Proceedings of the 56th Annual Meeting of the Association for Computational Linguistics (Volume 2: Short Papers).* Association for Computational Linguistics, Melbourne, Australia, pages 592–598. http://aclweb.org/anthology/P18-2094.

Meng Zhang, Yang Liu, Huanbo Luan, and Maosong Sun. 2017. Adversarial training for unsupervised bilingual lexicon induction. In *Proceedings of the 55th Annual Meeting of the Association for Computational Linguistics (Volume 1: Long Papers).* Association for Computational Linguistics, Vancouver, Canada, pages 1959–1970. https://doi.org/10.18653/v1/P17-1179.

Zhihao Zhou, Lifu Huang, and Heng Ji. 2017. Learning phrase embeddings from para-
phrases with grus. In *Proceedings of the First Workshop on Curation and Applications
of Parallel and Comparable Corpora*. Asian Federation of Natural Language Processing, Taipei, Taiwan, pages 16–23. http://aclweb.org/anthology/W17-5603.

Electronic resources for Livonian[1]

Valts Ernštreits
University of Latvia
Livonian Institute
Kronvalda 4-200, Rīga, LV-1010, Latvia
valts.ernstreits@lu.lv

Abstract

Livonian is a Finnic language indigenous to Latvia. Presently, Livonian, which is listed in UNESCO's Atlas of the World's Languages in Danger as critically endangered, is spoken fluently by just over 20 people. Despite its regional importance, Livonian remains underresearched in many areas and also has a limited number of available resources.
The core of the Livonian linguistic tools is formed by three databases that are entirely online-based and completely interconnected. The lexicographic database holds data of the Livonian-Estonian-Latvian dictionary (2012) and serves as the backbone for the morphology database and corpus; lemmas are also being added instantly from the corpus during the indexing process. The morphology database contains semi-automatically generated template forms for every declinable word found in the lexicographical database. This database is used for corpus indexing purposes, and – after indexation – for collecting morphological data from the corpus in order to statistically verify or point out differences in declination principles. The Corpus of Written Livonian contains a variety of indexed and unindexed Livonian texts and serves as a base for obtaining new lemmas for the dictionary as well as forms for the morphology database via the indexing process. The corpus has a dual purpose – it serves also as a repository of written texts in Livonian.
Taking into account the experiences and results acquired during the creation of linguistic resources for Livonian, the overall conclusion that can be drawn is that when available resources are minimal, solutions may be hidden in increasing workflow efficiency and data management in a way that allows one to extract maximum data with minimal effort. And also that sometimes simple manual on semi-automatic approaches may, in the long run, appear more efficient than fully automated solutions that are also more affected by everchanging technologies.

Kokkuvõte

Liivi keel on UNESCO Maailma keelte atlasesse kriitiliselt ohustatud keelena kantud Läti põliskeel, mida tänapäeval räägib umbes 20 inimest. Vaatamata regionaalsele tähtsusele on mitmed liivi keele aspektid endiselt piisavalt uurimata ning ressursid on piiratud.
Liivi keele elektrooniliste ressursside tuumiku moodustab kolm omavahel integreeritud andmebaasi. (1) Leksika andmebaas sisaldab Liivi-Eesti-Läti sõnaraamatu (2012) andmestikku ning on morfoloogia andmebaasi ja korpuse selgrooks; märgendamise käigus lisatakse sellele korpusest uusi lemmasid. (2) Morfoloogia andmebaas sisaldab osalt automaatselt genereeritud šabloonvorme iga leksika andmebaasis leiduva muutsõna jaoks.Andmebaasi kasutatakse korpuse märgendamisel vormide allikana ning märgendamise järel – morfoloogilise andmestiku kogumiseks korpusest olemasolevate vormide statistiliseks kinnitamiseks või erinevustele viitamiseks. (3) Liivi kirjakeele korpus sisaldab märgendatud ja märgendamata liivikeelseid tekste ning on uute märgendamise käigus saadud lemmade ja morfoloogiliste vormide allikaks. Korpust kasutatakse ka liivikeelsete tekstide koguna.
Liivi keele elektrooniliste ressursside loomise käigus saadud kogemused ja tulemused viitavad sellele, et minimaalsete ressursside puhul võib lahendus peituda tööjärje efektiivsuse tõstmises ühes andmetöötlusega nii, et minimaalsete vahenditega oleks võimalik hankida võimalikult palju erinevaid andmeid. Samuti võib lihtne käsitööd toetav poolautomaatne lähenemine pikas perspektiivis osutuda efektiivsemaks kui täisautomaatsed lahendused, mida rohkem mõjutab ka tehnoloogia pidev muutumine.

1 Introduction

Livonian is a Finnic language indigenous to Latvia. During the 12th century Livonian was spoken across vast territories in Latvia along the Gulf of Rīga, including the location of Latvia's present-day capital. Livonians have contributed greatly to the historical development of the Baltic region and over time have shaped various layers of modern-day Latvian language and culture. Livonian is currently listed in Latvia's language law (1999) as an indigenous language. The Livonian cultural space, including the Livonian language as its main component, has also been added to Latvia's list of intangible cultural heritage (2018), beginning the journey towards the inclusion of Livonian into the corresponding UNESCO global list.

Proceedings of the fifth Workshop on Computational Linguistics for Uralic Languages, pages 184–191,
Tartu, Estonia, January 7 - January 8, 2019.

Presently, Livonian, which is listed in UNESCO's Atlas of the World's Languages in Danger as critically endangered, is spoken fluently by just over 20 people. The number of Livonians according to the most recent Latvian national census is 250, but the influence and importance of Livonian language and culture, however, reaches far beyond the numbers of Livonian speakers, as it is an important research subject not only for those interested in the Uralic nations, but also for scholars researching various aspects of Latvian as well as Uralic and Indo-European contacts.

Currently, despite its regional importance, Livonian remains underresearched in many areas and also has a limited number of available language resources. Livonian also suffers from extremely limited human resources – in terms of competent scholars and people possessing Livonian language skills and the fact that, due to the complex historical reasons, Livonian collections, scholars, and the Livonian community itself are either scattered across Latvia or exist abroad. In these circumstances a modern set of various linguistic tools is a necessity for solving numerous problems associated with research of Livonian, language acquisition, and accessibility of language sources, in order to ensure the competitiveness and continued development of Livonian.

2 Background

The first primitive linguistic database – a source for the later published first Livonian-Latvian dictionary (Ernštreit 1999) – was created 20 years ago as a *FileMaker* database file. However, at that time Livonian faced far more basic challenges associated with the arrival of the digital age such as creating fonts with Livonian letters, overcoming fixed sorting strings to match the needs of the Livonian alphabet, getting keyboard drivers for different platforms, etc.

Although several minor digital collections had already existed earlier, serious work on creating linguistic databases started as late as 2012 following the publication of the Livonian-Estonian-Latvian dictionary (LELD; ca. 13 000 lemmas). During the following year, the dictionary was transformed from its original text format into a database and published online (E-LELD). Following that, in 2015, the indexing tool *Liivike* was created, which used E-LELD as a lemma reference source and enabled the creation of a corpus of Livonian texts in phonetic transcription within the Archive of Estonian Dialects and Kindred Languages at the University of Tartu (murre.ut.ee). The database used for E-LELD and the tables of morphological patterns published in that dictionary were also used in the University of Helsinki project "Morphological Parsers for Minority Finno-Ugrian Languages" (2013–2014).

All of the aforementioned linguistic instruments, however, had their problems, e.g., the web version of the dictionary was created as a static database and therefore was complicated to update and correct. The dialect corpus utilized Uralic phonetic transcription and so was suitable only for research purposes (rather than, for example, language acquisition), its indexing system also allowed only for fully indexed texts to be uploaded or edited. This lead in many cases to "forced indexation", especially for unclear cases, and indexation errors sometimes due to the poor Livonian language skills of the people doing the indexing. Also, due to the structure of the workflow, later corrections of various inadequate indexations were extremely complicated to correct, e.g., systematic indexation mistakes could be corrected in isolated textual units, but not across the entire corpus, etc. The morphological analyzer and other tools created by *Giellatekno* within the University of Helsinki project worked nicely, but were made using an existing set of morphological rules. As further developments have clearly shown, morphological rules for Livonian remain at a hypothetical stage in many cases, as they still need to be further clarified and/or adjusted based on information gained from the corpus. However, the most severe flaw of all these previously existing systems and linguistic tools was the fact that they used the same initial source (the LELD database), but were also isolated, not providing any feedback with updates or corrections, requiring all efforts for keeping databases updated to be fully manual, thus being quite ineffective and never consistently performed. As a result, the understanding that a new approach for linguistic tools is needed gradually began to be form.

An effort to create a new set of linguistic tools for Livonian started out as a different project – when the Estonian-Latvian Dictionary (ELD; ca, 52 000 lemmas) had to be compiled from scratch and published as a joint effort of the Latvian Language Agency and the Estonian Language Institute within a timeframe of two and a half years. Since existing compiling tools proved to be too slow and incapable of handling such a large and complicated task within such a narrow time limit, a new online compiling system was developed to meet the project's compiling needs. This system turned out to be extremely fast and productive, offering convenient opportunities for building dictionaries, shaping and reviewing word entries, executing various control tools (inverse dictionaries, compound controls, etc.), which ensured completion of this project on time.

In 2016–2017, this new system was developed further to suit the structure and needs of LELD (multilingual options, Livonian-specific sorting orders, source references, etc.), developing the online digital database of the Livonian lexicon (LLDB) based on LELD. It was then followed in 2017 by the online morphology database (LMDB) and the online corpus of Written Livonian (CWL) – these three databases form the core of the Livonian linguistic tools.

These databases are currently accessible for linguistic research purposes through registered-access modules. Their public part – mainly targeted towards language acquisition – is currently fully accessible in a separate section of the Livonian culture and language web portal *Livones.net* (lingua.livones.net). This section contains the online Livonian-Estonian-Latvian dictionary and word forms for each declinable word. In the future, it is planned to be supplemented with corpus data, a grammar handbook, and other linguistic tools to be developed on an ongoing basis.

3 Structure and work principles

All three databases forming the core of the Livonian linguistic tools – the lexicographic database, morphology database, and corpus of written Livonian – are entirely online-based and completely interconnected.

The general working principles within all the databases are based on simplified approaches – all necessary work is performed mainly by dragging, clicking, entering search criteria, or completing necessary fields. Workflow is made intuitive and no programming skills whatsoever are required by personnel involved in any of the processes. User controls are eased with visual attribution (e.g., color-indexed statuses, book-ready lemma articles, etc.).

The lexicon databases and corpus also include multilingual options – the possibility of adding translations of items into several languages (currently – Estonian and Latvian, but the addition of more languages is possible), in order to provide better use of materials by users with no Livonian skills.

The **lexicographic database** primarily holds updated data of the Livonian-Estonian-Latvian dictionary (LELD) and serves as the backbone for the morphology database and corpus; lemmas and variations are also being added instantly from the corpus during the indexing process and then developed further within the dictionary module.

The database contains lemmas and examples along with references to their sources, translations into several languages, basic grammatical data (word classes, declination, references). The system allows one to perform dynamic and creative changes within lemma articles (changing of meaning and example sequences, adding new meanings, cross-references, homonym identifiers, etc.). Book-ready lemma articles are displayed in this module dynamically during compiling in order to have an overview of the public presentation of data. In the compiling module, full grammar information is also displayed from the morphology database and in the near future it will be supplemented with a script that generates declinable word forms based on the indicated declination type.

The database also includes various statuses that allow one to identify the status of work performed (e.g., finalized, missing grammar, etc.) or to limit public access (e.g., technical lemmas from the corpus such as Latvian-like personal names or casual new borrowings). These may also be used for language standardization purposes.

This module also has several additional functions such as various search and selection options, a reverse dictionary, and also options for printing search results in the form of a pre-formatted dictionary.

The **morphology database** was initially built to ease work and the presentation of complex Livonian morphology, which contains a significant number of declination paradigms or types (currently 256 noun and 68 verb declination types).

The database contains full sets of paradigm templates (paradigm identifiers already served as grammar identifiers in the lexicographical database), example words and fields for all possible forms (separately for nouns and verbs). Based on these paradigm templates, semi-automated generation using simplified formulas (the initial form minus a number of letters to be deleted plus an ending according to the paradigm, e.g., Supine (*lā'mõ*) = Infinitive (*lā'dõ*) - 2 + *mõ*) was used initially to generate template forms for every declinable word found in the lexicographical database connecting these forms with corresponding lemmas of that database. Since these formulas are connected with a corresponding paradigm they are also used to generate template forms for new lexemes belonging to that paradigm and acquired from corpora while indexing. No template forms were generated in case of significant stem changes (e.g., NSg *õļaz* > GSg *aļļõ*) – these were entered manually. The same also applies to rare forms, for which rules or endings are still unclear.

The result is accessible in matrix form offering an overview of all forms of words included in the corresponding paradigm and the automatic generation process also helped to reveal inconsistencies and subsequently to create new sub-paradigms. Also, based on this database, an overview of paradigm patterns is available for further methodological grouping. Template forms of every declinable word can be moved to another – existing or new – paradigm retaining its current content, however content is fully editable as needed.

This database is used for corpus indexing purposes offering possible matches for indexation, and – after indexation – for collecting morphological data from the corpus in order to statistically verify word form templates or point out differences in declination principles. Although morphological paradigms linked to words in LELD and subsequently in the lexicography database have been collected over decades of field research, this statistical verification is done due to the fact that these paradigms still remain hypothetical to some extent, since there are many specific forms that are quite rare and may appear differently than initially assumed. This is the gap that feedback from the corpus can fill.

The database has already proven to be extremely useful and efficient for practical purposes in language acquisition. One of the key problems for people learning Livonian even after the publication of LELD has been that every time they needed to determine a particular form of a declinable word they had to use the paradigm number indicated in LELD and create the form themselves based on analogy with the corresponding example word in the morphological tables. This turned out to be very complicated and messy, especially for people with a Latvian background (including most of the Livonian community) not familiar with the "type word" approach used in Finnic languages. The morphology database allows one to abandon this entire process by providing a list of all necessary forms right in the lemma article by just clicking on the paradigm number.

The **Corpus of Written Livonian** contains a variety of indexed and unindexed Livonian texts and serves as a base for obtaining new lemmas for the dictionary as well as forms for the morphology database via the indexing process.

The corpus has a dual purpose – it serves as a linguistic source for research on Livonian, but also as a tool for researching other areas, e.g., folklore or ethnography. The corpus acts as a repository of written texts in Livonian. Sources used in the corpus are, therefore, quite varied. Although initially it primarily contained texts in literary Livonian (books, manuscripts, etc.), other written texts (folklore, texts in dialects, etc.) have been gradually added. The corpus also contains lots of metadata about the added texts, including their origin, dialect (if applicable), compiler or author, historical background, and other references. This data may also be used for narrowing searches – e.g., texts from a particular village, author, etc.

When texts are uploaded, they are split into subsections (e.g., chapters), paragraphs, sentences, and separate words, and then joined back together when the text is presented as whole. Previously uploaded texts are normalized so that they are represented using the unified contemporary Livonian orthography. Normalization mostly affects only orthographical representation, leaving, e.g., dialectal peculiarities intact. The same applies to texts written in phonetic transcription since there is no point in retaining phonetic details. This is, first of all, due to the fact that the purpose of the corpus is not phonetic research, second, that the Livonian contemporary orthography provides sufficiently detailed information on pronunciation, and, third and most importantly, due to the fact, that in the case of Livonian, instead of phonetic transcription one can speak of a phonetic orthography that displays texts according to certain rules of its own and not the actual pronunciation of those texts. This has also been confirmed by various later research projects revealing many important phonetic features found in Livonian, which are not reflected by texts written in phonetic transcription (e.g., length of various vowels, etc.).

During the indexation process a mandatory reference is made to the lemma and its form. In case of new lemmas or deviations from prior indexation, new records are generated in the lexical database and subsequently in the morphology database directly from the indexation module, using the default lemma form, reference to the form, and its source. Indexation itself is performed by selecting lexemes and their forms, and the lemma article view from the dictionary is available for the purposes of checking every form selected. For every word to be indexed, possible versions are offered based on either previous corpora statistics or the morphology database, and in most cases indexation can be performed by simply clicking to accept the offered combination or choosing a form from the list offered. It is also possible to search for a lexeme in the lexicographic database on the spot, choose a different, unlisted morphological form, or add a completely new lexeme. Indexed words and sentences are marked with color indicators in order to distinguish fully indexed, partially indexed, and unindexed parts.

All texts are available for searching as soon as they are uploaded and do not require to be fully or even partially indexed. While indexing, it is possible to leave an indexed word completely unindexed or marked as questionable, which does not limit the availability of texts for research. Since indexing languages with unclear grammatical rules involves lot of interpretation, it is also possible to add a completely independent second indexing interpretation (e.g., *piŋkõks* 'with a dog': substantive, singular, instrumental ~ substantive, singular, comitative) or a reference to a completely different lemma and form (*kõrandõl* 'in the yard': adverb ~ substantive, singular, allative).

It is possible to edit every sentence separately in order to eliminate possible mistakes in the original text, to add translations in several languages, and to set limitations for sentences, text parts, or entire texts with regard to public use for language standardization purposes. At every stage it is also possible to index texts or their parts, or to make corrections in existing indexations on the spot. This option is also available dynamically when entering the corpus from the search module.

4 Overcoming problems

Extremely small linguistic communities like Livonian are in quite a different position compared to larger language groups with more resources. Many linguistic instruments which seem entirely obvious to larger, or even not so large, language communities, simply do not work for much smaller languages, due to extremely limited resources – both in terms of people, and in terms of available legal, financial, and technical support. Also sometimes such communities face an entirely different set of problems to solve – problems, that at times are difficult to completely see and understand unless one is involved with such a community.

But there is also a bright side to this. Looking for solutions in unconventional cases may lead to unconventional approaches, which in the long run may appear more appropriate for the current situation. Below is a list of some of the problems addressed while building electronic resources for Livonian and solutions that may be of use also for other small linguistic communities.

The first of these is the fact that since the 1950s the Livonian community has been scattered across Latvia and also abroad. Likewise, Livonian researchers and resources also have traditionally been located across different institutions in various countries. This means that in creating and using any Livonian resources, people from very different backgrounds are involved working from different platforms and different locations across the globe. So the only obvious solution to suit all of their needs is to create completely and purely online-based resources, which would be consistent, simultaneously accessible wherever they are needed, and function technically in the same way regardless of local technical solutions (e.g., fonts, operating systems, programs, etc.). Also, this solution would allow people with different linguistic or educational backgrounds to be simultaneously involved in the same processes, complementing each other's efforts.

Secondly, when working with Livonian and presumably also other small languages, manual work is inevitable and only some processes can be fully entrusted to automated solutions, at least in their initial phases. For example, due to the existence of few and limited data, many automated features that are so common for larger linguistic communities cannot be applied – automated text recognition would not be effective since most of the texts are handwritten or printed at a poor level of quality. There is also considerable variation in orthographies. Automated indexing does not work because of a lack of clear and verified grammar rules and limited data. Machine translation cannot be executed properly due to a lack of those same grammar rules and limited data, etc.

Thus, when developing linguistic tools for small linguistic communities, the main focus should be on helping to maximize the efficiency of all areas of manual work, supporting semi-automated solutions instead of fully automated approaches, which – due to insufficient or occasionally incorrect input data – may lead in the long run to completely messing up the entire effort by, e.g., creating a large number of misinterpretations. Also, since linguistic sources for small languages are significantly smaller anyway, the creation of fully automated solutions may also be questionable from the perspective of the effort necessary to create them versus the actual benefits gained from their creation.

Thirdly, there is a disadvantage of limited sources that in the case of Livonian has actually been exploited as an advantage. For smaller linguistic communities there is the possibility to connect different language resources. In the case of more widely-used languages, such resources are usually developed by separate institutions. Smaller languages can unite such resources under one roof, interconnect them, make one resource supplement another without any great additional effort, and ensure overall data consistency, thus supplementing lack of quantity with quality.

Databases created for Livonian, for example, also allow one to simultaneously perform linguistic research on the language while dynamically setting the language standard (e.g., adjusting morphological templates, suggesting better lexemes, omitting from public view poor quality texts, etc.). And, last but not least, since language materials also contain important cultural value, it is important to retain their availability as textual units for research and use that may have nothing to do with linguistics.

Such an approach allows one to extract maximum data from limited sources with minimal effort. In a sense it is reminiscent of Livonian Rabbit Soup, which has nothing to do with rabbits and is made as an extra dish by simply not throwing out the water left over from boiling potatoes for dinner.

The fourth problem is a lack of personnel with sufficient linguistic and language skills. This is one of the most serious issues that is faced by any smaller language. In the case of databases created for Livonian, this problem has been addressed by two separate approaches. The first is to simplify work methods and technical solutions, bringing them down to simple familiar actions mostly performed using a computer mouse such as clicking, choosing from drop-down menus, dragging, etc., which also helps to contain possible mistakes. Secondly, and most importantly it is addressed by overall principles of database performance and workflow.

This means that people with lesser skills only perform actions matching their skill level. For example, they transcribe texts from manuscripts following a set of normalization rules, but final normalization prior to adding the texts to the database is performed by better-skilled scholars. This principle is also integrated into the corpus indexing principles where lesser skilled personnel only index simple items of which they are completely certain (such items also happen to make up most of the texts to be indexed), leaving complicated cases for more skilled personnel. Ultimately, this saves time and effort for everyone involved.

Closely connected to this is also fifth problem that is the finalization of database content. In most cases, content of databases is usually completely prepared and finalized before making it available for further use. However, in the case of Livonian and also perhaps in the case of many other small languages, such preparation and finalization of content is sometimes quite complicated. This is mainly due to a lack of sufficient people or time to perform the necessary work, but also due to unclear interpretations. Concerning mandatory need to finalize content in corpora, in many cases this leads to "forced indexation", which is a significant source of misinterpretations and leads to a later necessity for additional work involving elimination of such incorrect indexations. Also waiting for completion and finalization of content may limit or significantly postpone its use for research purposes.

In the Livonian case, this is addressed by making all content available immediately, e.g., texts are fully searchable right after they are uploaded and there is no requirement for them to be indexed at all. During indexation it is also possible to index the whole text, index it partially, mark it as questionable, or add different interpretations. At the same time, all actions (indexation, adding lemmas, etc.) can be performed at any stage of working with the databases, even during research of some other subject. However, indicators are used for marking completed workflows (completed lemma articles, completely indexed sentences, etc.). This means that all resources are fully usable, each to a certain extent depending on readiness, of course, and unclear cases, at the same time, can be left unclear until they can be resolved at some point in the future or indexed purely as an interpretation leaving it for final attention at a later time.

Taking into account the experiences and results acquired during the creation of linguistic resources for Livonian up to this point, the overall conclusion that can be drawn is that when available resources are minimal, solutions may be hidden in increasing workflow efficiency and data management in a way that allows for maximum output with minimal effort. And also that sometimes simple manual on semi-automatic approaches may, in the long run, appear more efficient than fully automated solutions that are also more affected by everchanging technologies.

5 Future plans
In the near future, there are plans to continue development of databases within several projects in Latvia and Estonia. Upcoming projects include addition of a Livonian folktale

corpus, which enables the handling of various subdialects of Livonian; transfer of the existing phonetic transcription-based corpus (E–LELD) to lingua.livones.net; and construction of a separate topographical map-based Livonian place names database that would eventually allow for the development of a universal tool for areal research and mapping of linguistic patterns, using information from other already existing Livonian databases.

Acknowledgements
This study was supported by the Latvian Ministry of Education and Science State research program "Latvian language" (VPP-IZM-2018/2-0002).

References
CWL= Corpus of Written Livonian (2017). Rīgõ: Līvõ kultūr sidām. Available online at <http://lingua.livones.net/lv/module/korpuss>. Accessed on 13.11.2018.
ELD =Ernštreits, Valts; Marika Muzikante, Maima Grīnberga (2015). Eesti-läti sõnaraamat=Igauņu-latviešu vārdnīca. Tallinn: Eesti Keele Instituut.
E-LELD = Viitso, Tiit-Rein and Valts Ernštreits (2013). Līvõkīel-ēstikīel-leţkīel sõnārõntõz. Liivi-eesti-läti sõnaraamat. Lībiešu-igauņu-latviešu vārdnīca (web version). Tartu, Rīga: Tartu Ülikool, Latviešu valodas aģentūra. Accessible online: http://www.murre.ut.ee/liivi/. Accessed on 13.11.2018.
Ernštreit, Valt (1999) Līvõkīel-leţkīel-līvõkīel sõnārõntõz=Lībiešu-latviešu-lībiešu vārdnīca. Rīga: Līvõ kutlūr sidām.
LELD = Viitso, Tiit-Rein and Valts Ernštreits (2012). Līvõkīel-ēstikīel-leţkīel sõnārõntõz. Liivi-eesti-läti sõnaraamat. Lībiešu-igauņu-latviešu vārdnīca. Tartu, Rīga: Tartu Ülikool, Latviešu valodas aģentūra.
LLDB= Viitso, Tiit-Rein and Valts Ernštreits (2016). Livonian Lexicographic Database. Rīgõ: Līvõ kultūr sidām. Available online at < http://lingua.livones.net/lv/module/vardnica/>. Accessed on 13.11.2018.
LMDB = Viitso, Tiit-Rein and Valts Ernštreits (2017). Livonian Morphology Database. Rīgõ: Līvõ kultūr sidām. Available online at <http://lingua.livones.net/lv/module/vardnica/list_vtipi>. Accessed on 13.11.2018.

The use of Extract Morphology for Automatic Generation of Language Technology for Votic

Kristian Kankainen
University of Tartu
Institute of Estonian and General Linguistics
`kristian@keeleleek.ee`

Abstract

The article presents a source code generating extension to Språkbanken's morphological dictionary building tool, the "Morphology lab". This is done for three reasons: 1) to include the speech community in the morphological dictionary making 2) to enable a time-resistant, human readable description of Votic morphology 3) source code generation minimizes the efforts keeping multiple language technologies in sync when the morphological dictionary is updated.

The morphological dictionary tool uses Extract Morphology that extracts the paradigm descriptions automatically from user input inflection tables. In this way the user's linguistic and technological knowledge is kept at a bare minimum.

The presented extension encodes both the lexical information and the procedural paradigm descriptions into the ISO standard Lexical Markup Framework (LMF). From this central representation program source code is generated for morphological analysis and synthesis modules in two language technological systems: the Grammatical Framework and the Giellatekno infrastructure.

Integration into the Giellatekno infrastructure is still work in progress, but the extension has allready been successfully used as a continuous integration platform for developing the morphology module of the Votic Resource Grammar Library in the Grammatical Framework.

In the end the article discusses four main implications of the presented approach: 1) the work on morphology is reduced to an interface similar to Wiktionary, 2) the lexical resource is put in the middle, 3) the general benefits of source code generation, 4) benefits of lemma form agnosticity inherent in the approach.

Teesid

Artikkel tutvustab koodigenereerimise laiendust Språkbankeni morfoloogiliste sõnaraamatute koostamissüsteemile. Laiendusel on kolm eesmärki: 1) kaasamaks kõnelejaskonda morfoloogilise sõnastiku koostamisprotsessi; 2) võimaldada arhiveeritava ja inimloetava morfoloogiakirjelduse koostamise; 3) koodigenereerimine minimeerib jõupingutused, et hoida mitut rööpset keeletehnoloogiat ajakohastena morfoloogilise sõnaraamatu uuendamise puhul.

Morfoloogilise sõnaraamatu koostamissüsteem põhineb ekstraktmorfoloogial, mis eraldab automaatselt paradigmakirjelduse tüüpsõna muutvormitabelist. Sellisel viisil viiakse kasutaja vajatud keelelised ja tehnoloogilised teadmised miinimumi.

Proceedings of the fifth Workshop on Computational Linguistics for Uralic Languages, pages 192–204,
Tartu, Estonia, January 7 - January 8, 2019.

Tutvustatud laiendus teisendab nii leksikaalse informatsiooni, kui ka paradigmade arvutuslikud kirjeldused rahvusvahelise standardi kujule ISO Lexical Markup Framework. Sellest kesksest kujust genereeritakse programmkood kahe keeletehnoloogilise raamistiku morfoloogiamoodulite jaoks: programmeerimiskeel Grammatical Framework ja Giellatekno infrastruktuur.

Integreerimine Giellatekno infrastruktuuri on pooleli. Ent tutvustatud laiendust on edukalt kasutatud vadja keele Grammatical Framework'i morfoloogiamooduli genereerimiseks.

Artikli lõpus käsitletakse neli teemat, mida tutvustatud lähenemine toob kaasa: 1) töö morfoloogilise kirjelduse kallal on taandatud muutvormide tabelite esitamisele, 2) töö keskseks osaks on leksikaalse ressursi loomine, 3) koodigenereerimise üldised hüved, ning 4) tutvustatud lähenemise lemmavormi valimise sõltumatuse hüved.

1 Introduction

The presented system is part of a broader work on defining a normative description of Votic morphology to be used in corpus planning, language teaching and language revitalization efforts.

There was no literature developed for Votic in the 1930s (unlike for Karelian, Veps, Ingrian and other languages in the Soviet Union). But still the Votic language has many linguistic descriptions, including grammars (e.g. Ahlqvist (1856), Tsvetkov (2008), Ariste (1968), Маркус and Рожанский (2011)) and big (electronic) dictionaries (Tsvetkov (1995), Grünberg et al. (2013)) but very few that gives definitive answers to language learners asking *how is lexeme xyz in genitive form?* For this a standardization or normative description of the morphology is needed. Metaphorically, the presented system tries to give the fishing rod instead of only the fish. That is, to give to the language community not only the normative morphology but a system where the normative can be altered. This is seen as crucial for the group of less than 20 active Votic language activists.

To minimize efforts, a morphological dictionary is compiled in such a way that it can be used both as a reference guide of the normative morphological description and as a basis for automatically generating the source codes implementing the morphological analysis and synthesis modules for two language technological platforms: the Giellatekno infrastructure and the Grammatical Framework.

Planned future applications for the generated morphological modules is proofing tools obtained from the integration with Giellatekno's infrastructure, and a bilingual Russian–Votic phrasebook application done in the Grammatical Framework.

The morphological dictionary is built with an existing tool called the "Morphology Lab". The presented method is not language dependent, but so far work has only been done with the Votic language. The most language dependent part of the system is the type system for the generated Grammatical Framework source code and this concerns only the optimization of computer memory usage.

The system has been successfully used for continuous integration when working on the morphology module of the Votic Resource Grammar Library in the Grammatical Framework. New paradigm functions has continuously and automatically been added to the morphology module when the corresponding words' inflection tables have been added to the dictionary through the Morphology Lab.

Initial work for generating source code and integrating with the Giellatekno infrastructure is presented. This is work in progress that has not been deployed nor fully tested.

The article first presents the Morphology Lab tool's workflow for working on the Votic morphological dictionary and how it uses Extract Morphology for paradigm extraction. Section 3 introduces source code generation and section 3.1 how the morphological dictionary's data is used as its ontology represented in the Lexical Markup Framework. Section 3.2 explains the source code generation for GF and section 3.3 for Giellatekno. Lastly, section 4 discusses the advantage and main implications of using the presented approach. Generated source code examples are added at the end.

2   Workflow: Morphology Lab and Extract Morphology

The Morphology Lab is a separate online tool for working with morphological dictionaries. It was created as a prototype to integrate Extract Morphology into Språkbanken's lexical infrastructure Karp. It uses Extract Morphology to predict correct paradigms for new lexical entries, and to extract new paradigms not yet existing in the system from user input example inflection tables. It also integrates with the corpus tool Korp and shows frequency counts for wordforms in the inflection tables.

The workflow for building the Votic morphological dictionary with the Morphology Lab has been straight forward. Although no users from the Votic speech community has yet been found, the tool is seen simple enough to encourage their inclusion.

For a new entry, the user first inserts the new word (or any of its wordforms) and chooses the correct paradigm(s) for it. The paradigm can be specified either by inserting another word that shares the same paradigm or by reviewing the generated inflection tables and choosing the appropriate one(s). The generated inflection tables show for each wordform also their frequency count in a corpus.

If a correct paradigm does not yet exist in the system, the user has to input all wordforms in the inflection table which is then saved as a new paradigm. The user can do this by filling a blank inflection table or by editing wordforms in a generated (wrong) inflection table. The newly saved paradigm is directly reflected in the system and can be chosen when adding the next new entry to the system.

Next we will introduce Extract Morphology. The paradigm extraction facility of Extract Morphology has been proposed as a more natural way for a linguist to define a computational morphology (Forsberg (2016)) as it doesn't rely on any specific knowledge other than wordforms. It has been presented in detail in (Ahlberg et al. (2014)) and (Ahlberg et al. (2015)). Extract Morphology has been used for deriving morphological guessers as weighted and unweighted finite state transducers (Forsberg and Hulden (2016)). The design of its extraction techniques in finite state calculus has been presented more thoroughly in (Hulden (2014)).

At the core, Extract Morphology's paradigm extraction finds the longest common subsequence (LCS) across all wordforms in an inflection table. These common parts are used as a technical stem for defining the lexeme. The common and non-common parts make up concatenation patterns for each wordform.

As a simplified example, consider the two wordforms *tšiutto* and *tšiutod* ('shirt'). Their longest common subsequences are highlighted in table 1.

The common parts are abstracted away into variables and thus define concatenation templates for the paradigm's wordforms, such as: $x_1 \oplus t \oplus x_2$ and $x_1 \oplus x_2 \oplus d$.

It is obvious that replacing the variables with the values x_1=**tšiut** and x_2=**o** recreates the inital inflection table. Furthermore, other words sharing the same paradigm

Wordform	MSD	LCS
tšiutto	Sɢ Nᴏᴍ	<u>tšiut</u> t <u>o</u>
tšiutod	Pʟ Nᴏᴍ	<u>tšiut</u> <u>o</u> d

Table 1: Inflection table with morphosyntactic descriptions and underlined longest common subsequence.

can also be instantiated, for example x_1=**kat** and x_2=**o** instantiates the lexeme's *katto* paradigm.

The technical stem creates a too low-level interface for any practical human use. But by choosing one wordform to be used as lemma, the concatenation pattern can be used to construct a dispatch function that segment the complete lemma wordform into the needed technical stem parts. This approach is illustrated in the Grammatical Framework source code generation in section 3.2.

Since the technical stem is independent of any wordform in the paradigm, it is also independent from the choice of what is used as the dictionary lemma.

This has several implications. The choice of lemma form in the dictionary meant for human consumption can be post-poned after analysing the principal parts of the paradigms or consulting the end dictionary users. Also, the choice of lemma form used in the generated language technology need not be the same and can be chosen in accordance to specific needs of each generated software individually. Ideally though, the same form is used in all systems, but the point here is that this choice can be made on-the-go, or when enough data has been collected.

This kind of lemma agnosticity in the work flow is seen as a good thing for languages that lack a lexicographic tradition and is discussed more closely in section 4.

3 Source code generation

Source code generation is a loose term used here to designate the automatic process where program source code is generated from a description or ontology. The ontology describes the *what*, not the *how* of the morphological knowledge, whereas the generators transform this knowledge into a program implementation. The implementation is a derived kind of *how*, trying as close as possible to resemble the original *what* of the ontology.

In our work we represent the ontology using the ISO standard Lexical Markup Framework (LMF). All the data recorded by the Morphology Lab is converted into LMF form and this is used as input for the source code generator.

Two source code generators are presented below, one for the Grammatical Framework and one for the Giellatekno infrastructure. The source code generators are implemented with the XQuery programming language.

A shared architectural feature of both code generators is the use of translation tables for translating terms used in the LMF ontology to their corresponding terms used in the host environment. For example the names of paradigms are prefixed with as in the LMF (e.g. `asTšiutto`), but named like actions in the GF (`mkTšiutto`), and prefixed by their part of speech in Giellatekno (`N_TŠIUTTO`). Also the terminology for grammatical features differ between the environments.

In this way different terminological traditions are supported and respected.

3.1 Lexical Markup Framework

The Lexical Markup Framework (LMF, ISO 24613:2008) is an ISO standard for natural
language processing lexicons and machine readable dictionaries. It provides a common model for managing exchange of data and enables merging of different resources.
(Francopoulo, 2013).

The LMF standard consists of a core model and several extensions. In our work we
use two extensions: the *NLP Morphological Pattern* extension to model the extracted
paradigm information, and the *Morphology* extension to represent each lexeme's inflected wordforms.

Representing the lexeme's morphology with both paradigms (describing in inten-
sion) and inflected wordform tables (describing in extension) might seem superfluous.
But both representations serve their own purpose.

Listing extensionally all inflectional wordforms for each lexeme is in this work
considered part of documentation and what adds value to the work's 50-year perspective (discussed in section 4).

Recording lexeme's all inflected wordforms extensionally also creates the possibility to further annotate the individual wordforms, such as real attested corpus attestations, or other meta-linguistic information such as judgements.

Listing wordform information explicitly is also beneficial for the dictionary system, enabling quick searches and statistics.

Next, we will introduce our data and how it is represented in the LMF.

3.1.1 Representing the lexical entries

All lexical entries carry information about their part of speech, their paradigm(s), the
(chosen) lemma form, and the inflected wordforms together with their morphosyntactic descriptors. Also some additional information specific to Karp and the Morpholoy
Lab is stored.

The lexical entry for our simplified example is shown in figure 1.

3.1.2 Representing the paradigms

The extracted paradigms are represented as LMF Morphological Patterns. These hold
information about their part of speech and are name-tagged with an ID. The names
follow the LMF tradition and are prefixed with as, such as asTšiutto.

The LMF Morphological Patterns model all the information extracted by Extract
Morphology. The attested variable values, i.e. the technical stems, of all lexemes
added in the Morphology Lab is saved. This information could be utilized to integrate prediction models into the generated source code, as have been demonstrated
by Forsberg and Hulden (2016). This has not been done, as the work has focused on
integrating the lexical resources as a first stage.

The extracted paradigm's concatenation patterns are represented as LMF Transform Sets. These hold, for each inflected wordform, the morphosyntactic description
and an ordered list of Processes which model the concatenation of constant strings
(e.g. the non-common parts) and instantiable variables (e.g. the common parts, the
LCS).

Furthermore, the full LMF Lexical Resource also holds global meta information
such as language name and language code. This is used mainly to name the generated
source code files.

Thus, for our simplified example we get its extracted paradigm represented as shown in figure 2.

3.2   Generating Source Code for the Grammatical Framework

Grammatical Framework (GF) is a special purpose programming language for grammars (Ranta, 2011). It can treat grammars as software libraries called Resource Grammar Libraries (Ranta, 2008) and the aim of the work presented here is to generate the source code that implements the morphology module for the Votic resource grammar library.

GF's concept of a paradigm is similar to that of Extract Morphology, and writing the source code generator has been intuitive.

3.2.1   Generating the lexicon

GF is a multilingual framework and each application is expected to define their own semantics in an abstract grammar. No attempt is made to include semantic pivots to the Votic resource, instead a simple monolingual word list is generated as a lexicon.

This lexicon specifies for each entry in the resource its lemma, which is appended with its part of speech and a call to the paradigm function. In the case a lemma has multiple paradigms, each one is declared as variants.

The GF developer could use this word list when translating the application-specific vocabulary names of the abstract grammar.

The source code of the generated word list is illustrated in figure 3.

3.2.2   Generating the paradigm functions

In GF, a paradigm is a function that produces an inflection table. To generate the function for an extracted paradigm description, we need to specify its name, interface and body.

The name of the function is the paradigm's ID from the LMF, where the prefix as is simply replaced with mk.

The function's interface is declared in the oper section and parameter types in the param section. The names and values of the parameters reflect the attributes and values of the grammatical features in the lMF, with minor modifications. The oper definition is largely templatic, reflecting only the parts of speech from the LMF.

To help readers navigate the code, the paradigms are ordered by their part of speech and headers are generated in the form of comments for each part of speech section. These are the only comments generated at the moment.

Every paradigm is split into two separate functions a high-level dispatch function (mkTšiutto, and low-level to mkTšiuttoConcrete). This is to allow a developer to use the low-level function for debugging or testing purposes.

The high-level function takes a string with the chosen lemma form as its input and splits it into the technical stem parts, which are then simply delegated to the low-level function. An error message is thrown in case the input string is not able to match.

The names of the variables holding the technical stem parts are taken from the paradigm's name.

The low-level, or concrete, function is the one that generates the inflection table. On the left-hand side of the table is the grammatical features and on the right-hand side are the concatenation patterns that instantiates the wordforms.

Note that GF's implementation of regular expressions is non-greedy as opposed to many other programming languages. Because of this the expression `@(-(_+"t"+_))` is appended to the last part of the pattern. This expression is automatically created and makes the `` `t` `` match the last letter t in the wordform. This matching strategy is suspect to be language dependent.

The source code of the generated morphology module for our example is shown in figure 4.

It can be noticed that the language code is used for naming the module (`MorphoVot`).

3.3   Giellatekno infrastructure source code integration

The Giellatekno infrastructure has been characterized in Moshagen et al. (2013) to be a *development environment infrastructure* (as opposed to a resource infrastructure), offering a framework for building language-specific analysers and directly turn them into a wide range of useful programs.

From the point of view of our work on Votic morphology, the programs of interest are proofing tools and morphological analyzers.

For the integration with Giellatekno's infrastructure, several components are needed: a lexicon, paradigm descriptions in FST, automatic test declarations, and a Makefile that binds all the components together.

At the work's current stage all but the Makefile is being generated. Because of this, each component has only been tested on its own but not integrated in the infrastructure.

We don't include any examples of generated code for the Giellatekno infrastructure because of space considerations. We will only present and discuss the main design choices made.

3.3.1   Generating the lexicon

Instead of generating the lexicon straight into FST representation, we use Giellatekno's Sanat XML format. This is achieved by simple XML transformations from the LMF format.

The Giellatekno infrastructure uses the Sanat XML to generate its own source codes.

In its essence, the Sanat XML contains the lexical entry's lemma, the name of the paradigm (e.g a FST continuation class) and the technical stem needed by the continuation class.

What is crucially missing from our implementation is the Finnish translation equivalents used as interlingual pivots in the Giellatekno infrastructure. These equivalents will be generated when our work on the Votic morphological dictionary resource has reached the stage of adding them.

3.3.2   Generating the paradigm functions

The FST source code generated for the paradigm functions follow the general structure for realizational morphology introduced in (Karttunen, 2003). This differs from Giellatekno's tradition of using two-level rules as introduced in Koskenniemi (1983). This choice should not reflect any ideological stance, it was chosen only for pragmatic reasons.

A design decision was made so that currently only the low-level paradigm functions are generated. The segmenting of the lemma is done when generating the dictionary.

3.3.3 Generating tests

Tests are optional but used in Giellatekno's infrastructure for verifying that the paradigm functions work as intended.

For verifying generated wordforms they need to be matched with known to be correct wordforms. For this purpose the inflected wordforms stored in the original dictionary are used.

Note that the "correct" wordforms are currently the ones generated by the Morphology Lab. This means that the tests now only validate the performance of the generated FST paradigm functions. This could in the future be enhanced when information about corpus attestations or prescriptive information has been added to the Votic dictionary.

3.3.4 The Makefile

Giellatekno's template for the Makefile that orchestrates the building of all the components uses two-level of the Giellatekno infrastructure. It is currently not generated by the presented system and will not be discussed here.

4 Discussion

It is not yet known, which way of building language technology is the best or most beneficial for different stakeholders. The key points that will be discussed here, with regard to the presented work, is centered around the following four aspects: 1) work on morphology is done through an user interface similar to Wiktionary 2) work on a lexical resource is put in the middle 3) the general benefits of source code generation 4) inherent lemma form agnosticity.

The work on morphology is reduced to an interface similar to Wiktionary. In the presented approach, all that is needed by the user working on the morphological resource is knowledge of *wordforms*, not *morphology per se*.

This interface brings together the work on creating a normative morphology for Votic, but opens the process up for collaboration with the Votic language community.

Setting up a project in this way, the computational linguist could earlier start working on a higher level (e.g. describing the syntax) and delegate work on the morphology to language activists. By developing traditional GF applications, like the city or foods phrasebooks, the linguist could show the direct effect of the activists adding words to the dictionary and how the words show up in multiple phrases of the phrasebook. This direct connection is hoped to motivate the activists.

Other "motivators" are the benefits gained from integration with Giellatekno's infrastructure, mainly the proofing tools. Even though this is an indirect link, it is a parallel and simultaneous benefit.

Advantages of putting the resource in the middle. The key advantage of the presented approach springs out of putting the lexical resource in the middle. Here we keep in mind the LMF representation of the lexical resource. This centrality has several implications.

One aspect is the technological neutrality this brings. The resource models the procedural (or operational) knowledge of morphology, but this is not reflected in the shape of the resource. The resource does not use terminology from Finite State Transducers, nor from functional programming, even though the resource is used as an ontology for source code generation into both these programming paradigms.

Because of this neutrality, the lexical resource is believed to be readable and understandable in a 50 year perspective, whereas any program code implementing the same kind of knowledge might not be. In fact, a working platform for executing the code will most likely not even exist after 50 years.

The advantage of this self-documenting aspect is believed to be situated somewhere between the areas of computational linguistics, descriptive linguistics and documentational linguistics. Because of the close connection to language documentation, further research in this area is believed to be a worthwhile endeavor by the authors, especially for small and under-resourced languages.

Another advantage of putting the resource in the middle is that any faults found during the usage of the generated language technology, will get fixed up-streams in the lexical resource itself. In this way it is the resource that gets worked on, not only the language technology.

This is highly connected to the benefits of source code generation, discussed next.

General benefits of source code generation The general benefits of using source code generation is that changes need only be done in one place. The usefulness of this gets larger for every added target platform, our work comprises only two.

By only needing to change faults in one central place might also encourage in the future to keep what is then considered "old" software functioning and up to date.

Not only fixing any found faults or simply improving the resource needs to be done in one central place. The centrality of code also ensures consistent style in the generated source code. Changing style throughout all the generated code is done by changing only in one place: in the source code generator.

Benefits of lemma-form agnosticity. The lemmaform agnosticity of the presented approach is seen beneficial to languages that lack a lexicographic tradition. Since Extract Morphology is independent of the choice of which wordform is used as lemma, this choice can be post-poned. This could permit more time and resources to investigate appropriate forms by linguists or lexicographers, or simply give more time to the real dictionary users to get acquainted using the dictionary.

Acknowledgments

Acknowledgments should be un-numbered last section. Do not include acknowledgements in anonymised review version.

References

Malin Ahlberg, Markus Forsberg, and Mans Hulden. 2014. Semi-supervised learning of morphological paradigms and lexicons. In *Proc. of EACL.* pages 569–578. http://www.aclweb.org/anthology/E/E14/E14-1.pdf#page=595.

Malin Ahlberg, Markus Forsberg, and Mans Hulden. 2015. Paradigm classification in supervised learning of morphology. In *HLT-NAACL.* pages 1024–1029. http://www.aclweb.org/old_anthology/N/N15/N15-1107.pdf.

August Ahlqvist. 1856. *Wotisk grammatik jemte språkprof och ordförteckning: (Föredr. d. 15 Oktober 1855)*. s.n, [Helsingfors.

Paul Ariste. 1968. *A grammar of the Votic language*. Number vol. 68 in Indiana University publications. Uralic and Altaic series. Indiana University ; Mouton, Bloomington : The Hague.

Markus Forsberg. 2016. What can we learn from inflection tables? In *BAULT 2016*. Helsinki. http://blogs.helsinki.fi/language-technology/news/bault-2016/.

Markus Forsberg and Mans Hulden. 2016. Deriving Morphological Analyzers from Example Inflections. In *LREC*. http://www.lrec-conf.org/proceedings/lrec2016/pdf/1134_Paper.pdf.

Gil Francopoulo. 2013. *LMF lexical markup framework*. ISTE Ltd ; John Wiley & Sons, London; Hoboken, NJ.

Silja Grünberg, Ada Ambus, Georg Grünberg, Roman Kallas, Tatjana Murnikova, Tatjana Nikitina, Agnia-Agnes Reitsak, Savvati Smirnov, Indrek Hein, Esta Prangel, and Esta Prangel, editors. 2013. *Vadja keele sõnaraamat =: Vaďďaa tšeelee sõna-tširja = Словарь водского языка*. Eesti Keele Sihtasutus, Tallinn, 2., täiend. ja parand. tr edition.

Mans Hulden. 2014. Generalizing inflection tables into paradigms with finite state operations. In *Proceedings of the 2014 Joint Meeting of SIGMORPHON and SIGFSM*. pages 29–36. http://aclweb.org/anthology/W/W14/W14-2804.pdf.

Lauri Karttunen. 2003. Computing with realizational morphology. In *Computational linguistics and intelligent text processing*, Springer, pages 203–214.

Kimmo Koskenniemi. 1983. Two-Level Model for Morphological Analysis. In *IJCAI*. volume 83, pages 683–685. http://ijcai.org/Past%20Proceedings/IJCAI-83-VOL-2/PDF/020.pdf.

Sjur N. Moshagen, Tommi A. Pirinen, and Trond Trosterud. 2013. Building an open-source development infrastructure for language technology projects. *In: Proceedings of the 19th Nordic Conference of Computational Linguistics (NODALIDA 2013). Volume 16 of NEALT Proceedings Series. (May 22–24 2013)* pages 343–352.

Aarne Ranta. 2008. *Grammars as software libraries*.

Aarne Ranta. 2011. *Grammatical framework : programming with multilingual grammars*. Studies in computational linguistics. CSLI Publications.

Dmitri Tsvetkov. 1995. *Vatjan kielen Joenperän murteen sanasto*. Suomalais-ugrilainen seura ;Kotimaisten kielten tutkimuskeskus, Helsinki.

Dmitri Tsvetkov. 2008. *Vadja Keele Grammatika*. Eesti Keele Sihtasutus, Tallinn.

Елена Борисовна Маркус and Федор Иванович Рожанский. 2011. *Современный водский язык: тексты и грамматический очерк. Том 2, Грамматический очерк и библиография: [в 2-х томах]*. Нестор-История, Санкт Петербург.

```
<LexicalEntry morphologicalPatterns="asTšiutto">
  <feat att="partOfSpeech" val="nn"/>
  <feat att="karp-lemgram" val="tšiutto..nn.1"/>
  <Lemma>
    <feat att="writtenForm" val="tšiutto"/>
  </Lemma>
  <WordForm>
    <feat att="writtenForm" val="tšiutto"/>
    <feat att="grammaticalNumber" val="singular"/>
    <feat att="grammaticalCase" val="nominative"/>
  </WordForm>
  <WordForm>
    <feat att="writtenForm" val="tšiutod"/>
    <feat att="grammaticalNumber" val="plural"/>
    <feat att="grammaticalCase" val="nominative"/>
  </WordForm>
</LexicalEntry>
```

Figure 1: LMF representation of the (toy example) lexical entry for *tšiutto*.

```
<MorphologicalPattern>
  <feat att="id" val="asTšiutto"/>
  <feat att="partOfSpeech" val="nn"/>
  <AttestedParadigmVariableSets>
    <AttestedParadigmVariableSet>
      <feat att="first-attest" val="tšiutto..nn.1"/>
      <feat att="1" val="tšiut"/>
      <feat att="2" val="o"/>
    </AttestedParadigmVariableSet>
  </AttestedParadigmVariableSets>
  <TransformSet>
    <GrammaticalFeatures>
      <feat att="grammaticalNumber" val="singular"/>
      <feat att="grammaticalCase" val="nominative"/>
    </GrammaticalFeatures>
    <Process>
      <feat att="operator" val="addAfter"/>
      <feat att="processType" val="pextractAddVariable"/>
      <feat att="variableNum" val="1"/>
    </Process>
    <Process>
      <feat att="operator" val="addAfter"/>
      <feat att="processType" val="pextractAddConstant"/>
      <feat att="stringValue" val="t"/>
    </Process>
    <Process>
      <feat att="operator" val="addAfter"/>
      <feat att="processType" val="pextractAddVariable"/>
      <feat att="variableNum" val="2"/>
    </Process>
  </TransformSet>
  <TransformSet>
    <GrammaticalFeatures>
      <feat att="grammaticalNumber" val="plural"/>
      <feat att="grammaticalCase" val="nominative"/>
    </GrammaticalFeatures>
    <Process>
      <feat att="operator" val="addAfter"/>
      <feat att="processType" val="pextractAddVariable"/>
      <feat att="variableNum" val="1"/>
    </Process>
    <Process>
      <feat att="operator" val="addAfter"/>
      <feat att="processType" val="pextractAddVariable"/>
      <feat att="variableNum" val="2"/>
    </Process>
    <Process>
      <feat att="operator" val="addAfter"/>
      <feat att="processType" val="pextractAddConstant"/>
      <feat att="stringValue" val="d"/>
    </Process>
  </TransformSet>
<MorphologicalPattern>
```

Figure 2: LMF representation of the (toy example) paradigm common for both *tšiutto* and *katto* (the concatenation patterns $x_1 \oplus \mathbf{t} \oplus x_2$ and $x_1 \oplus x_2 \oplus \mathbf{d}$).

```
fun
  lin tšiutto_N = mkTšiutto "tšiutto" ;
  lin katto_N = mkTšiutto "katto"
```

Figure 3: Generated source code for the Votic GF lexicon.

```
resource MorphoVot = {

param
  Number = singular | plural ;
  Case = nominative ;
  NForm = NF Number Case ;

oper
  Noun : Type = {s : NForm => Str} ;

  ----------------------------------------------------
  -- Start of Noun section
  ....................................................

  mkTšiutto : Str -> Noun = \tšiutto ->
    case tšiutto of {
      tšiut + "t" + o@(-(_+"t"+_)) => mkTšiuttoConcrete tšiut o ;
      _ => Predef.error "Unsuitable lemma for mkTšiutto"
    } ;

  mkTšiuttoConcrete : Str -> Str -> Noun = \tšiut,o ->
    { s =
      table {
        NF singular nominative => tšiut + "t" + o ;
        NF plural nominative => tšiut + o + "d"
      }
    } ;
}
```

Figure 4: Generated source code for the Votic GF morphology module.

Author Index

Association for Computational Linguistics
209 N. Eighth Street
Stroudsburg, Pennsylvania 18360

ISBN 978-1-5108-8132-7